D1558081

Clinical Research Handbook

An Analysis for The Service Professions

Edited by
Charlotte Brasic Royeen Ph.D., O.T.R., F.A.O.T.A.

SLACK Incorporated, 6900 Grove Road, Thorofare, New Jersey 08086

Harry Benson — Publisher
Lynn Borders — Managing Editor
Phyllis Leggoe — Editor
David Murphy — Production Coordinator
Susan Hermansen — Design

SLACK International Book Distributors

In Europe, the Middle East and Africa.
  John Wiley & Sons Limited
  Baffins Lane
  Chichester, West Sussex PO19 1UD
  England

In Canada:
  McAinsh and Company
  2760 Old Leslie Street
  Willowdale, Ontario M2K 2X5

In Australia and New Zealand:
  MacLennan & Petty Pty Limited
  P.O. Box 425
  Artarmon, N.S.W. 2064
  Australia

In Japan:
  Central Foreign Books Limited
  1-13 Jimbocho-Kanda
  Tokyo, Japan

In Asia and India:
  PG Publishing Pte Limited.
  36 West Coast Road, #02-02
  Singapore 0512

Printed in the United States of America

Library of Congress Catalog Card Number: 86-42961

ISBN: 1-55642-011-0

Published by: SLACK Incorporated
              6900 Grove Rd.
              Thorofare, NJ 08086

Last digit is print number: 10 9 8 7 6 5 4 3 2 1

Contents

Preface

Just as no individual research investigation serves to "prove" a theory or fact, it is not presumed that this book is a "definitive" statement on clinical research design, procedure or analysis. Instead, it is hoped that this book will further stimulate development, reflection, refinement, and originality in clinical research in the fields of occupational therapy, physical therapy, clinical psychology, nursing, and other practice based service disciplines. Examples in the book are all from the field that I know best occupational therapy so that the validity of the methodological examples can be assured. However, application of the research issues discussed in this book can extend far beyond the scope of the field of occupational therapy and apply to almost any other practice based discipline. In the same way that the hallmark of good research is consideration of how much continued research it generates, so too is my personal hallmark for the success of this book based upon how much continued research it influences. It is my goal that this book be considered not simply in isolation, but in context of how much research, reflective thinking, and even controversy it generates and influences. Thus, each chapter has been developed and influenced in response to identified issues or needs within the scope of clinical research.

I have been fortunate enough to have studied or collaborated with all of the authors contributing to this book. These authors were asked to contribute based upon their recognized expertise in particular areas. Therefore, over half of the contributing authors are outside of any clinical practice profession and are in the disciplines of statistics or research. The fact that each of them labored intensely to share their expertise in a manner meaningful for a clinically based practitioner/researcher or research therapist is laudable and significant. It is significant because it puts the burden of responsibility on those of us in the practice disciplines to work to understand their contributions, and to make informed decisions or judgments about how their thoughts will or will not be incorporated into clinical research practice.

Great Falls, Virginia
Charlotte Brasic Royeen
    Winter, 1989

Introduction

Part one of this book consists of chapters one through five and is organized to begin to address the process of conducting research by sequentially addressing areas to be considered in the conceptualization and implementation of research. Thus, part one is oriented to applications of concepts presented in clinical research. All of the chapters in part one may be considered to deal with issues and areas to be considered prior to data analysis. That is, part one deals with what the researcher might consider prior to inferential statistical testing. It is assumed that the reader of this section will have some degree of familiarity with research. However, for the reader's convenience, a listing of Greek symbols and corresponding meaning is presented.

Variables are considered in the context of distributional characteristics in chapter one, "Distributions and Variables in Clinical Research" by Marilyn Lichtman, Judy Barokas, Susan Heling Kaplan and Charlotte Brasic Royeen. Part of the development of a body of knowledge in any practice or service discipline should include specification and analysis of the variables of interest. This chapter provides the background for a researcher to do so.

Suggested procedures and methods for determining (a) how to sample, and (b) number of subjects to sample in clinical research are provided in Chapter Two, "Provisional Guidelines for Sampling in Clinical Research" by Jim C. Fortune and Mary Bender. The first part of the chapter is more conceptually oriented and the latter part offers practical solutions in the form of formulae.

Chapter Three, "Measurement Considerations in Clinical Research" by Theodore R. Cromack, offers an overview of measurement issues to be considered by the clinical researcher. In addition, practical guidelines for use when considering what and how to measure variables of interest are provided. Statistical methods for evaluating measurement issues such as validity and reliability are addressed and examples provided in Appendix A.

Chapter Four "The Role of Exploratory Data Analysis in Occupational Therapy Research" by Charlotte Brasic Royeen and Leigh Geiger provides a definition for this set of statistical procedures, a rationale for their role in clinical research, and presents procedures for calculations. Additionally, examples of exploratory data analysis are interspersed throughout the chapter as well as in the Appendix B.

Chapter Five "Provisional Guidelines for the Process of Data Analysis" by Charlotte Brasic Royeen, presents a sequential process as a framework to follow for data analysis. Additionally, reference figures are provided to serve as resources when gathering information regarding what statistical procedures to employ in data analysis of clinical research.

Part Two of the book is a combination of issues to be considered by a clinical researcher (should I use a parametric or a nonparametric statistic for data analysis?) and application to be considered by a clinical researcher (what is a repeated measure design and how can I use it?). As in part one, it is assumed that the reader has some degree of statistical and research background.

Chapter Six, "Comparison of Parametric versus Nonparametric Statistical Procedures" by Charlotte Brasic Royeen, addresses the issue of what class of statistical procedure with actual occupational therapy data sets. However, findings and implications therein may apply to most research in clinically based investigations.

The subsequent Chapter Seven, "Nonparametric Data Analysis Procedures for Clinical Research" by William L. Seaver, presents rationale for using nonparametric statistical procedures in clinical research. It also offers procedural delineation of selected nonparametric statistics which could meet the analysis needs of a fair portion of clinical research. Statistical reference tables accompanying this chapter are presented in Appendix C.

Chapter Eight, "Statistical Significance Testing: Rationale and Alternative in Occupational Therapy Research" by Kenneth J. Ottenbacher and Bette R. Bonder offers the clinical researcher a variety of procedures to use instead of or in addition to the arbitrary standard of a set alpha level.

In Chapter Nine, "Design and Analysis of Repeated Measures Data in Clinical research," Gabriella M. Belli explains this type of research design and statistical procedure. She bolsters these explanations with examples from rehabilitation. Examples are presented in the chapter, some of which are subsequently illustrated using computer code to run the analysis in Appendix D.

Greek Alphabet

A α	alpha		N ν	nu
B β	beta		Ξ ξ	xi
Γ γ	gamma		O o	omicron
Δ δ	delta		Π π	pi
E ε	epsilon		P ρ	rho
Z ζ	zeta		Σ σ	sigma
H η	eta		T τ	tau
T τ	theta		Y υ	upsilon
I ι	iota		Φ φ	phi
K κ	kappa		X χ	chi
Λ λ	lambda		Δ ψ	psi
M μ	mu		O o	omega

Reproduced with permission from G.E.P. Box, W.G. Hunter, and J.S. Hunter: *Statistics for Experimenters: An Introduction for Design, Data Analysis and Model Building,* © 1978, Addison-Wesley Publishing Co., Inc.

Acknowledgement

Parts of Chapter Four are adapted from C.B. Royeen " The Box Plot: A Screening Test For Research Data," in the *American Journal of Occupational Therapy, 40 (8), 569-571.* Used with permission. Parts of Chapter Six are based upon (a) a paper presentation to the Educational Statisticians Special Interest Group of the Annual Meeting of the American Educational Research Association, April 16, 1986 in San Francisco, California, and (b) a doctoral dissertation, "An Exploration of Parametric versus Nonparametric Statistics in Occupational Therapy Clinical Research" submitted to Virginia Polytechnic and State University, Blacksburg, Virginia, April 1986.

Parts of Appendix B are based upon C. B. Royeen. *An Exploration of Parametric versus Nonparametric Statistics in Occupational Therapy research,* 1986, Ann Arbor, MI: University Microfilms International.

This book was originated and edited by the author in her private capacity. No official support or endorsement by the U.S. Department of Education is intended or should be inferred.

The Editor

Charlotte Brasic Royeen, Ph.D., O.T.R.,F.A.O.T.A. is a Research Analyst with the Division of Innovation and Development, Office of Special Education Programs, U.S. Department of Education. She graduated Summa Cum Laude with a B.S. degree in occupational therapy from Tufts University, an M.S. degree in occupational therapy from Washington University School of Medicine, and a Ph.D. degree in educational evaluation and research from Virginia Polytechnic Institute and State University. Dr. Royeen's research activities and publications have centered upon the organization of sensory processing in children and the refinement as well as the development of methodologies for clinical investigation.. Dr. Royeen serves on the editorial review board of several journals and is a faculty member of Sensory Integrational International. She has recently authored another book on research entitled, *Research Tradition in Occupational Therapy: Process, Philosophy, and Status* Due to her work in research, Dr. Royeen was honored to become a Fellow of the American Occupational Therapy Association in 1988.

The Authors

Judy Barokas, M.A., is a Senior Associate with Caliber Associates of Oakton, VA. She is currently researching the interrelationships of family, work, and community for the Department of the Army. Ms. Barokas' fifteen year career as an educator and consultant has included experience with students and projects across three continents. Her primary areas of interest are research methodology, applied demography, and evaluation of programs and institutions.

Gabriella M. Belli, Ph.D., is an Assistant Professor of Educational Research and Evaluation at Virginia Polytechnic Institute and State University, where she teaches graduate level statistics and research courses. She received her master's degree in measurement and evaluation and her doctoral degree in statistics and research design from Michigan State University. Her scholarly work centers on the valid use and application of multivariate test statistics for repeated measures analyses.

Mary Bender, Ph.D., is a Faculty Research Analyst in the Department of Family and Child Development at Virginia Polytechnic Institute and State University. Dr. Bender received her doctorate from Virginia Polytechnic Institute and State University in educational research and evaluation with a concentration in statistics. She has served in various capacities as a specialist in survey design, implementation and analysis. Her recent work focuses on the stress levels of airline pilots and their spouses.

Bette R. Bonder, Ph.D., OTR, is an Adjunct Assistant Professor at the University of Illinois at Chicago. She received a B.S. in occupational therapy from Washington University, an M.A. in guidance and counseling from St. Louis University, and a Ph.D. in counselor education from Northwestern University. She is currently involved in research on factors contributing to maintenance of independence in elderly individuals.

Theodore R. Cromack, Ed.D., is an independent consultant working with several clients in the field of measurement and evaluation. He has taught courses in psychology, research, evaluation, and testing and worked on and managed a number of large scale research projects. In addition to presentation of numerous papers on theoretical and practical issues of measurement, he has several publications in measurement in educational journals and books.

Jim C. Fortune, Ed.D., is a Professor of Research and Evaluation at the College of Education at Virginia Polytechnic Institute and State University. He received his doctorate in education from Stanford University and has served on the faculties of Memphis State University, University of Massachusetts and Educational Testing Center. He has authored the text *Understanding Testing in Occupational Licensure* and several articles and chapters on program evaluation and research methodology. He takes particular pride in having chaired or co-chaired over 150 dissertations during his career.

S. Leigh Geiger, Ph.D., is an independent computer consultant and evaluation specialist. She received a B.A. in psychology from Allegheny College, an M.A. in Education from Antioch College, an M.S. in Speech Pathology and

Audiology from Bowling Green State University and her Ph.D. in educational research and evaluation from Virginia Polytechnic Institute and iv State University. Dr. Geiger currently provides consulting services to numerous clients and has conducted national research projects designed to evaluate special education services in the public schools.

Marilyn Lichtman, Ed.D., is currently an Associate Professor of Educational Research and Evaluation at Virginia Polytechnic Institute and State University. Dr. Lichtman received her doctorate from George Washington University. She has served on the faculties of George Washington University, The Catholic University of America, and Boston University. She teaches graduate courses in statistics, research design, survey research, and evaluation. She has directed various survey and evaluation efforts at federal, state, and regional levels on such topics as evaluation of occupational and physical therapy departments at the Woodrow Wilson Rehabilitation Center. She is currently studying factors influencing women's occupational preference.

Susan Heling Kaplan, M.H.S.,OTR, is an Associate Professor and Acting Chairperson of the Occupational Therapy Department of Florida International University where she teaches research design. Her research interests include the use of microcomputers.

Kenneth J. Ottenbacher, Ph.D., OTR, F.A.O.T.A. is currently Associate Professor of Occupational Therapy and Coordinator of the Graduate Program in Theraputic Science at the University of Wisconsin. He received training in both occupational and physical therapy in addition to receiving a M.S. degree from the University of Tennesse, and a Ph.D. in special education from the University of Missouri. Dr. Ottenbacher's research interests include the effectiveness of various intervention strategies for children with developmental delays and the refinement of clinical research methods. He has published numerous articles in a variety of professional journals and is currently the Editor of *The Occupational Therapy Journal of Research*.

William L. Seaver, Ph.D., is an Assistant Professor in Statistics at Virginia Polytechnic Institute and State University, where he teaches graduate courses in statistics across such disciplines as engineering, business, and education. He received his B.B.A. and M.B.A. from the University of Texas and his doctorate in statistics from Texas A and M University. He has been a statistical consultant to the U.S. Department of Energy and the U.S. General Accounting Office. His research articles cover the application of specific statistical methodologies (linear regression, multivariate statistics, outliers, nonparametrics, and fuzzy analyses) in diverse areas such as meteorology, economics, business, finance, science, banking, and sports.

PART I

CHAPTER 1

DISTRIBUTIONS OF VARIABLES IN CLINICAL RESEARCH

Marilyn Lichtman
Judy Barokas
Susan Heling Kaplan
Charlotte Brasic Royeen

Chapter Overview

This chapter addresses a number of factors concerning distributions of variables. First, definitions of variables, levels of measurement, and the role of variables in clinical research are considered. Second, methods of presenting data about variables are discussed. Third, measures of central tendency, measures of variability, measures of symmetry, and measures of kurtosis are identified. Fourth, and finally, a section on the transformations of variables in terms of distributional characteristics is presented.

Definition of Variables

A variable is a representation of a characteristic, trait, or behavior that encompasses a range of values. Characteristics, traits, or behaviors are either variables or constants depending on their range within a given research study. Although a variable may take on any number of values, it must have at least two values. For example, gender is a variable when both females and males are included in an investigation; as such, gender is a variable that has two possible values. Conversely, a characteristic that takes on only one value is really not a variable at all. Rather, it is referred to as a constant because, by definition, it does not vary. To illustrate, if all members of a sample are female then gender is not a variable; it is a constant.

Of course, a variable may take on more than two values. For example, when a research study includes individuals of varying intelligence, then intelligence is a variable having a range of values. Scores on an intelligence test may range from 90 to 130, or 75 to 100, or any variety of possibilities depending on the sample being measured. Under such conditions, intelligence is a variable taking on a multiple range of values. Many variables can take on two, three, or an infinite number of values depending on the nature and purpose of the particular study. In a study in which a researcher is interested in making comparisons among major ethnic groups, the variable of race/ethnicity might take on four values: white, black, Hispanic, or other. In contrast, another researcher might be interested in examining differences among various racial/ethnic subgroups. If so, the racial/ethnic variable might be classified into numerous categories, such as white, black, Mexican-American, Puerto Rican, Cuban, other Hispanic, American Indian, Korean, Vietnamese, and other. In the first example, Hispanics are grouped together because the researcher's purpose is to make general conclusions about the racial/ethnic groups under study. In the latter case, specifying multiple subgroups of Hispanic and Asian populations is germane to the research question and allows the researcher to make more refined comparisons within and between ethnic subgroups.

In another example, an occupational therapist, physical therapist, or other professional wishing to study the relationship between sensory integration therapy and the motor planning ability of learning disabled children might classify the variable of sensory integration therapy in one of two ways: either as the presence of sensory integrative therapy or the absence of it. Or, in another investigation, the variable of motor planning ability could be grouped along two dimensions: demonstrated praxis ability or absence of praxis ability. Another therapist might decide upon a different study by classifying sensory integration therapy into specific categories that more accurately describe the varying amounts of therapy, such as none, once a week, twice weekly, or daily. Or, in yet a different investigation, motor planning ability might be categorized into more than two dimensions that might include: inability to plan, slight ability to plan, moderate ability to plan, and considerable ability to plan.

This example illustrates how classification of variables into two, or more than two categories, is guided by the nature and purpose of the research study.

Dimensions of Variables

Because variables differ on a number of dimensions, researchers distinguish among them in a variety of ways. One dimension on which variables differ is whether a variable can be thought of as qualitative or quantitative. Variables also can be delineated according to their function in the research design: descriptive or explanatory, dependent or independent, or attribute or treatment.

Variables also differ along the dimension of level of measurement. To illustrate, variables can be classified according to a categorical or continuous dimension or along four levels of measurement. These dimensions overlap to some extent and thus may create problems when trying to distinguish among them. This is discussed more fully in a following section.

Qualitative and Quantitative Variables

As previously stated, one dimension on which variables can be considered relates to whether or not they are qualitative or quantitative. Many variables can be measured along both dimensions, although some are more likely to be measured in a qualitative manner and others quantitatively. Variables that are measured qualitatively can be characteristics of an individual, a school, a residential treatment center, a region, or a group, among others. They usually include such areas as gender, place of birth, nationality, or type of client served. Qualitative variables also can be considered as measures that focus on the use of words to describe people, events, or characteristics. The quality of the environment, setting, or location of an occupational therapy clinic might be described as warm, open, and relaxed. Qualitative data usually refer to measures using words to describe characteristics or traits, whereas quantitative data are characterized by numbers or amounts. Rather than using verbal descriptions to characterize traits, people, or events, quantitative measurements rely on numbers to do so. Variables measured quantitatively can include such factors as age, ability, aptitude, or intelligence.

Function of Variables in the Research Design

Other dimensions of variables relate to the role or function of variables in a research design. Variables can be classified as either descriptive or explanatory, dependent or independent, or attribute or treatment. These classifications refer to the role or function of the variable in the research design. These classifications represent another way of describing variables. It is essential to have a solid understanding of the ways in which variables of interest can be categorized or described.

Variables take on certain functions in a research study, depending in part on the nature of the design. A variable is said to be descriptive only if it plays no function in the design beyond a mere account of its existence; it becomes explanatory when it is used to look for causes of circumstances or events. In a study of disabilities of clients and amelioration of those disabilities, the disabilities themselves might be a descriptive variable only. To illustrate, the researcher could report the percentage of cases with head injuries, spinal cord injuries, and post-surgical injuries without trying to relate those disabilities to effects of treatment. In such a study, the variable of disabilities can be considered a descriptive variable. If, on the other hand, the researcher designed a study looking at the effects of different types of treatment procedures on the various classes of disabilities, then the variable of disabilities can be considered an explanatory variable.

Another way to classify variables is to look at whether or not they can be considered as independent or dependent variables regarding the research design. An independent variable is presumed to be the cause or the variable manipulated by the examiner. A dependent variable is considered the effect or outcome. To illustrate, in a study of postrotary nystagmus, variables could be identified for the length of time vestibular stimulation was provided and for the duration of nystagmus after stimulation. In this case the independent variable (the variable manipulated by the examiner) is the length of time vestibular stimulation was provided, whereas the dependent variable (or response variable) is the duration of the nystagmus.

Kerlinger (1973) breaks down the independent variable even further. He suggests that an independent variable may be an attribute either of an individual or a treatment. Attributes are variables such as age, ability, type of disability, or sex. These variables cannot be manipulated by the researcher, but can be effectively used in a research design. A treatment variable, on the other hand, is an independent variable that can be manipulated by the researcher. Examples of treatment variables include duration of training, type of program, and materials used in teaching, among others. Regardless of how a quantitative variable is classified, one can consider it in terms of the level at which it is measured. This is termed "level of measurement," which leads to the next section of this chapter.

Levels of Measurement

An important consideration regarding variables is the kind of data generated when the variables are measured. Data can be measured in various ways. It is important to be clear about the manner in which such data are measured because future use of the data for descriptive or inferential analysis is affected by the type or level of measurement. Statisticians usually think of data measurement in one of two ways. One way to measure data is to think of it as representative of either discrete categories or categories that could be represented on an underlying continuum. Another way to measure data is to identify four levels of measurement. Each approach, i.e., categorical and levels of measurement, will be discussed.

Categorical and Continuous Data

Another dimension of variables relates to the way in which variables are classified and the kind of data that are generated. As previously mentioned, many statisticians consider that variables can be measured in one of two ways: categorical or continuous.

Categorical variables are measured in such a way that characteristics, traits or behaviors can be assigned to any one of a number of discrete categories. Patients may be classified according to causes of disabilities such as spinal cord injury, trauma, or neurologic dysfunction. In contrast, continuous variables are measured in such a way that the values range along a continuum with an inherently underlying numerical distribution. For example, patients can be measured on a scale rating the amount of muscle movement where zero represents no movement and ten represents maximum movement. Goniometric measurements of range of motion and recordings of muscle strength or duration of nystagmus are examples of continuous variables in rehabilitation.

Categorical variables can be either dichotomous or polytomous. This principle is illustrated in one study where a variable "level of handicap" is

placed into a simple dichotomous condition such that an individual is classified as handicapped or non-handicapped. If a researcher's purpose suggests
that multiple classifications are more desirable, the researcher might enu-
merate handicaps such as physically handicapped, mentally retarded, emo-
tionally disturbed, or developmentally disabled. However, in this latter case,
the variable may no longer be termed dichotomous. In another example, a
therapist studying patient performance in activities of daily living might
classify the variable "level of independence" into the dichotomous categories
of dependent or independent or into the polytomous categories of dependent, maximal assist needed, minimal assist needed, and independent.

Determination of whether a variable should be dichotomous or polytomous depends on the purpose of the research, the nature of data being
collected, and the types of statistical techniques to be used. It is essential that
sufficient categories are included at the onset of an investigation to allow the
research analyst to obtain the optimum information available. Should a
decision to collapse categories be made at some later point in an investigation,
the analyst has the option available. However, if insufficient categories have
been used to classify variables, one cannot easily add categories after the data
have been collected.

Often when categorical variables are used, a researcher elects to assign
numbers to the various categories. It is important to remember, however, that
the assignment of numbers is purely arbitrary and without arithmetic meaning. In the study described above, 0 or 1 (or 1 and 0) can be assigned to the
dichotomous variable of handicap or non-handicap. Note that the choice of
which number to assign to which condition is arbitrary. The same is true in
the polytomous example. The numbers 0 through 10 (or 10 through 0) or any
other numbers can be assigned to the handicapping conditions. Again,
whether variables have been dichotomized or placed into multiple categories,
the assignment of numbers to categories is solely for the purpose of labeling
and arithmetic calculations are meaningless. Somewhat differently, continuous variables are measured in such a way that numbers assigned to them have
real meaning. For example, if achievement levels of students are measured,
values can range along a continuum from zero to the maximum score on a
test. Thus, if Case A receives a score of 80 on one test, Case B receives a score
of 60, and Case C receives a score of 40, it can be said that Case A scored
higher than Case B and Case C, and Case B scored higher than Case C. Case
A's and Case B's scores cannot be arbitrarily reversed without losing inherent
meaning.

Another example of a continuous variable involves a researcher studying
the degree to which a student met an educational goal. Case workers might
be asked to rate the degree to which a student met the goal. Using a three-
point scale of "did not meet," "met," and "exceeded," numbers such as 1, 2,
and 3 can be assigned to this scale. Although the order of the assignment of
the numbers could be reversed, the numbers take on values representing
more or less of the characteristic of goal-meeting behavior. In this example,
the variable of meeting the educational goal is assumed to be measured with
some continuous underlying distribution.

Clinicians sometimes may use continuous variables in studying the effects of a treatment on a certain type of condition. For example, a therapist studying the effects of neurodevelopmental therapy on the development of spasticity in a hemiplegic patient might rate the spasticity according to a scale of 1 (spasticity not appreciable), 2 (minimal spasticity), 3 (moderate spasticity), and 4 (severe spasticity). Similarly, in a study of sensory techniques applied to patients in a coma, the Glasgow Coma Scale might be used to classify patient arousal (Umphred, 1985). In these examples, the numbers are assumed to indicate an underlying continuous distribution even though only some of the points on the distribution are measured. The numbers also are assumed to represent an amount or quantity of the variable under study. The important concept to understand is that categorical variables fall into discrete categories in contrast to continuous variables that range along a continuum.

Four Levels of Measurement

Instead of considering the dichotomous distinction of categorical or continuous variables, the categories of nominal, ordinal, interval, or ratio level of measurement can be used for variable classification.

Nominal. Nominal variables can be classified according to discrete or categorical conditions. To illustrate, the value of "one" can be assigned to blue eyes, the value of "two" to brown eyes, and the value of "three" to all other eye colors. While numbers have been assigned to these values, the assignment is done arbitrarily. It would have been equally valid to assign the value of "one" to blue eyes, "three" to brown eyes, and "two" to all other eye colors. The numbers represent labeling schemes and can be interchanged because they have no inherent meaning. Researchers usually assign numbers to nominal variables for ease in analysis, especially when using a computer. Typical variables measured at the nominal level are geographic area of birth, religion, or color of eyes.

Ordinal. A second level of measurement used to classify certain variables is the ordinal level. Ordinal variables are classified according to rank. When numbers are assigned to categories dependent on the ordering of "more to less" or "first to last," the numbers have real meaning beyond mere labels. Thus, we can assign the rank of "one" to the winner of a horse race, "two" to the horse that comes in second, and "three" to the third place finisher. Measurement at the ordinal level is at a higher level than nominal measurement. Thus, the numbers represent more than simple labeling schemes; rather they represent ranks and cannot be interchanged.

Ordinal scales demand that the categories be mutually exclusive and that each level be classified in terms of relative magnitude when compared with the others. The intervals between each category, however, cannot be assumed equal. Consider the following Likert scale measuring frequency of occurrence:

1 = almost never
2 = seldom
3 = occasionally
4 = regularly but infrequently
5 = regularly and often

In this scale, the interval between 1 and 2, for example, is probably not equal to the interval between 2 and 3 or that between 3 and 4. Surveys frequently use a ranking mechanism for the measurement of ordinal varia-bles. For example, a respondent might be asked to rank the types of splints used most often, the types of patient education techniques used, or the relative effectiveness of several group tasks.

Interval. A level of measurement that goes beyond either nominal or ordinal is that of interval measurement. Interval variables can be classified according to a particular system of ordering that includes both order and known and equal intervals between the points. Thus, when Case A received a score of 80 on a test, Case B received a score of 60, and Case C a score of 40, the 20-point difference between Case A's score and Case B's score is equal to the 20-point difference between Case B's score and Case C's score. These 20-point differences probably represent equal numbers of correct items. Thus, interval level of measurement represents both order and equal distances between the points.

Test scores as well as scores on psychological attribute scales often are measured on an interval scale. The numbers obtained represent equal units with an arbitrary zero point. What does an arbitrary zero point mean? To illustrate, think of a zero score on an IQ test. A score of zero on an intelligence test does not mean that the examinee has no intelligence; it only means that on that specific sampling of intelligence, no score was achieved. The zero point was set arbitrarily by the test developer. Another example of interval scale data is that of temperature. Temperature is measured in equal units or degrees. The equal intervals between the units can be added or subtracted. Again, the zero point is arbitrary and does not mean total absence of heat.

Ratio. The highest level of measurement according to this classification scheme is at the ratio level. Ratio variables are somewhat different from those previously mentioned. They can be classified according to all of the same criteria, but they have one additional characteristic. Measurement assumes an absolute zero point. Typical measures on a ratio scale might include weight, range of motion, two-point tactile discrimination, and grip strength.

Typically, measures of intelligence, attitude, or abilities are measured at only the first three measurement levels. In many of the clinically based disciplines, ordinal level of measurement is widely used. Variables such as a therapist's ranking of clients who are in need of treatment, identification of schools with regard to number of students served, or selection and ranking of students with behavior problems are all examples of variables measured at the ordinal level.

Some variables in the social sciences are measured at the interval level. Variables frequently measured at this level include teacher-constructed tests, intelligence levels, achievement measures, or incidences of misbehavior.

Although most variables are measured at only one level, some variables can be thought of as being measured at either the ordinal or the interval level. These typically include variables that are measured using a Likert-type scale. They often include such measures of attitude or behavior as self concept or locus of control. There is some disagreement as to whether these Likert distributions fall within the realm of ordinal or interval measurements because of the inability to assume equal distances between values. The dis-tance from "strongly disagree" to "disagree" may be different than the dis-tance from "disagree" to "agree," thus raising the question of whether or not it is appropriate to classify these kind of measures as interval level. The researcher should be aware of potential problems of statistical analysis of these types of data at the interval level.

It is desirable to measure a variable at the most sensitive level. Therefore, a therapist designing a study should measure a variable in the most precise way so as not to lose information. For example, a therapist may conduct a study where range of motion is a variable. Any of the following types of classifications could be used. At the nominal level, measurement of range of motion may be designated as either normal or abnormal. At the ordinal level, measurement of range of motion can be in the following categories or ranks: 1 = 0 to 20 degrees, 2 = 21 to 40 degrees, 3 = 41 to 60 degrees, and 4 = 61 to 80 degrees. At the interval or ratio level, the actual measurement of degrees of movement would be recorded. Upon inspection one can readily see that the interval or ratio level of measurement conveys the most information.

As previously mentioned, it is important that one decide on the level of measurement when first designing a study. While it is easy to convert more sensitive levels of measurement to less sensitive levels, it is impossible to convert low level data to a higher level. As an example, consider a therapist who wants to study the effectiveness of a sensory program on return of tactile discrimination. It would be desirable to measure tactile discrimination on a ratio scale (that is, record the actual two-point discrimination measurement) rather than use a ranking of the measurement. One cannot, however, take the ranking of a measure and convert it to an actual numerical measurement. In contrast, the actual measurement can be converted easily to a ranking at a later date.

Scale	Characteristics	Examples
Nominal	Mutually exclusive categories. Numbers do not reflect any order and have no inherently meaningful mathematical qualities.	Sex, race, diagnosis such as gravitational insecurity, tactile defensiveness, left side body neglect, etc.
Ordinal	Numbers do indicate relative magnitude or order. However, it cannot be assumed that intervals are equal between numbers.	Percentile ranks, income rankings, level of awareness, muscle strength, grades, IQ scores
Interval	Numbers represent magnitude with equal intervals between numbers and an arbitrary zero point.	Temperature, IQ scores
Ratio	Has all of the characteristics of interval level data and, in addition, has a meaningful zero point.	Weight, range of motion, time, distance, height

Figure 1.1. Characteristics of the four levels of measurement (Hopkins, Glass, Hopkins: *Basic Statistics for the Behavioral Sciences* (2nd ed) (1987) (Adapted by permission of Prentice Hall, Inc.)

Table 1.1
Frequency Count of Intelligence Test Scores for a Group of Students who are Handicapped (n=100)

Test Score	Frequency
52	4
66	4
67	3
69	3
71	5
73	4
77	3
78	3
79	2
80	5
82	3
83	5
84	4
85	4
87	1
88	6
89	5
90	6
91	7
92	6
93	5
98	1
100	2
104	2
107	4
110	3

A chart showing the four levels of measurement is provided in Figure 1-1.

In reviewing this figure, one might wonder why intelligence quotient scores are classified as both ordinal and interval. These scores are clearly of a higher level than ordinal scores because more than a ranking number is achieved. Intelligence quotient scores, however, do not necessarily represent equal units between numbers as is required of interval level data. For example, the difference in intelligence level between intelligence scores of 60 and 100 probably is not the same as the difference between scores of 90 and 130 (see Hopkins and Glass, 1978, for an interesting discussion of this problem). To summarize, nominal measurement shows difference in type, ordinal in rank, and interval or ratio in amount (Kovacs, 1985).

Presentation of Data

Whatever methods the researcher chooses to measure data, the manner in which the data and organized and summarized is important. Data can be summarized in two ways: graphically and numerically. Each method will be discussed in turn. There are a variety of ways in which data can be displayed graphically. In this section, several means to present data are considered.

Frequency Tables and Distributions

Frequency distributions are among the most common ways of displaying data. A frequency table is a count of the number of times a given characteristic or behavior occurs. Table 1-1 displays a frequency count of intelligence test scores for a group of 100 handicapped students.

Sometimes it is preferable to group data before displaying a frequency table. Table 1-2 shows how these same scores may be grouped to display the data more meaningfully.

As another example, in a study of splint effectiveness on the increase in active wrist flexion, the therapist might have range of motion as a ratio level dependent variable. Table 1-3 shows a frequency distribution for such measurements.

Table 1.2
Cumulative Frequency Distribution of Intelligence Test
Scores for Students who are Handicapped (n=100)

Score Interval	Frequency	Cumulative Frequency	Cumulative Percentage
50-59	4	4	4%
60-69	10	14	14%
70-79	17	31	31%
80-89	33	64	64%
90-99	25	89	89%
100-109	8	97	97%
110-119	3	100	100%

Table 1.3
Cumulative Frequency Distribution of Degrees
of Active Wrist Flexion (n=48)

Measurement (in degrees)	Frequency	Cumulative Frequency	Cumulative Percentage
5	1	1	2.08
7	1	2	4.17
8	1	3	6.25
10	1	4	8.33
13	3	7	14.58
15	5	12	25.00
25	7	19	39.58
35	9	28	58.33
42	5	33	68.75
55	4	37	77.08
62	5	42	87.50
67	3	45	93.75
70	3	48	100.00

Table 1.4
Cumulative Frequency Distribution of Degrees of Active
Wrist Flexion Using Intervals (n=48)

Measurement (in degrees)	Frequency	Cumulative Frequency	Cumulative Percentage
0-9	3	3	6.25
10-19	9	12	25.00
20-29	7	19	39.58
30-39	9	28	58.33
40-49	5	33	68.75
50-59	4	37	77.08
60-69	8	45	93.75
70-79	3	48	100.00

For ease of presentation, the measurements are grouped into intervals in Table 1-4. Also included in these tables are the cumulative frequency and the cumulative percentage.

These last two columns are useful for quick, informal data analysis. For example, Table 1-4 readily reveals that 28 out of 48 subjects (or 58%) had a measurement of wrist flexion of 39 degrees or less. Thus a cumulative frequency table is one method of organizing and displaying data in a meaningful way.

Graphs and Charts

Sometimes a frequency table does not provide a clear picture of the distribution of scores. It might be preferable to display the data through means of a histogram, a bar chart, or a frequency polygon. A histogram is the presentation of data in graphic form where the frequencies are represented by means of connected bars, while bar graphs have spaces inserted between the bars. If categorical data are to be displayed, a bar graph is preferred. In contrast, if the researcher is graphing continuous data, a histogram is usually used.

The data described in Tables 1-1 and 1-2 can be constructed into a histogram or bar chart to illustrate more clearly the characteristics of the distribution. Figure 1-2 is a histogram of the data provided in Table 1-1.

For some readers, this graphic display of the distribution of intelligence scores is more easily understood than the numerical displays in Table 1-2. Bar graphs and histograms are of special value when displaying data to a group of therapists in an oral presentation. Specification of the units on a graph can greatly influence the visual effect and, therefore, require special attention. The graphs shown in Figures 1-3 and 1-4 depict identical information, although the graph in Figure 1-3 appears to show a significant difference in revenue for each therapist, while Figure 1-4 does not.

These figures represent different interpretations of the same data depending upon the units of revenue.

Similarly, in Figure 1-5, it can be seen that the data in Figure 1-6 show a

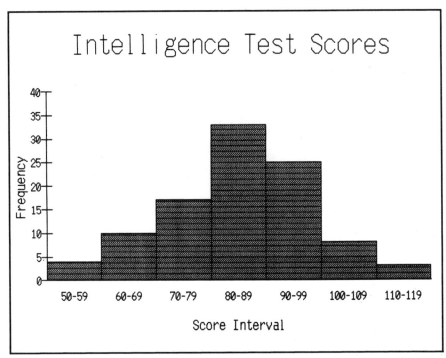

Figure 1-2. Histogram of intelligence test scores of students who are handicapped (n=100).

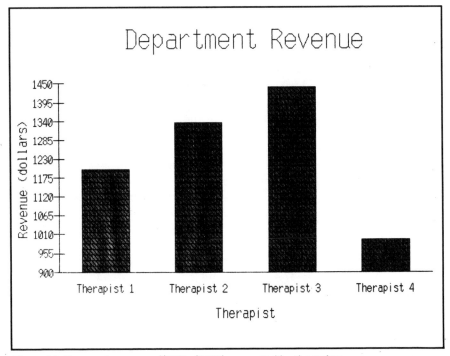

Figure 1-3. Bar graph revenue ($900 - $1450) generated by therapists.

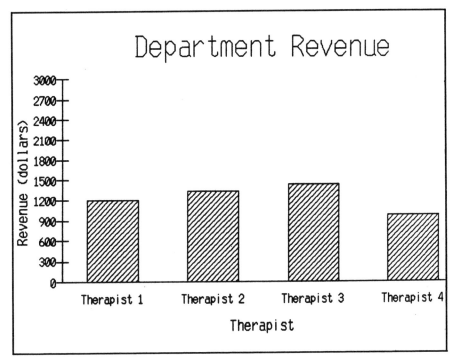

Figure 1-4. Bar graph of revenue ($0 - $3000) generated by therapists.

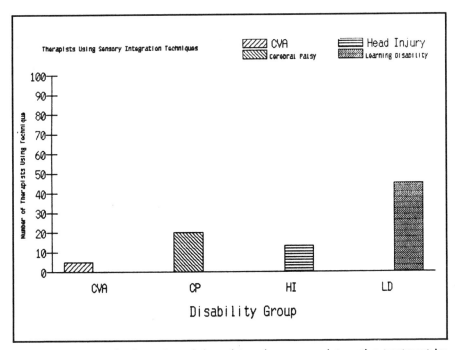

Figure 1-5. Bar graph of number of therapists using sensory integrative treatment by disability group (n=86).

Table 1.5
Percentage of Therapists by Speciality Area of Practice (n=112)

Specialty Area	Number	Percentage
Pediatrics	43	38.39%
Neurology	34	30.36%
Orthopedics	19	16.96%
General Medical/Surgical	6	5.36%
Psychiatry	10	8.93%
Total	112	100.00%

seemingly larger difference in terms of the numbers of therapists using sensory integration techniques with specified disability groups compared with Figure 1-5.

One must consider carefully the range of units given on the vertical axis. Although there is no absolute method of determining the correct proportions, a clear and appealing graph has dimensions where the vertical axis is approximately three-fourths as long as the horizontal axis (Hayes, 1981). For a complete discussion of the manipulation of graphs, see Huff (1954). Nominal data, such as the data representing percentage of therapists by specialty area as shown in Table 1-5 can best be displayed in a bar graph or pie chart, as demonstrated by Figures 1-7 and 1-8, respectively.

Recognize that because this data is not continuous, it makes no sense to attempt a continuous graph, such as a histogram or frequency polygon.

An alternative method for displaying data is to use a frequency polygon or line graph. A frequency polygon is the presentation of data in graphic form whereby the frequencies are represented by means of lines connecting the midpoint of each interval. Figure 1-9 illustrates the use of a frequency polygon to display the data on intelligence scores summarized in Table 1-1.

Figure 1-10 shows the use of a line graph as another possible means of depicting data.

In this graph, two sets of data are shown: the use of computers and the use of standard techniques for perceptual retraining. One of the distinct advantages of a line graph is that several sets of data or representations of numerous variables can be overlayed on the same graph, thus allowing for easy comparison. Although any type of data can be displayed in graphic form, a distribution cannot be formed unless the data has an implied or actual numerical underpinning. The manner in which data are displayed depends on the nature of the data and the uses to be made of such data.

Distribution of Variables

As mentioned previously, a variable can take on many different values. The distributions of these values can be characterized along many dimensions, the sum of which constitutes the shape of a distribution.

The distributions of the values representing variables can be thought of

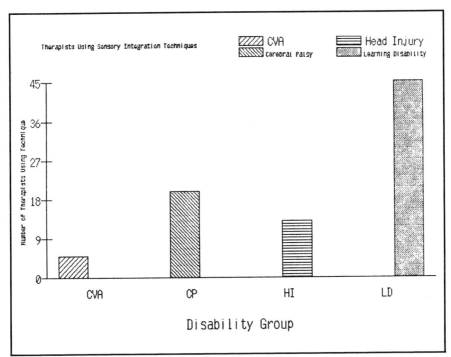

Figure 1-6. Bar graph of number of therapists using sensory integrative treatment by disability group (n=86).

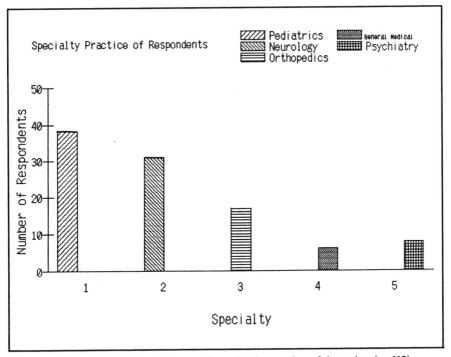

Figure 1-7. Bar graph of specialty area of practice by number of therapists (n=112).

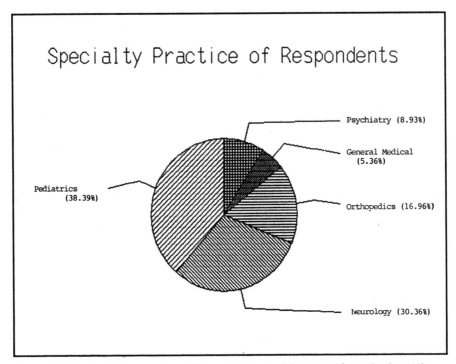

Figure 1-8. Pie chart of percentage of therapists in specialty areas of practice (n=112).

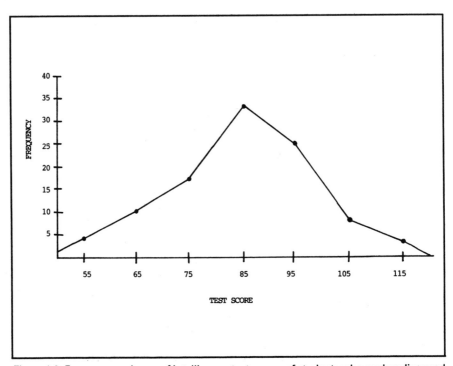

Figure 1-9. Frequency polygon of intelligence test scores of students who are handicapped (n=100).

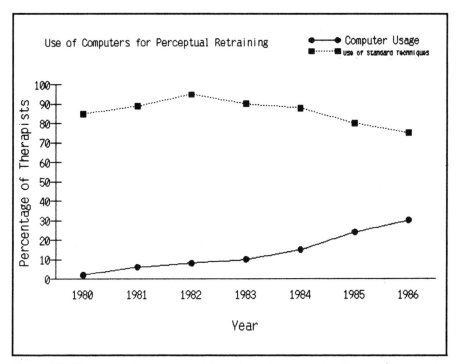

Figure 1-10. Line graph of percentage of therapists using computers for perceptual retraining.

along four dimensions. The first dimension, or moment, is a description of the central tendency of a distribution. Central tendency is considered the single most descriptive information about a distribution. The second dimension of a distribution is the variability of the distribution about its center. This is sometimes referred to as the second moment. The third moment is represented by the symmetry of a distribution and refers to the equality of distributions of scores on each side of its center. Kurtosis is the fourth property, or fourth moment, of a distribution. It refers to the peakedness or flatness of a distribution.

Many research studies in occupational and physical therapy as well as those in education, health, and the social sciences assume certain properties of the moments that are actually properties of normal distributions. Figure 1-11 represents the familiar normal or bell-shaped curve.

All normal curves have certain unique properties or characteristics. Normal curves have a single mode and are symmetrical and smooth. Normal curves change shape from convex to concave at the exact point represented by one standard deviation on either side of the mean; and, the equal length tails of a normal curve approach, but do not touch, the horizontal axis as they deviate from the mean.

It has been assumed by social scientists that many variables are normally distributed. If that is true, then the standard of comparison for distributions is the normal curve. Treating a particular variable as being normally distributed permits the researcher to make many assumptions about certain

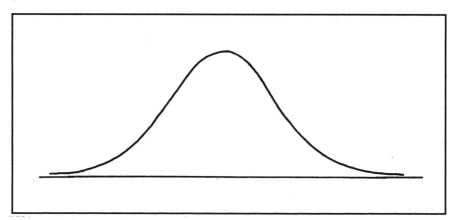

Figure 1-11. The normal curve.

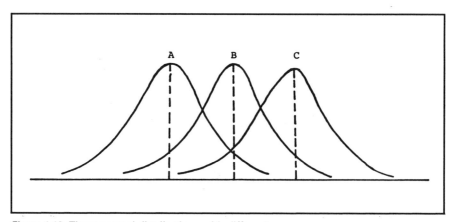

Figure 1-12. Three normal distributions with different means.

characteristics of the variable. However, not all variables are normally distributed and, in some data sets, it is difficult to determine if the distributions approximate normality.

Most inferential statistical techniques, that is parametric statistical techniques that are used to make inferences about a population, require an assumption of normality about the variable in the population. This is an important assumption, because those statistical techniques use the known mathematical properties of the normal distribution. A careless decision to "assume normality" when the distribution is actually skewed or otherwise misshapen, may greatly affect the validity of the results when inferential statistics are used.

When distributions do not approximate normality, alternate means of identifying and decribing the location, spread, and shape of these variables must be used. This topic is discussed more fully in Chapter Seven.

There are various statistics that can be used to describe each of the four moments of a distribution. The next section considers examples of each of these.

Measures of Central Tendency

A measure of central tendency summarizes in a single index one of the most important characteristics of a distribution. This characteristic often is a measure of the location of the majority of data. Although measures of central tendency are appropriate statistics to describe the centrality of the distribution, such measures may be misleading for asymmetrical or non-normal distributions.

The most commonly used measures of central tendency are the mean, the median, and the mode. The mean of a distribution is a summarizing statistic, defined as the sum of all values in a single distribution divided by the number of cases in that distribution. It is commonly referred to as the arithmetic mean or average and is expressed mathematically by the following:

$$\mu = \frac{\Sigma X_i}{N}$$

where:
μ = the population mean
ΣX_i = the sum of all observations
N = the total number of observations

Figure 1-12, after Ferguson (1976), displays three normal distributions with identical shapes and different measures of central tendency.

It can be seen that the mean of distribution A is lower than the mean of distributions B and C. The only difference among the three figures is the location of the mean. To relate this figure to a clinical example, distribution A might represent a control group of patients who received no treatment, distribution B might represent a group of patients who received an inferior treatment method, and distribution C would represent those patients who received the more effective treatment method.

The median of a distribution is another summary statistic representing a central position of a distribution. It is defined as the point in a distribution at which half of the observations fall above, and half fall below. Thus, by definition, in any distribution there will always be an equal number of observations above the median and below it.

The mode of a distribution also is a summary statistic representing the most frequently occurring value or values. Distributions can be unimodal, bimodal, or even multimodal. In all likelihood, many distributions of variables in clinical research will be bimodal or multimodal.

The "Best" Measure of Central Tendency

Determination of the "best" measure of central tendency depends on what one is trying to accomplish. In a normal curve, the mean, median, and mode are in the same location, in the exact center of the distribution. Because inferential statistics make use of the mean, it is then the best measure to use when a variable is normally distributed. If a normal distribution cannot be assumed, then nonparametric analysis should be used. In nonparametric tests, the median rather than the mean often is used as the preferred measure to describe the central tendency of the data.

In using a measure of central tendency as a "best guess" about a population parameter or value, the mean is the recommended measure of central tendency when one wants to be as close as possible "on the average" and when one also wants to consider the signs and magnitudes of the errors. Over a number of guesses, the signs and magnitudes of the errors will cancel out, resulting in the smallest average signed error. On the other hand, if one wants to guess as closely as possible on the average without regarding average signed error, the median is the best indicator because it is the middle score (Hayes, 1981).

As an example of the bias created by an inappropriate measure of central tendency in a small, skewed sample, consider the following situation. An occupational therapist is interviewing for a position in a department with four other therapists. She is told that, although her exact salary has not yet been determined, the average salary in the department is $31,600. Thinking that this salary is attractive, the therapist agrees to take the position. She is rudely awakened when she discovers that, in actuality, the salaries follow the following distribution:

Administrator: $90,000
Chief O.T.: $20,000
Staff O.T.: $16,000
Staff O.T.: $16,000
Staff O.T.: $16,000 (her position)

In a skewed distribution such as the one above, the mean is quite different from the median and mode. In this example, although the mean salary is $31,600, both the median and mode are $16,000. It is evident that either the median or mode present a more accurate picture of the salary distribution.

The three most common measures of central tendency have been described in this section. It is important that a researcher determine the purpose of the research and the nature of the data before selecting which measure of central tendency best describes the central location of the data.

Measures of Variability

The mean, median, or mode are the best indicators of the central tendency or similarity in a distribution of scores; however, it is insufficient to rely on these measures of central tendency to give an accurate portrait of a distribution. To more fully describe a distribution, measures of variability are also necessary. Variation exists in many distributions, resulting in scores being dispersed or scattered about some point or points. The most commonly used measures of dispersion are the range, the variance, and the standard deviation.

The range is the simplest of all indices of variability. It is defined as the difference between the highest and lowest values of the distribution. Because it is based on the minimum and maximum values, the use of the range as the sole measure of variability can be misleading. One data point that is extremely distant from the rest of the points in the distribution can yield a range that is not representative of a distribution as a whole. For example, consider the two frequency distributions, distribution A and distribution B, shown in Table 1-6. Although both look similar, distribution A has one value of 10, which is far different than the other values.

Table 1.6
Frequency Distributions A and B

Distribution A

Number	Frequency	Cumulative Frequency	Cumulative Percentage
10	1	1	2.22
50	5	6	13.33
55	7	13	28.89
57	10	23	51.11
62	8	31	68.89
65	9	40	88.89
70	5	45	100.00

Distribution B

Number	Frequency	Cumulative Frequency	Cumulative Percentage
50	3	3	6.82
53	6	9	20.45
57	11	20	45.45
61	9	29	65.91
67	10	39	88.64
70	5	44	100.00

Such a value may be referred to as an outlier. An outlier is an unusually high or low data point that might be legitimate, or might represent error in the measurement or recording of data. Because distribution A has the value of 10 as an outlier, the range for distribution A is 10 to 70, while the range for distribution B is 50 to 70. The presence of this outlier suggests that in certain circumstances the range is an unstable and misleading index of variability, and a more sensitive measure should be used.

A somewhat related measure of variability divides a distribution into four equal portions. The distance between the first and third portions is referred to as the interquartile range. Some researchers further elaborate on this concept and calculate a semi-interquartile range or the quartile deviation, which is the midpoint of the distance between the first and third quartiles. Both these measures of variability are more stable than the range because they exclude the values at the extreme of the distributions. However, there are other measures of variability that provide even more stability than the range, interquartile range, or quartile deviation.

Variance and standard deviation are the two measures of variability thought to be most stable. They are usually used with normally distributed, interval-level data. The variance is best thought of as the sum of the squared differences of each individual value from the mean divided by the number of cases in the distribution. Stated another way, the variance is an average squared deviation about a mean. The standard deviation is the square root of the variance and often is preferred to the variance as a measure of dispersion.

This is so because standard deviation is expressed in the same metric as the data whose spread it is representing, making its interpretation more intuitively comprehensible. The mathematical formulae for variance and standard deviation are provided below.

Variance

$$\sigma^2 = \frac{\Sigma(X_i - \mu)^2}{N}$$

Standard Deviation

$$\sigma = \sqrt{\frac{\Sigma(X_i - \mu)^2}{N}}$$

where:

σ^2 = the population variance
Σ = the sum of
X_i = each observation
μ = the population mean
σ = the population standard deviation
N = the number of cases

Figure 1-13 displays three distributions with the same mean and different dispersions.

The variability of scores is clearly much greater in distribution C than in either of the other two distributions. In other words, distribution A might represent patients who were all very homogeneous on the variable being measured, and distribution C represented patients who were heterogeneous on the variable being measured. If these curves represented the amount of spasticity in three groups of patients, distribution A would represent those patients who all had approximately the same amount of spasticity, distribution B would represent a group of patients with more variability in the amount of spasticity, and distribution C would represent a group of patients where a wide variety of spastic conditions was encountered.

As another example, concepts of variability may be understood easily if one considers the difference between the grade point averages (GPA) of graduate students versus undergraduate students. A distribution of GPAs for third-year graduate students would be much less variable than a distribution for undergraduate students. Graduate students are a much more homogeneous group, because a certain amount of selection has already taken place. There is, therefore, a much less variable performance in grades obtained.

Because the variance and the standard deviation are measures of the distance of each individual value from the mean of a distribution, both measures are somewhat sensitive to extremes in the data. However, they are not as sensitive to extreme scores as the range. Even though these measures of variability are the most sensitive of the measures of variability, their use for data that are not normally distributed has been questioned by some.

As suggested earlier, the key to determining which statistic to use to describe the central tendency and variability of a distribution rests with the researcher. There is no one best measure of variability, just as there is no one best measure of central tendency. The researcher must be guided in the

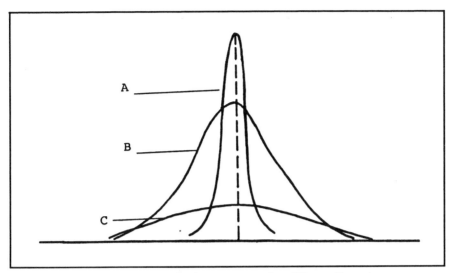

Figure 1-13. Three distributions with the same mean but different dispersions.

selection of an appropriate statistic by the nature of the research purpose and the nature of the available data.

Measures of Symmetry

In addition to measures of central tendency and measures of dispersion, the third moment that defines a distribution of a variable is skewness, or the degree to which a distribution departs from symmetry. Symmetry is one of the characteristics of the normal curve. The departure from symmetry, or the degree of symmetry of a distribution, is defined as its skewness.

A distribution can be skewed positively or negatively. A positive skew indicates a preponderance of scores below the mean of a distribution, with fewer scores at the upper end of the distribution. Figure 1-14 is a representation of a positively skewed distribution.

Many types of samples may yield a positively skewed distribution. Examples of positively skewed distributions that may be familiar to the clinical investigator are a sample of dynamometer measurements for grasp in a group of patients with median nerve damage, scores on tests of visual perception for a group of stroke patients with right hemisphere damage, and scores on an assertiveness scale for patients with low self-esteem. All of these examples show a greater proportion of scores at the low end of the distribution. An extreme case of positive skewness yields a "J-curve" (Ferguson, 1976; Walberg, Strykowski, Royal and Hung, 1984).

Conversely, a negative skew indicates a majority of scores above the mean with fewer scores at the lower end of the distribution. A negatively skewed distribution is depicted in Figure 1-15.

Some examples of negatively skewed distributions are as follows: dynamometer readings for a group of weight trainers, muscle strength measurements for a group of aerobic instructors, and the scores of 12-year-old children on a perceptual test that is designed to test 5-year-old children. The

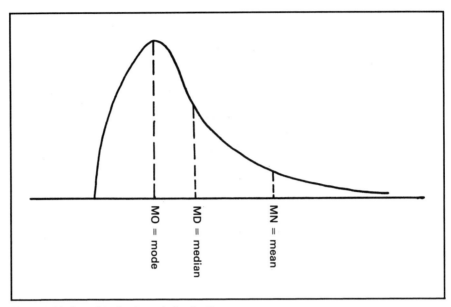

Figure 1-14. A positively skewed distribution.

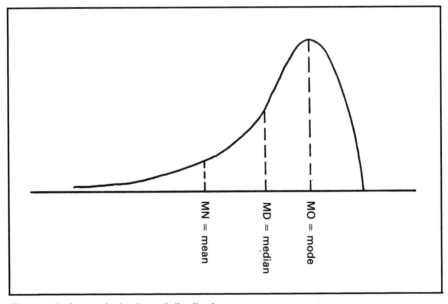

Figure 1-15. A negatively skewed distribution.

underemphasis on normality of distributions can lead to errors of interpretation of data in clinical research (Royeen, 1986). Evidence is beginning to accumulate that the numbers and varieties of known distributions with positive skews have been understated and underidentified by researchers (Walberg, Strykowski, Royal and Hung, 1984). The degree of skewness of a distribution is most important in any calculation involving means and variances because of the undue weight of the preponderance of values at one or the other end of the distribution. The more a distribution is skewed, the more the distance increases between the mean, median, and mode (Glass and Hopkins, 1984).

In distributions that are skewed, medians and interquartile ranges are more representative measures than means and variances, but not perfect solutions. In cases of extreme skewness, no measure of location or spread accurately reflects the shape of the distribution. Only a visual representation will reveal the true characteristics of such a distribution. Hartwig and Dearing (1979) suggest stem and leaf displays or box and whisker plots as two possible visual representations. Those procedures will be described in Chapter Four.

Kurtosis

Kurtosis is the fourth moment defining the nature of a distribution. It is a measure of the peakedness or flatness of a distributional curve compared with that of a normal distribution. Technically, kurtosis measures the degree to which the rate of acceleration of the frequency of scores in a distribution differs from the inflection of the normal curve that is located exactly one standard deviation above and below the mean (Cooley and Lohnes, 1968). Kurtosis examines whether the values in a distribution concentrate either at the center of a distribution or at the tails, and to what degree those concentrations are different from those of the normal curve.

Thus, a normal curve is said to be mesokurtic or of medium kurtosis (Ray, 1962). Departures from the normal are measured and can be either positive or negative. Measures of positive kurtosis indicate peakedness, while negative kurtosis indicates distributions flatter than normal.

A peaked distribution is shown in Figure 1-16. The leptokurtic (slender or narrow curve) distribution portrayed in this figure has some data points at the center of the distribution and some in the tails.

The distribution has fewer data points in the area between the center and the extreme, where the bulk of the data would fall in a normally distributed sample.

Figure 1-17 shows a variety of platykurtic or flat distributions.

To one degree or another, the data points in these curves fall in a wider, more even band around the mean than they would in a normal distribution. Clinically, one might see a distribution such as this in a case where a test of visual perception designed for children ages six to eight was given to a large group of children ages three to ten. This type of group would have a wide variety of scores with the distribution being more spread out and flatter.

Transformations

Because parametric statistical tests assume the presence of normally distributed populations with equal variances, in certain cases it may be desirable to transform non-normally distributed variables. Sometimes, these data can be transformed into a normal distribution through non-linear transformations (Edwards, 1985).

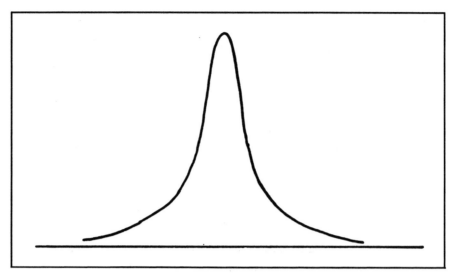

Figure 1-16. A leptokurtic distribution.

Linear vs Non-Linear Transformations

A linear transformation of the type Y = ax + b, where a = the new mean, b = the new standard deviation, X = the z score, and Y = the transformed score is commonly used to convert a z score (a standard deviation score) into a more convenient form. Because z scores are numbers that have a mean of zero and a standard deviation of one and can be positive or negative, their usefulness for communication of test scores may be limited. For example, on an IQ test a person may have scored exactly one standard deviation above the mean (z = +1.0). However, it is intuitively unappealing and uninformative to speak of a person's IQ as 1.0. One approach is to transform this score without changing its inherent meaning. The score is transformed by the equation Y = (100 × 1.0) + 16. This equation follows the format Y = ax + b, and the new mean is 100 with a standard deviation of 16. In this specific example, the transformed score would be 116. One could then speak of a person's IQ as 116 rather than 1.0, a metric that is more understandable.

In contrast to a linear transformation, which results in a new distribution that has the same shape as the original, a non-linear transformation results in a distribution with a new shape. To determine the appropriate type of transformation to use, one must determine the mean, variance, and standard deviation of the original distribution. The following classes of transformations may be useful.

If the mean is proportional to the variance for each treatment group, a square root transformation may be used successfully to obtain a normal distribution. This can be expressed by:

X' = X + 0.5
Where: X' is the transformed number

If the mean is proportional to the standard deviation, then a logarithmic transformation may be helpful in obtaining a normal distribution. This can be expressed mathematically by: $X' = \log X$.

If there is heterogeneity of variance when the dependent variable is time, a reciprocal transformation may be useful: $X' = (1 \div X)$.

The first two transformations deal with the problem of normality, the last transformation helps to assure homogeneity of variance where that assumption cannot be met using the original distribution. After performing a transformation, statistical tests are then done using the newly transformed data. Although these transformations may sound formidable, they are not as troublesome as they appear because most major statistical packages (Norusis,

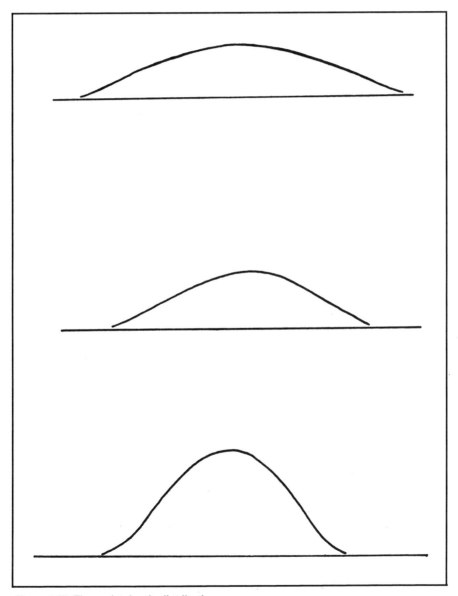

Figure 1-17. Three platykurtic distributions.

1983; Helwig, 1985) will transform data in the desired way and a manual transformation is relatively simple with small data sets.

Summary

This chapter has considered the central theme of distributions. Definitions of variables and their various dimensions were discussed, and alternative means of measuring variables were covered. The graphic and tabular display of data were presented. A discussion of distributions of variables with regard to measures of central tendency, measures of dispersion, symmetry, and kurtosis followed. The chapter ended with a section on transformation of variables.

References

Cooley, W., and Lohnes, P. (1968). *Introduction to statistical procedures: With computer exercises.* New York: Wiley.

Edwards, A. (1985). *Experimental design in psychological research.* (5th ed.). New York: Harper and Row.

Ferguson, G. (1976). *Statistical analysis in psychology and education.* New York: McGraw Hill.

Glass, G., and Hopkins, K.D. (1984). *Statistical methods in education and psychology.* Englewood Cliffs, N.J.: Prentice-Hall.

Hartwig and Dearing (1979) *Exploratory data analysis.* Beverly Hills: Sage Publishing Company.

Hayes, W. (1981). *Statistics.* (3rd ed.). New York: Holt, Rinehart and Winston.

Helwig, J. (1985). *SAS introductory guide.* Cary, N.C.: SAS Institute.

Hopkins, K., and Glass, G. (1978). *Basic statistics for the behavioral sciences.* Englewood Cliffs, N.J.: Prentice-Hall.

Huff, D. (1954). *How to lie with statistics.* New York: Norton Press.

Kerlinger, F. (1973). *Foundations of behavioral research.* New York: Holt, Rinehart and Winston.

Kovacs, A. (1985). *The research process: Essentials of skill development.* Philadelphia: F. A. Davis Company.

Norusis, M. (1983). *SPSSX introductory statistics guide.* Chicago: SPSS, Inc.

Ray, W. (1962). *Statistics in psychological research.* New York: Macmillan.

Royeen, C. (1986). *An exploration of parametric versus Nonparametric statistics in occupational therapy clinical research* (Doctoral dissertation). Blacksburg, Virginia: Virginia Polytechnic Institute and State University. (University Microfilms, Ann Arbor, MI: No. 8620659).

Umphred, D. (Ed.). (1985). *Neurological rehabilitation.* St. Louis: The C.V. Mosby Company.

Walberg, H., Strykowski, B., Royal, E., and Hung, S. (1984). Exceptional performance. *Review of Educational Research* 54(1):87-112, 1984.

CHAPTER 2

PROVISIONAL GUIDELINES FOR SAMPLING IN CLINICAL RESEARCH

Jim C. Fortune
Mary M. Bender

Chapter Overview

Research typically is conducted using only a part of the overall population to which the researcher wishes to generalize the results. This chapter addresses the issues that exist in choosing the part of the population to be studied: sampling in clinical research. The first part of the chapter discusses types of research and corresponding differences in sampling needs. Typical problems and difficulties concerning sampling in clinical research also are identified and discussed. The middle part of the chapter offers practical guides in the form of statistical formulae for calculating acceptable sample sizes appropriate for different types of research. The final part of the chapter suggests innovative solutions or procedures for sampling problems specific to experimentally based clinical research.

Introduction

Research in clinical settings contains ample opportunity for both reward and challenge. The design of research in a clinical setting must take into account the characteristics of the setting as well as the intent of the researcher and the unique attributes of the study population. The characteristics of the setting pose difficulties in research design due to a) a social expectation that clinics provide the loci of treatment and healing; b) the use of clinical diagnosis (identification of dysfunction) for the definition of client problems, which often form the basis of subject selection in a research study; c) natural nesting of small groups of clients within clinics; and d) unique differences in policies and interpretations of theory among clinics. The social expectation that clinics exist to remedy problems of individuals who come to clinics for treatment raises legal and ethical issues in the establishment of control groups. Rights of clients must be protected by having them sign "permission" waivers.

The design of research among clinics often must be compromised to include special interests of different clinic administrations. The necessity of obtaining individual agreements to participate in a study may establish dispositions on the part of the clients that affect their reactions to the experimental conditions, thus threatening the internal validity of the study. The necessity of negotiating cooperation among clinics introduces into the study the influence of volunteers, thereby threatening the external validity of the study. Internal and external validity of research are used here in the sense defined by Campbell and Stanley (1966). Internal validity refers to the ability of the researcher to reject the null hypothesis and accept the experimental hypothesis. External validity refers to the ability of the researcher to generalize the results of the study to the population of interest.

The use of diagnosis in defining client eligibility for a study introduces the potential of error in the definitions of study populations. Seldom in clinical practice can diagnosis be considered certain. Differences in the application of specific aspects of theory and in techniques used in diagnosis produce variance within clinical classifications. Some of this variance can be construed as normal variation or individual differences within the client group; however, a part of the variation can be attributed to incorrect diagnosis or incorrect problem identification. Due to the relation of diagnosis to research criteria or to an interaction between diagnostic error and treatment, the incorrect diagnosis can become a causal factor in the invalidation of research efforts.

Frequently, diagnosis involves the use of measurements, where relative status or the location of the client score with respect to a devised cut score is the basis for inclusion in the population. To illustrate the concept of the cut score, relative status age or intelligence quotient (IQ) may be used as examples. Should a 5-year-old child whose birthday is next week be considered a 5-year-old or a 6-year-old for research purposes? Even if there is a convention for handling some variables such as age within a research group, there should be some assurances that other related research groups and test developers use the same convention. With regard to IQ, is the child with a 140 IQ any more intelligent than the child with a 139 IQ? Probably not, but one child may qualify for the benefits of education programs for the gifted and the other may not. The cut score is the point on a continuous measure where a dichotomous decision for inclusion is made. With the lack of the reliability of many social science measures, the exactness of a cut score for a decision using a continuous variable is questionable. The necessity of the researcher having to determine a point or cut score for defining inclusion in a study population can bring about uncertainty that is not present in the use of nominal measurement for placement and population definition. In the latter case, the client either has or does not have the attribute of interest. There are no degrees of the attribute of interest.

The nesting or grouping of small groups within individual clinics adds complexity to research designs, even if across-clinic studies can be implemented. Individuals nested within a single group are apt to share some common attributes or experiences not shared by individuals within another nested group. Individual clinics provide situational variance that must be accounted for in research studies. Too often, the clinician-researcher limits the population of the study to those clients within a specific clinical setting. When this occurs, sample size and generalizability become major research limitations.

The differences among clinics with regard to policies and interpretations of theory provide a basis for situational variation and selectivity bias. For instance, some clinics may promote the use of drugs in treatment, while other clinics may discourage the use of drug-aided therapy. The use of drugs by a given clinic establishes a systematic client history in that particular setting that is not present in the other clinical settings included in the study, where drugs are not part of treatment. Situational variation also can be caused by the location of the clinic, leading to the presence of a unique client group, such as charity cases or exclusive clients; by the reputation of the clinic, causing self-selection on the part of the clients, such as those clients also suffering from heart disease; and by differential treatment of clients due to differences in clinical equipment or personnel. The difference in policy may result in exclusion of certain types of clinics and clients from research study.

Research opportunity in most clinical settings is enriched by the dependency of practice on research results. To some extent, communication networks and constructs are crystallized in clinical settings, creating a rich and rewarding support system for research. Benefits of research results often can be observed by the researcher in changes in practice and in progress of individual clients.

A critical dimension of any research study involves the composition and origin of those studied. If the subjects in a study comprise a population or universe of interest to the researcher, then the differences and relationships observed in the study are actual and no inference is needed. If the subjects are only members of a larger population to which the researcher wishes to infer or generalize the results of the study, then both the selection and configuration of those studied are important to the validity of the study.

This chapter will explain the role and function of sampling in clinical-based research, advance an argument for special considerations that a clinician should make in selecting research samples, and offer some cautions with regard to selected practices of questionable validity that can be found in clinical research literature. Most of the information presented in this chapter can be derived from any introductory research methodology text, but the discussion of the information is directed specifically toward application in a clinical setting.

Purpose of Research by Clinicians

Research can be defined as a systematic process of gathering and synthesizing empirical data so as to generate knowledge about a given population for a selected topic. The use of a sample in this research permits the researcher to establish a linkage between the subjects studied and the population about which knowledge is to be generated. The purpose of the research interacts with the characteristics of the population to determine the nature of the linkage and to establish the requirements for appropriate sample design.

Classification of Clinical Research

Generally, clinical research can be categorized into three classifications based on the purpose of the research. Researchers in clinical settings may seek to establish the incidence and/or intensity of one or more attributes in the general public, or the "normal" population, as illustrated by Royeen (1984). Here, the "normal" population refers to the group that includes individuals with and without the pathologic characteristics common to clients. In other studies, researchers may seek to study the relationships among an array of variables for a given clientele, as illustrated by Yerxa and Baum (1986). Finally, researchers may seek to validate the effects of a given treatment or the applicability of a given theory as Fisher, Mixon, and Herman (1986) have done. Descriptive studies in a clinical setting are conducted to establish the prevalence or the variability of a given set of conditions in society or in a defined subset of society. Associational studies in clinical settings often are conducted to identify or establish the degree of relationship between selected variables and client characteristics for a given population. Experimental studies are conducted to determine the reaction of clients to a defined program of treatment.

In the last two applications of clinical research (associational and experimental), study is directed toward developing information about a population defined by a common dysfunction, usually identified through clinical problem identification diagnosis. Clinical researchers seldom, if ever, wish to generalize to the public or to a "normal" population, except in studies where incidence or intensity is to be estimated. In most associational studies the clinical researcher wishes to expand knowledge about trait/experience configurations of the universe of individuals who share a profile of related symptoms, i.e., a syndrome. In other associational studies the researcher may wish to see how a tailored line of treatment works across selected demographics of individuals identified as having the same syndrome. In both cases the population to which inference is to be made is one of clients, rather than the "normal" population. Experimental studies generally are designed to direct inference to the population for which the treatment was designed.

In cases where the intent of the research is to establish incidence or intensity, the investigator does wish to infer to a population that goes beyond the client group. This population to which inference is directed may be the entire general population; but, more likely, it is a carefully defined subgroup of the general population, such as adolescents, tactually defensive elementary school aged children, overweight teenage females, or stroke victims.

In studies in which generalizability to global populations are sought, it is often impractical to assume that resources are available that will permit the researcher to draw the study sample systematically from the referent population. Instead, the researcher should attempt to choose from a more convenient population whose characteristics may be described and then argued, for all practical purposes, to be the same as the global target population. Seldom do studies go beyond the bounds of a nation or a language group, because the politics and management requirements of such single study expanse exceed the potential benefits or expanded utility of the research. Usually, the "normal" population is defined in terms of a national population or a common language group. Convenient subgroups of this type of population that appear to be valid for most incidence and intensity investigations are state or county delimited populations. In studies to establish incidence, the sample should be taken from the confines of a governmental unit such that a meaningful statistic may be derived. The referent population then should be contrasted to the global population with regard to key demographics to help provide a logical relationship.

Studies that seek to estimate the incidence or level of intensity of a variable use sampling to gain representation and to control accuracy of estimation. The researcher requires that the sample studied possesses the same profile of characteristics as the population of inference, so that valid estimates of the parameters of interest may be calculated. The researcher also requires that the sample studied be large enough to permit estimation of the parameters of interest within a preset level of accuracy. Both characteristics may be controlled through the use of survey sampling methods.

In studies where the researcher wishes to study the interrelationships among variables, the referent population often is of clientele. When choosing a sample or a part of the population to be studied in a correlational study, it is important that the population be carefully defined with a focus on representativeness. In clinical studies of interrelationships among variables, the population of clientele may be expected to be more homogeneous than the global population, especially with regard to the variables of interest. The homogeneity of the population will tend to reduce the sample size required, but the reduction is countered by the potentiality of restricted ranges for the variables in question. Restriction in range may be expected to occur when most of the population targeted by the study have similar values on a given variable, but the total range of the variable is not represented in the population. Restriction in range frequently results in erroneous estimates of correlation between variables.

The same survey sample techniques are as appropriate for associational studies as they are for descriptive studies. Because the survey sampling techniques are in their simplest form applicable to the estimation of a single variable, joint probability techniques that take into consideration the sampling distributions of both variables taken simultaneously should be considered when precise estimation of two or more variables is important. For correlational studies involving an array of variables, required sampling sizes may be derived through size requirements of the statistical technique used to test for the probability of a relationship. This technique is usually a regression procedure. When size requirements are estimated in this manner, the researcher should still use the selection procedures of one of the survey sampling techniques to assure representativeness of the sample.

Experimental study in clinical settings usually seeks inference to a clientele population. The researcher, in inferring to the population, first must focus on the assurance of an efficient and fair comparison to achieve valid results. The quality of the experimental comparison depends on the assurance of both treatment manipulation and adequate analytic power. In this case, analytic power is defined as one minus the probability of failing to reject the null hypothesis when it is false. Random assignment or the establishment of group comparability through quasi- experimental research designs is essential for clinical studies. In most experiments designed in clinical settings, random assignment can and should be used to establish the groups to be compared. In some cases delayed administration of treatments may be used to meet legal or professional obligations to the control group members. In this application the researcher, after completing the experiment, administers the treatment to the individuals who served as the control group and who had not received the treatment as part of the research design. This second administration of the treatment generally offers the benefits of the treatment to all and provides the researcher with an additional data point for half of the study sample.

In studies where treatments are administered to clientele groups, the use of a sample from the "normal" population as a control group is inappropriate. The researcher cannot create comparability between these two groups. Inference is to be made to the clientele group; the "normal" population is involved only as the group with characteristics that the clinician wishes to develop in the clientele through treatment. The desired comparison should be a sample from the clientele population.

Purpose of Sampling

Most researchers wish to study populations that extend beyond their span of control and immediate proximity. The applicability of the results of a study to a population not limited by geographic bounds or by a single individual's sphere of influence is essential to the importance and utility of most research. Limited resources make it impossible or impractical to include every member of an extended population in a given research study. Hence, the researcher studies a part of the population and infers the findings to the entire population. The part of the population that is studied is referred to as the sample.

The method through which the sample is selected is important to the inference process. In descriptive and associational studies the researcher wishes to link the sample to the population so as to maximize correspondence between the two. In other words, the researcher wishes to maximize the representativeness of the sample. The researcher requires that the sample include members whose attributes and characteristics closely resemble those of the population (United States General Accounting Office, 1986). In experimental studies, the researcher wishes to establish a set of probability conditions such that a fair comparison may be made across subdivisions of the sample and the results of this comparison inferred to the population. Subdivisions of the sample are achieved through random assignment or through methods dictated by quasi-experimental design. These subgroups receive different treatments, the effects of which are under investigation. The statistical concept of a sampling distribution of the parameter of interest provides the method for establishing the probability conditions.

The Central Limit Theorem provides the basis for both linkages desired by the researcher. This theorem states, "As the sample size 'n' becomes large, the sampling distribution of the sample mean can be approximated by a normal distribution with a mean of μ and a standard deviation of σ divided by the square root of 'n', where μ is the mean of the population and σ is the standard deviation" (Mansfield, 1986, p. 241). This theorem can be applied directly to estimate key parameters in survey sampling, or can be applied to establish a test statistic through its application to the distribution of a selected parameter of the sample, such as the mean, in repeated samples from the same population. In the second application of the theorem, it is the sample parameter, not the variable being sampled, that is normally distributed.

Sampling for Descriptive and Associational Studies

In sampling for descriptive studies, the researcher wishes to control the estimation of population values for one or more variables. This control involves a) setting the degree of accuracy at which the parameter of the variable of interest is to be estimated; and b) maximizing the representativeness of the sample. In associational studies the researcher wishes the same control, except for the estimation of parameters for two or more variables.

Both descriptive and associational studies in clinical research may be conducted on populations that are either pooled, so as to ignore clinical associations, or nested within several clinics. In the latter case, the individual effects of clinic associations should be addressed in the sampling design. It is unlikely that a descriptive or associational study using a sample can be designed within a single clinic setting due to limits in sample size. In this case, it is more likely that either of these studies would be conducted using the entire clinic clientele as a population, making inference unnecessary.

In the discussion of appropriate models, a method will be given for estimating required sample sizes that will provide a formula for a 95% confidence interval. These estimates can be converted to 99% confidence intervals by replacing the number 4 in the formulae with 6.75. This conversion represents the difference between twice the variance and 2.6 times the variance, as indicated by values on a t distribution.

Simple Random Sampling

For descriptive and associational studies that do not take into account effects from subjects associated with individual clinics, the selection of subjects can best be achieved through simple random sampling. A useful definition of simple random sampling is given by Mansfield: "A simple random sample is a sample chosen so that the probability of selecting each element in the population is the same for each and every element, and the chance of selecting one element is independent of whether some other element is chosen" (1986, p. 219).

Selection by simple random sampling requires listing all members of the population, numbering them on the list, and using a random number table or a computer program with a random number algorithm to select the desired number of members or elements. Descriptive and associational studies require sampling without replacement and a correction for a finite population.

Estimation of the Required Sample Size

The selection process maximizes representativeness of the sample to the population and allows the researcher to set "B" as the acceptable error for the estimation of the mean of the variable, whose variance is represented in the formula for estimating required sample size:

$$n = \frac{4 * N * (\sigma^2)}{(N-1) * B^2 + 4 * (\sigma^2)}$$

where:
  n = the required sample size,
  N = the number of elements or members in the population,
  σ^2 = the population variance, and
  B = the required precision (Mendenhall, Ott and Scheaffer, 1971).

The use of this formula can be illustrated by a study of 34,000 pensioners residing in 170 nursing homes in a state in the Western United States. The researcher wishes to estimate the daily average grams of protein intake of these geriatric patients. Although the parameters of the variable are not known for the state population, national figures are available that establish that persons over 65 years of age have a daily average protein intake of 52 grams with a standard deviation of 9.82. Because there is no reason to assume that the state population differs from the national averages, these figures will be used as population values in choosing the sample. The desired sample is for a 95% confidence interval with a precision bound of one gram of protein. Substitution in the formula produces the following:

$$n = \frac{4 * 34000 * 96.43}{33999 * 1 + 4 * 96.43}$$

$$n = \frac{13114480}{33999 + 385.72}$$

n = 381.40 or 382 patients.

For a sample with a 99% confidence interval and a precision of one gram, substitution into the formula is as follows:

$$n = \frac{6.75 * 34000 * 96.43}{33999 * 1 + 6.75 * 96.43}$$

$$n = \frac{22130685}{33999 + 650.90}$$

n = 638.69 or 639 patients.

A narrower confidence bound dictates an increase in the required sampling size. Similarly, less precision dictates smaller sampling sizes. For a sample with a 95% confidence interval and a two grams precision, the substitution is:

$$n = \frac{4 * 34000 * 96.43}{33999 * 4 + 4 * 96.43}$$

$$n = \frac{13114480}{135996 + 385.72}$$

n = 96.16 or 97 patients

After the researcher has obtained the required sample size, the population is listed and numbered. The researcher then applies a table of random numbers to select the required number of subjects. It is likely that the selected sample would be scattered over the entire state and would include nearly all of the nursing homes.

Estimation of a Proportion of a Population

A variation of this model can be used in estimating the proportion of the population possessing a given attribute. The formula for the estimation of the sample size required to estimate a proportion is:

$$n = \frac{4 * N * p * q}{(N-1) * B^2 + 4 * p * q}$$

where:
   n = the required sample size,
   N = the number of elements in the population,
   p = the proportion of the sample having the attribute,
   q = 1 - p, and
   B = the required precision (Mendenhall, Ott and Scheaffer, 1971)

The following example will illustrate the use of this formula. An investigator is interested in estimating the proportion of geriatric patients over 75 years of age in a Midwestern state that regularly take a diet supplement. Unfortunately, no records on diet supplements have been kept, but there are a total of 800 eligible patients in the state. A sample of patients is needed to estimate the proportion of the population (p) with a bound on the error of estimation of b = 0.05. Substitution into the formula is as follows:

(When no prior information is available to estimate p, set p = 0.5, and then q = 1 − p or 0.5. These values for p and q maximize the variance of the distribution.)

$$n = \frac{4 * 800 * 0.5 * 0.5}{799 * 0.0025 + 4 * 0.5 * 0.5}$$

$$n = \frac{800}{1.9975 + 1}$$

n = 266.89 or 267 patients.

Estimating Differences in Percents of Subgroups

In cases where a simple random sample is desired, but the researcher has no information on the population variance, the researcher may conceptualize the problem as one estimating differences in percents of subgroups. Within this conceptualization, the sample for the estimation of differences in proportions may be used as a method. In cases where population totals are unknown, the researcher should use an approximate figure that is probably better if the error is on the side of overestimation. A second option is available when there is inadequate researcher information for sample selection: to define the population to a smaller group from which the sampling information can be gained.

Models Accommodating Nesting of Clients

Three models exist for the selection of a sample for either descriptive or associational studies that include design accommodations for the nesting of clients within clinics. Each of these models include both advantages and disadvantages that somewhat depend on the purposes of the researcher.

Systematic Selection with a Random Start

The model that provides for perhaps the greatest ease of selection is systematic selection with a random start. A useful definition of this method is as follows: "A sampling method in which a given sample size is divided into the universe size in order to obtain a sampling interval. A random starting point between one and the sampling interval is obtained. This item is selected first; then every item whose number or location is equal to the previously selected item plus the sampling interval is selected, until the universe is used up" (General Accounting Office, 1986, p. 149).

The effects of association with particular clinics can be controlled for by ordering the list of population members by clinic, and then dispersing the selected sample proportionally across clinics. This selection method produces an unbiased estimate of the mean of a given attribute, but the precision of the estimation of this parameter depends on the relationship between the selected interval and the attribute (Anderson and Sclove, 1986). This may occur if the listing of clients by clinics is not random. Generally, the calculations used to control the error of estimation and to estimate sample size for systematic sampling with a random start are the same as those used for simple random sampling.

Stratification Model

A second survey sampling model appropriate for selecting a sample for descriptive or associational studies that controls for the nesting of clients within clinics is the stratified random sample model. There are several ways this model can be used. The number of clients served by a clinic most likely will be the criterion for nesting in most studies; however, emphasis on certain theoretical perspectives or service community characteristics could be used as stratification criteria. The model could be applied simply by setting different fractions of selection across varying strata of clinics, using the clinic universe in the sample. This application, however, does not appear to be the most effective use of the model. The most useful application appears to be based on a two-stage approach.

In the two-stage application, a random sample of clinics is selected in the first stage, and a random sample of clients from the selected clinics is selected in the second stage. Again, options are available for selecting both clinics and clients. In the selection of clinics, clinics can either be chosen proportionally across strata, or selection can be made using a fraction proportional to the number of clients nested within a stratum. The first option maximizes the contribution of clinics, whereas the second maximizes the coverage of clients. In the second stage, the researcher may choose clients proportional to their membership in the clinics, or clients may be chosen in equal lots from each clinic.

Self-weighting should be considered in the specification of the model. To establish self-weighting the researcher must choose each member of the sample with the same probability. If this is done, then each member of the sample contributes equally to the estimation process. Jessen (1978, pp. 184-210) provides a helpful discussion of this topic. If the researcher does not have or cannot estimate the information needed to implement one of the models to control for the nesting of subjects, then the researcher should revert back to the simple random sample. Sample size requirements may be estimated using the following formula:

$$n = \frac{4 * \Sigma_1{}^L[N(i)^2 * \sigma(i)^2/w(i)]}{(N * B)^2 + 4 * \Sigma_1{}^L[N(i) * \sigma(i)^2]}$$

where
  n = the required sample size,
  N(i) = the number of elements in the population in the ith stratum,
  $\sigma(i)^2$ = the population variance of the ith stratum,
  L = the number of strata,
  w(i) = the fraction of elements allocated to stratum i,
  B = the required precision (Mendenhall, Ott and Scheaffer, 1971).

The earlier example used to illustrate the simple random sampling formula can be used to illustrate this one. This case involves the study of the 34,000 pensioners residing in 170 nursing homes in a Western state. The researcher wishes to estimate the daily average grams of protein intake of these geriatric patients.

In selecting a stratification model, the researcher is indicating a belief that either the patients differ systematically across nursing homes or that resources dictate that the scatter of the sample across the state must be controlled by choosing from only a part of the nursing home. If the former is the reason for adopting stratification, the researcher would choose a single-stage model and most likely would choose proportionally across strata. If the latter is the reason for the choice, the researcher most likely would use a two-stage model, choosing first a sample of nursing homes and then a sample of patients from each selected nursing home. In this application it is likely that a larger fraction or percentage of homes containing the most patients would be selected than would homes that contain fewer patients.

Although the parameters of the variable are unknown for the state population, national figures are available that establish that persons over 65 years of age have a daily average intake of 52 grams with a standard deviation of 9.82. Because there is no reason to assume that the state population differs from the national averages, these figures will be used as population values in choosing the sample. To properly implement the model, the researcher would have to know or be able to estimate the variance of protein intake for the different sized nursing homes. Suppose that the researcher had evidence that feeding in the larger homes was more controlled and consequently more homogeneous with regard to protein intake. The variance for the largest nursing homes was estimated to be 88.00, for average sized homes 95.50, and for smaller homes 99.87. In the state where the nursing homes are located, there are 28 nursing homes that house more than 300 patients, 56 homes that house between 150 and 300 patients, and 86 homes that house less than 150 patients. Enough information has now been developed to permit the researcher to build the sampling frame and to sort nursing homes into strata.

The desired sample is for a 95% confidence interval with a precision bound of one gram of protein. Substitution in the formula produces the following:

$$n = \frac{4*[10000*10000*88.00/0.3333 + 13000*13000*95.50/0.3333 + 11000*11000*99.87/0.3333]}{(34000*1)*(34000*1) + 4*[88.00*10000+95.50*13000 +99.87*11000]}$$

$$n = \frac{444329673000}{1168880280}$$

n = 380.13 or 381

where n = the required sample size

N(1) = 10000,	L = 3,
N(2) = 13000,	w(1) = 0.3333
N(3) = 11000,	w(2) = 0.3333
$\sigma(1)^2$ = 88.00,	w(3) = 0,3333, and
$\sigma(2)^2$ = 95.50,	B = 1.
$\sigma(3)^2$ = 99.87,	

When the correlation between the variable of primary interest and the variable on which the stratification is based is high, the required sample size is often reduced. In this example the relationship of protein intake to the size of the nursing home was not adequate to reduce the required size of the sample: 380.13 to 381.40. If the relationship was higher, the use of stratification may be expected to reduce the required sample size. The model also can be used to reduce the number of nursing homes that will include members of the sample by choosing a sample of homes in the first stage and then estimating the required sample size for the second stage, with the potential of some small loss in generalizability.

Cluster Sampling Model

The third survey sampling model that is appropriate for selecting a sample for descriptive or associational studies that control for the nesting of clients within clinics is the cluster sampling model. In the application of this model clinics make up the sampling unit in which the clients are clustered. This model appears to be efficient with regard to the number of clinics to be included in the study. Kish (1965, pp. 148-212) provides an excellent discussion of this model and the options and complexity of its applications.

Sampling for Experimental Studies

In experimental studies the intent of the clinician is often to validate one or more treatments with a specific client group. Here, emphasis is on the appropriateness of the comparison. For the comparison to be appropriate, the following five conditions must exist: a) the sample studied must be drawn from the population to which the inference is to be made, so that unbiased estimates of the parameter of interest (usually the mean) may be gained; b) an appropriate probability model and test statistic must be established; c) random assignment or a quasi-experimental model must be employed so as to assure manipulation of the treatments across the groups being compared; d) nuisance variables that may confound the estimation of effects must be controlled; and e) there must be a large enough sample in the study to detect possible differences at the level hypothesized.

Concepts of Sample Selection

Several concepts are involved in the selection of a sample for an experimental study. One of the key concepts is the use of the Central Limit Theorem and repeated samples from the population of interest, with the intent of defining the distribution of the test statistic and establishing the probability model for testing the comparative hypothesis.

Use of the sample distribution permits the researcher to calculate the variance of the test statistic. This variance permits the researcher to establish for the sample the probability of a Type II error (i.e., failing to reject the null hypothesis of no difference when a difference exists) once the probability level of a Type I error (i.e., rejecting the null hypothesis when it is true) has been set by the researcher. The probability of rejecting the null hypothesis when it is true is referred to as the significance level of the study, or α. For a fixed sample size, the Type II error is increased when the Type I error is decreased.

Four factors are required to estimate the power of a study, which can be defined as one minus the probability of a Type II error (again, failing to reject the null hypothesis when it is false). They include a) the effect size or the size of the difference between the true value of the parameter in question and the hypothesized value; b) the significance level α or the probability of rejecting a true null hypothesis; c) the standard deviation of the sampled population or the test statistic; and d) the sample size drawn from the population (Kachigan, 1986, p. 185).

The standard deviation is fixed by the characteristics of the population to which the inference is directed. The significance level α is set by the researcher depending on the consequences of the error of accepting a false research hypothesis. To maximize power of the test of the hypothesis, sample and effect sizes are left to be determined. The sample size may be too small to observe any effect at all. This frequently happens when the researcher becomes overly concerned with costs or physical barriers preventing access to a large part of the population.

The sample size also may be too large, such that the design is capable of detecting trivial or slight, unpractical differences through the comparison. The conjecture here is that the researcher should fix the effect size at a level that has meaning for practice. Establishing a meaningful effect size in clinical research holds face validity for the improvement of practice with regard to healing endeavors. Determination of the effect size then establishes the sample size required to maximize power, consequently minimizing chances of error in the experiment.

Power curves and probability tables enable the researcher to maximize the utility of the results of an experimental study. Cohen (1969) offers an indepth discussion of the topic. For simple two-group experiments, the estimation of required sample size is very straightforward. The effect size is defined as $[\mu 1 - \mu 0] \div \sigma$. The formula for the estimation of required sample size is given by Kirk (1982):

$$n = \frac{[z\alpha - z\beta]^2}{[\mu 1 - \mu 0]^2 / \sigma^2}$$

where

   $z\alpha$ = the normal curve ordinate at the significance level for sampling distribution of $\mu 0$,
   $z\beta$ = the normal curve ordinate at the required power for sampling distribution of $\mu 1$,
   $\mu 0$ = the untreated population mean,
   $\mu 1$ = the mean required for the treatment to be meaningful,
   σ^2 = the variance of the population, and
   n = the required sample size.

Suppose a clinician had a population of 900 clients who were to be treated for short attention spans. On a spatial search task the population was found to have an average attention span of 3.2 minutes, with a standard deviation of 0.77. The clinician desired to validate an experimental treatment designed to expand the attention spans of these clients. The estimate of the required sample size for the study assuming a confidence level of 0.95 and power of 0.80 was needed. An extension of the memory span that the clinician judged to be of practical significance was 0.30. The effect size for the study can then be calculated by subtracting 3.2 (the mean under the null hypothesis, $\mu 0$) from 3.5 (the mean under the experimental hypothesis, $\mu 1$) and then dividing the result by 0.60, which is σ^2. The effect size is calculated to be 0.5. Under the null hypothesis $z\alpha = 1.645$ for 0.05. Under the experimental hypothesis $z\beta = -0.84$ for 0.20 to the left of the mean. To find the values for $z\alpha$ and $z\beta$ using a normal curve probability table, which provides for the positive half of the curve, first one finds the ordinate for the area of 0.45 (0.50, the area under the right half of the normal curve minus 0.05, the area in the critical region), then finds the ordinate for the area of 0.30 (0.50, the area under the left side of the normal curve minus 0.20, the area denoted by the required power) and affixes a minus sign to the last result. The required sample size for the study is: $n = 24.43$ or 25 clients.

If the power specification is increased to 0.90, then the values of the ordinates are 1.645 and -1.28, and the estimated sample size is $n = 34.22$ or 35 clients. If the amount of expansion is changed to 0.1, then the effect size changes to 0.1667, and for power of 0.90 the estimated sample size is $(n = 307.88)$ 308.

The selection of clients for the experimental study should be drawn from the population to which inference is to be made. In selecting a sample for an experimental study, the researcher must deal with the compromise between practical reality and ideal experimental conditions. In many cases, the reality is that the population to which the researcher wishes to infer is not available for selection, but some defendable (large enough) part of it is available. For these cases, the researcher should describe the study population (the part of the larger population that is available) and permit the consumer of the research to risk inferring to the hypothetical target population. This case represents the worst selection of an inferential sample that is permissible. If the researcher does not have the information needed to fix a sample for an experimental study, a pilot study would be in order to estimate the needed information.

In more favorable conditions, the population to which inference is directed is available and selection can be made. It should be noted that an experimental model calls for selection of a sample and then assignment of members to the groups required by the design. Random selection from different populations will not set up the desired comparison.

Actual selection can be made using the random sampling model discussed earlier, or selection methods may be used to permit blocking of the sample for control of nuisance variables. One method that controls for the presence of a given value of a nuisance variable is the exact sampling method.

The exact sampling strategy provides a method of unit selection that allows the researcher to choose a sample from the population systematically over a prespecified set of variables. The set of variables are chosen based on their relationship to the dependent variable in the study and desired control of the dispersion of the sample with relation to that of the population.

To illustrate the exact sampling strategy, consider the study of the anxiety symptoms of speech-handicapped adolescents. Sex, age, and socioeconomic status have been selected as the control variables based on their hypothetical

VARIABLES: SEX — AGE — SOCIO-ECONOMIC STATUS

SEX	Male								Female								
AGE	12-13			14-15			16-17			12-13			14-15			16-17		
SOCIO-ECON STATUS	L	M	H	L	M	H	L	M	H	L	M	H	L	M	H	L	M	H
Cell No.	1	2	3	4	5	6	7	8	9	10	11	12	13	14	15	16	17	18

Figure 2-1: Number of cells produced by the controlling variables in the exact sampling strategy illustration.

relationship to anxiety symptoms. It is desirable to choose a sample that would include subjects that exhibit variation in these variables. To begin the exact sampling process the variables over which control is desired are converted into categoric measures. Sex would have only two values, male and female. Age, most likely collected directly, could be divided into three intervals of interest: 1 = 12 to 13 years, 2 = 14 to 15, and 3 = 16 to 17. Socioeconomic status is to be defined by family income levels: 1(low) = $3000 to $12000, 2(average) = $12001 to $30000, and 3(high) = $30001 to $60000. A quick multiplication of the levels of each variable ($2 \times 3 \times 3$) shows that the population is to be broken down into 18 subdivisions.

Figure 2-1 shows the breakdown created by the three variables. The next step is to sort the population of clients into the eighteen cells, estimate the required sample size, and select randomly a whole number nearest, but greater than or equal to, the quotient of the estimated sample size divided by the number of cells in this case, which is eighteen. Empty cells and cells that contain fewer than the number required by the quotient result in increasing proportionally the number selected from the larger cells. If a cell contains fewer than the required number, then all clients in that cell should be selected.

Other Considerations in the Clinical Setting

To prepare for the development of this chapter, a selection of 20 articles were chosen and read from nine issues of three journals that were reviewed for types of statistical applications by Royeen (1986). The journals were: *American Journal of Occupational Therapy, Occupational Therapy in Mental Health,* and *Occupational Therapy Journal of Research.*

Of the twenty studies, only two could be classified as experimental, fourteen as associational, and four as descriptive. All four descriptive studies sought to discern incidence of a measured attribute, but three of the four studies suffered from inadequate sample size (i.e., 16, 15, and 12 clients).

Four of the associational studies involved the reliability of clinical measures. Measurement study models such as generalizability analysis appear more appropriate for this type of study. Analyses used in these studies were t-tests and analyses of variance. Of the ten remaining associational studies, three were completed using comparisons rather than the more appropriate correlational analysis. Four studies appropriately used comparisons to identify relationships. One of the three correlational studies appeared to have an inadequate sample (11 clients).

One of the two experimental studies appeared to have adequate selection and design. In the other, what appears to be an inappropriate control group was chosen from the "normal" population rather than from the client population to which inference was directed. Observation of the pretest variances revealed that the client group, obviously a subset of the "normal" population, had a higher variance than the "normal" group. A conjecture was made that the treatment group was comprised of two or more distinct subsets of the "normal" population rather than simply one subset. As far as could be discerned without reanalysis of the original data, reaction to treatment verified client differences within the experimental group. It is likely that these differences were due to variance in either the diagnostic process or the underlying constructs to the malady.

In reaction to the observed heterogeneity within the client population, two other examples were found in special education literature. It is believed that blocking on the basis of this heterogeneity would improve the potential of treatment validation. Suspicion of potential client population confounding may be raised when the variance of the client sample clearly exceeds the variance of the group on which the measure was normalized. Other bases for suspicion include distinct variations with regard to diagnostic methods and different theoretical expectations in client reaction to treatment due to variation in client configurations of active constructs.

Two methods appear useful in tracking this source of difficulty in experimental design. It is assumed that information on both the diagnostic process and on the underlying constructs is available at the time of selection. If not, this information, although somewhat limited as far as selection to set up blocking is concerned, could be gathered during pretesting. The two methods that appear to have potential are cluster analysis of the underlying constructs, and application of the Box-Scheffé test for homogeneity of variance across groups designated by the two methods of diagnosis. The application of the cluster analysis procedure is described by McKinney, Short and Feagans (1985) in the classification of handicapped children. Kirk (1982, p. 80) describes the application of the Box-Scheffé in his design methodology textbook. Both methods seem to offer value in addressing this potential design deficiency.

The problem addressed by these two methods is directly related to how a treatment may work on a particular client group. The inexactness of the definition of a study population may result in the researcher mistakenly mixing two populations for study. One population may contain a host of members that react differently to the treatment than do the majority of the second population. The existence of the two populations in the same study serves to increase the error term of the statistical test and reduces the ability of the researcher to see the effects of the treatment.

The first method, by identifying the source of error in the definition of the study population, does not address the problem directly. Instead, a sample of members of the population are sorted into categories based on similarities of their profiles with regard to characteristics judged to be significantly related to their reactions to the proposed treatments. Failure to obtain a cluster solution with more than one group suggests that a single population is being studied.

The second method directly addresses the population definition problem. To apply this method, a sample of members of the proposed population would be subdivided by a potential source of error in the definition of the population. The subdivisions would then be tested for homogeneity of variance. If the variances were found to be homogeneous, this potential source of error is not a cause for concern. If the method is repeated for the primary potential sources of error, and in all of the tests the variance is found to be heterogeneous, then it is likely that the definition of the population is adequate.

References

Anderson, T. W., and Sclove, S. L. (1986). *The statistical analysis of data*. Palo Alto: The Scientific Press.

Campbell, D. T., and Stanley, J. C. (1966). *Experimental and quasi-experimental designs for research*. Chicago: Rand McNally Publishing Co.

Cohen, J. (1969). *Statistical power analysis for the behavioral sciences*. New York: Academic Press.

Fisher, A. G., Mixon, J., and Herman, R. (1986). The validity of the clinical diagnosis of vestibular dysfunction. *Occupational Therapy Journal of Research*, 6(11), 3-20.

Jessen, R. J. (1978). *Statistical survey techniques*. New York: John Wiley and Sons.

Kachigan, S. K. (1986). *Statistical analysis*. New York: Radius Press.

Kirk, R. E. (1982). *Experimental design*. Belmont: Brooks/Cole Publishing Company.

Kish, L. (1965). *Survey sampling*. New York: John Wiley and Sons.

Mansfield, E. (1986). *Basic statistics*. New York: W.W. Norton and Company.

Mendenhall, W., Ott, L., and Scheaffer, R. L. (1971). *Elementary survey sampling*. Belmont: Duxbury Press.

McKinney, J. D., Short, E. J., and Feagans, L. (1985). Academic consequences of perceptual-linguistic subtypes of learning disabled children. *Learning Disabilities Research*, 1(1), pgs 6-17.

Royeen, C. B. (1986). An exploration of parametric versus non-parametric statistics in occupational therapy clinical research. (University Microfilms International, no. 86206590).

Royeen, C. B. (1984). Incidence of atypical responses to vestibular stimulation among behaviorally disordered children. *Occupational Therapy Journal of Research*, 4(3), 59-60.

United States General Accounting Office (GAO) (1986). *Using statistical sampling: Transfer paper 6*. Washington: Program Evaluation and Methodology Division, United States General Accounting Office.

Yerxa, E. J., and Baum, S. (1986), Engagement in daily occupation and life satisfaction among people with spinal cord injuries. *Occupational Therapy Journal of Research*, 6(5), 271-284.

CHAPTER 3

MEASUREMENT CONSIDERATIONS IN CLINICAL RESEARCH

Theodore R. Cromack

Chapter Overview

This chapter will provide a step-by-step guide concerning the decisions that are required in considering the measurement issues in a research project. For each of the decisions, some guidance concerning the implications is provided. Emphasis is given to considerations of developing an instrument. The chapter concludes with a discussion designed to caution the reader that, as yet, all of the implications of measuring human capabilities are not fully known.

Introduction

An eminent psychologist once said that if something exists, it can be measured. Since that time, people have gone about measuring nearly every aspect of human behavior. Much discussion and debate has occurred about the "mismeasure" of behavior (Gould, 1981). There can be little doubt that measurement has been misused, and even more, misinterpreted. In spite of the misuse, however, measurement is essential. To illustrate, automobiles are misused, but it is people who misuse them. Elimination of automobiles is not advocated, but rather, teaching people how to use them properly. Similarly, computers make mistakes. One is told, "it was a 'computer error," but it is people who make the errors due to misprogramming of the computer or improper data entry. Despite these errors, computers are considered to be valuable to society and necessary to manage the enormous amounts of information society needs processed. Like automobiles and computers, measurement has its place in today's society in spite of the potential for misuse.

Measurement of human behavior, or testing, is especially important to researchers. Without measurement, researchers would be unable to collect useful information about human behavior. Without measurement, researchers would understand far less about human functioning and would be far less able to predict behavior or change human function.

Definition of Measurement

Brown (1983) defines measurement as "...the assignment of numerals to behavior according to rules" (p.11). In other words, following a given set of rules or operations, a characteristic demonstrated in a behavior is assigned a quantitative value. One often hears: "How would you rate that on a scale of 1 to 10?" Perhaps the rules are not clearly stated, but some general idea of the rules is understood and the person is being asked to assign a numerical value based on a judgment; that is to measure an object using a judgmental scale.

It is important to distinguish between measurement and evaluation. Measurement stops at assignment of the number. Evaluation is the interpretation of that number. This chapter deals with measurement and will address interpretation only to the degree necessary for an understanding of measurement issues.

Role of Measurement

Clinical research in occupational therapy as well as other practice based disciplines is conducted for at least two purposes; extension of knowledge and evaluation of practice (Gilfoyle, 1986). In either case, some aspects of the phenomenon under investigation will require measurement. On an informal level, one measures many things every day; however, rules are seldom established. If clear rules are not established for measurement, failure to measure as objectively or consistently as possible may result. For example, consider a householder who purchases a roast at the market. He or she looks over several roasts and selects one. On what basis has this person selected a roast? He or she has not assigned a number to each roast and selected a "7" or a "85," but has measured the leanness, size, shape, color, and texture, and has evaluated the roast in comparison with others or with experience. This is an example of informal measurement. Would that same householder select the same roast tomorrow or next week? One does not know! However, with a rating scale, that is a formal set of rules, the selection of a roast could be made more consistent.

It seems trivial to consider devising a rating scale for the selection of a roast. However, for selection of a job applicant or a patient for treatment, such a rating scale would be quite useful. The rating scale is the set of rules or procedures for making a measurement and represents a measurement instrument. Of course, rating scales are only one form of instrument. Instruments may be in the form of a test, an interview schedule, a questionnaire, or any set of procedures that make judgments explicit.

There are many questions that may best be answered by the use of a standardized set of rules in the form of rating scales or tests.

- Does this child need treatment?
- What kind of treatment does an injured homemaker need?
- What services best meet the needs of a developmentally delayed adult?
- To what degree has the treatment been beneficial?
- In what way has the treatment been beneficial?

In most research the object is to collect data that may be analyzed to test hypotheses or to confirm theories. Analysis of data implies the use of numbers, although this is not necessarily so. Because measurement involves the assignment of numbers to behavior, it follows that in most cases measurement is vital to research.

Options in Measurement

There are a number of decisions that must be made as one proceeds with measuring variables in a research study. Figure 3-1 is a flow diagram of a number of these decisions. Before establishing the rules for assigning numbers to behavior (measuring), one must determine the goal or objective of the measurement. This first step generally emerges as a statement of the problem. This statement guides all decisions on measurement. Until it is clear what variables are being examined and whether these variables are to be described, related, or compared, no decision can be made about measurement.

The second step is to decide at what point to assign numbers or whether to measure at all. Essentially there are three options: 1) to measure at the point of data collection; 2) to measure after data collection; or 3) to use entirely narrative, descriptive data. If one elects to measure at the point of data collection 1), some sort of instrument is needed. It may be a test, an observation scale, an interview schedule, or another instrument. If one elects to measure after collecting data 2), an instrument again will be necessary, although it may be somewhat different than the instrument under the first option. In this case, one merely collects descriptive notes of behavior and/or conditions, often referred to as field notes or ethnographic notes, then assigns quantities to these phenomena at a later time. Under the final option 3) numerical data are never assigned, but ethnographic methods are used to develop case studies, and interpretation is directly from narrative descriptions. Although in some cases the third option may be considered measurement, it usually is referred to as qualitative data or ethnographic methodology and will be addressed only briefly in this chapter.

Ethnographic Methods

In option two if the data are to be assigned quantities at a later time, there are several decisions to be made. Who initially collects the descriptive data and in what form? Who will assign the numbers, an individual or a panel? Who will interpret the data, an individual or a panel? What types of analysis will be performed? What kinds of scales are appropriate? Answers to these

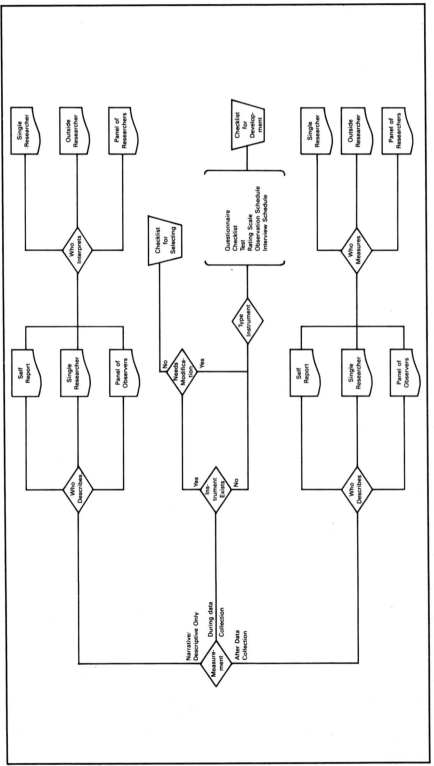

Figure 3-1. Flow chart of measurement decisions.

questions and others are needed as one proceeds to develop instruments for quantifying narrative data. For anyone choosing this option, there are a number of references that may be helpful, such as Glaser and Strauss (1967), Spradley (1980), and Yin (1984).

Measurement at Point of Data Collection

Regarding option one, if measurement is to occur at the point of data collection, there are many decisions to be made. One must determine whether an appropriate instrument already exists, whether it will be necessary to construct one, whether an existing instrument can be modified, or, one may find portions of an existing instrument appropriate for use. Each of these possibilities will be considered in turn.

Selecting an Existing Instrument. In selecting an existing instrument, it may be helpful to look at the checklist provided as Figure 3-2. Each item on the checklist should be answered.

First, return to the problem statement and confirm the purposes and uses of the data. Next, consider that the instrument must have reasonable technical qualities; in particular, it must be valid for the intended purposes and conditions. The technical manual should report acceptable levels and types of reliability suitable for this particular research project. If this research requires normative comparisons, the instrument must have appropriate normative data. In the area of usability, the administration and scoring must be considered as well as the practical aspects of cost and availability of the instrument.

It is always advisable to look at reviews of the instrument and how it has been used in similar research. Excellent sources for such reviews are the *Mental Measurements Yearbook* by Buros, which has been published every five years since 1940, and *Test Critiques,* Volumes I through V, published by Test Corporation of America (Keyser and Sweetland, 1984, 1985, 1986). More recent reviews may be found in journals.

Sources of existing measurement instruments generally are endemic to the problem under study and therefore may be found during the review of literature preparatory to undertaking the research. However, references are provided for a number of instruments that may be appropriate for some studies.

Tests in Print, published by the Gryphon Press in two volumes, will provide many sources for tests (Buros, 1974). Many tests are not published in the sense that they are commercially available, but may be available from either the test author or another source. In addition to the reviews mentioned above, which will yield sources of instruments, there are at least three other sources:

- Robinson, J.P., and Shaver, P.R. (1973).. *Measures of social psychological attitudes* (Rev. Ed.) Ann Arbor: Institute for Social Research, University of Michigan.
- Simon, A. and Gil Boyer, E. (1974). *Mirrors for behavior III: An anthology of observation instruments* (3rd Ed.). Philadelphia: Communication Materials Center.
- Educational Research Information Center (ERIC) documents.

Checklist for Selecting a Published Instrument

1. **What are the purposes and uses of the data?**
   a. Are comparisons to be made?
      On individuals?   On groups?
      Simultaneously?   Across time?
   b. Are individual scores to be used?
      Was the instrument standardized for individuals?
   c. Are part (sub−) scores to be used?
      Are part scores valid?
      Are part scores reliable?

2. **Is the instrument valid for your purposes?**
   a. Does it have content validity?
      Is the table of specifications complete?
      Do the items match your needs?
      Do the items appear appropriate?
   b. Does it have criterion related validity?
      What was the outside criterion used to validate it?
      Is the outside criterion appropriate for your needs?
      What is the claimed validity coefficient(s)?
   c. Does it have construct validity?
      Is the theoretical approach pertinent/appropriate?
      What is the basis for item selection?
      Do the items appear appropriate?

3. **Is the instrument sufficiently reliable?**
   a. Does it have internal consistency?
      What type of internal consistency measures are given?
      What is the reliability coefficiency for internal consistency?
   b. Does it have stability?
      What type of stability measures are given?
      What is the reliability coefficient for stability?
   c. What is the standard error of measurement?

4. **Are the items appropriate for your use?**
   a. Do the items have face validity?
   b. Are the items of appropriate variety?
   c. Are the item statistics reported?
      What is the general level of difficulty?
      What is the general level of discrimination?

5. **Are norms to be used?**
   a. What are the characteristics of the norm group?
      Are they appropriate for this group?
   b. What scales are provided?
      Are the scales suitable for the type of analysis to be done?
      Is there information on subtest scores?
      Are there interpretative aids available?

6. **Are there likely to be problems in administering and scoring?**
   a. Are there special requirements for administering?
      Is special training required?
      Are special equipment or facilities needed?
   b. Are standard instructions available and clear?
   c. How is the instrument scored?
      Can it be machine scored?
      Is it easily manually scored?
      Are scoring masks provided?

Checklist (continued)

7. **What are the practical aspects of the instrument?**
   a. What is the cost?
      What is the cost of the instrument?
      Are separate answer or recording sheets extra?
      What does it cost to score the instrument?
   b. What is the availability?
      Can it be obtained in time to meet schedule?
   c. What are the time issues?
      How long does it take to administer?
      How long does it take to score?
   d. Is the format and layout acceptable?

8. **Is there any other information available on the instrument?**
   a. Has it been reviewed?
      Is the review favorable?
      Are the weaknesses identified important for this particular use?
   b. Has the instrument been used for other research?
      Were the results pertinent to this research?
      Has the author of the research been consulted?

Figure 3-2. Checklist for selecting a published instrument.

Modifying an Existing Instrument. An instrument may be found that appears to be close to what is to be measured. It may be worthwhile exploring whether a portion of that instrument can be used or whether it could be modified to meet the particular needs of the research being considered. In either case, there are several factors that must be considered before adapting an instrument. Every element of that instrument was considered when it was standardized: the content, the format, the instructions, etc. If a portion of the instrument is to be used or adapted to meet a particular need, the validity and reliability of the instrument may be affected. In effect, the portion of the instrument being used should be treated as a new instrument unless the portion being used has been standardized in such a manner that it may be used alone.

Most published instruments have been copyrighted, and care should be taken to clear modifications or changes with the publisher of such instruments.

Instrument Development. If no standard or published instrument is available, it may be necessary or advisable to develop one. In many respects, developing an instrument is a research study in itself. Furthermore, the care and attention devoted to instrument development may make the difference between significant and nonsignificant findings in the final research. Therefore, particular attention should be paid to the aspects of instrument development discussed below. In most respects, it doesn't matter what type of instrument is being developed, the characteristics of a good instrument are similar. Therefore, the sections that follow will apply whether one is developing a test, an observation scale, a rating scale, an interview schedule, or a questionnaire. Figure 3-3 is a checklist for guiding the development of an instrument.

Checklist for Instrument Development

(Answers to the appropriate questions below, will increase the confidence in instrumentation and are generally appropriate for including in the research report.)

If Content Validity claimed, answers needed to these questions:
Source(s) of items?
Panel of content experts used?
Statistical technique(s) used (e.g., Factor Analysis)?
Item-total correlation (r and N)?

If Criterion Validity claimed, answers needed to these questions:
Outside criterion used?
Standardization (validity) group used?
   (Describe characteristics, size, etc.)
Correlation with criterion?

If Construct Validity claimed, answers needed to these questions:
Theoretical basis? (Describe)
   Source(s) of items?
Panel of experts used?
Statistical technique(s) used (e.g., convergent-divergent)?
Item-total correlation (r and N)

Reliability Claimed	**Coef**	**N**	**No. Items**
Internal Consistency			
Split-Half			
Coefficient Alpha			
KR-20/KR-21			
Stability			
Test-Retest			
Equivalent Forms			
Generalizability			
Standard Error of Measurement			
Item Analysis Performed			
Difficulty			
Discrimination			
H − L/H + L			
r(bis)			

Figure 3-3. Checklist for instrument development.

Components of Measurement Devices

What is the hallmark of a good measurement instrument? A good measurement instrument will help the user to attain a specific goal consistently and with a reasonable expenditure of time, energy, and money. First and foremost, an instrument must be valid for the specific purpose or goal the user intends to achieve through the measurement. Reliability is another word for consistency and is a crucial prerequisite for validity, but is not in any way a substitute for it. A reasonable expenditure of time, energy, and money is usually referred to as usability of the instrument.

Before discussing the issues of validity, reliability, and usability, it may be useful to consider the concept of "true score." Any measurement of human behavior is merely a sample from which the quantity, frequency, degree, or amount of the phenomenon under study possessed by an individual is estimated. The test or other instrument samples only a limited portion of the entire domain of the phenomenon for only a limited amount of time.

As with any sample, a certain amount of false readings or error is expected in the observations. Therefore, one may postulate that any measurement taken, which is called observed score, is made up of true score plus error score. This is often given in formula as:

$X = t + e$

where

X = observed score,

t = true score, and

e = error score.

Obviously, one cannot know with any exactness the true score, but the goal is to reduce or identify the controllable error to establish confidence that the observed score approximates the true score. The concepts of validity and reliability deal with identifying elements of error and controlling those elements that are not chance or random elements resulting from sampling.

Validity.   The validity question is always specific: How well does this instrument assess the characteristic, construct, or behavior the user desires to measure? A test may be valid for one thing and totally invalid for another. A joint committee of the American Psychological Association, American Educational Research Association, and National Council on Measurement in Education has prepared a set of guidelines for test publishers and others to aid in clarifying and understanding the concept of validity (APA, 1985). These recommendations classify validity as falling within three categories: content, criterion-related, and construct validity. Each of these categories are addressed below.

*Content Validity.*Certification or licensure tests such as the Sensory Integration and Praxis Tests (SIPT) Certification Examination, which is in the process of development, must have content validity. Certification examinations are types of achievement tests and all achievement tests must have content validity. That is, they must be a representative sample of the topical areas being assessed and of the cognitive processes required.

How does one determine the content validity of a test? The "Table of Specifications" will confirm whether the test has been constructed carefully and logically. Examine the table and the test items to determine that the test measures what one intends to measure. Content validity is determined by looking within the test and the testing materials. This is not to be confused with face validity, which merely says that the test appears to deal with appropriate material. Content validity means that one can demonstrate a logical encompassment of the appropriate topics in terms of overall coverage of the material and appropriate proportions of subtopics. Although almost never used in a formal manner, the same procedure would apply for determining the content validity of any other type of measurement instrument such as rating scales, surveys, etc.

To establish content validity, one begins with a task or domain analysis. If we are speaking of a certification test, this seems rather straightforward and clear. But what about content validity of other types of instruments? Borrowing from the domain specifications developed by Royeen (1985), we could construct a scale for measuring tactile defensiveness that would have content validity. Royeen first defined the construct tactile defensiveness, then collected a variety of behaviors related to the construct. She next submitted this list of behaviors to experts for review and developed descriptors of statements that a child might make based on those behaviors. At this point, the domain has been defined and described. A "Table of Specifications" can easily be made by listing these behaviors, and a rating scale (observation or interview) can be devised from the specifications. This rating scale could claim evidence of content validity.

It may be worth noting that Royeen had a pertinent point to make with the article cited above (Royeen, 1985), which is that the majority of constructs of interest in occupational therapy, as is true in many other fields, are not well defined. Research in this developing field of occupational therapy will need to be particularly concerned with domain specifications. Consider, for example, how one would devise an instrument that was intended to be an operational definition of domains such as gravitational insecurity or occupational engagement adaptive response.

Criterion-Related Validity. As opposed to content validity, where the validity rests on a judgement of the user as to whether the test has been logically developed to assess the content desired, criterion-related validity looks outside of the test in an empirical fashion. As the name implies, criterion-related validity requires demonstrating that the test results relate in some way to an outside criterion. For example, predictive validity is a type of criterion-related validity and requires that one demonstrate that the results of a test predict some future outcome. A reading readiness test in kindergarten should predict how well a child will do when he or she enters the reading program in the first or second grade. As a general rule then, we would expect those who score highly on the predictive test to do well on the future performance measure (the criterion).

Criterion-related validity may not necessarily refer to predictive validity of some future performance. It may refer to a more immediate criterion, in which instance it is called concurrent validity. If one is interested in substituting one measure for another, concurrent validity may be the most pertinent type of validity to demonstrate.

An example of concurrent validity appears in a study conducted by Harrison and Kielhofner (1986). These two researchers were interested in whether the "Preschool Play Scale" (PPS) would be a valid measure of the developmental level of play for handicapped children. To validate this scale, data were collected with the PPS, the Parten Social Play Hierarchy, and the Lunzner Scale of Organization of Behavior. The instrument being validated was the PPS; therefore the other two instruments were "outside criteria." In reporting the intercorrelations among various parts of the PPS and each of the other instruments, Harrison and Kielhofner confirmed that the scales of the PPS were valid, i.e., the validity coefficients were significant.

Of particular concern regarding criterion-related validity is the characteristic of the criterion. The instrument can be no more valid than the criterion. For example, in the study described above, components of the "Preschool Play Scale" were reported to correlate between 0.50 and 0.76 with the Lunzner Scale. This can be interpreted that those components of the PPS measure approximately the same as the Lunzner Scale. The claim for validity of the PPS now rests on the validity of the criterion, the Lunzner Scale.

Furthermore, the reliability of the criterion will also restrict the validity. A reliability coefficient squared (multiplied with itself) is known as the coefficient of predictability, because it represents the percentage of one variable predicted by the other variable. For example, when Harrison and Kielhofner (1986) reported, above, that the PPS correlated 0.76 with the Lunzner Scale, it is proper to infer that the PPS predicted 58% (0.76 times 0.76) of the variance in the Lunzner Scale scores. Because the reliability coefficient estimates how well the score of a test predicts itself, then the square of the reliability of the criterion is the uppermost limit of how well the instrument can predict the criterion. If a criterion does not predict itself, i.e., it is not reliable, the instrument cannot predict it.

Construct Validity. The third type of validity may well be the most important for the users of this book. Constructs are an abstract or unobservable trait or ability postulated from theory. A theory is an explanation of something that may not be observed, and the construct is the result of that explanation. People facing similar situations behave differently; therefore it is said that they possess more or less of a characteristic than others, for example, intelligence, anxiety, critical thinking, dominance, and achievement motivation are all psychological constructs.

Stanley and Hopkins (1972, p.112) suggest that the process of developing a measure of a psychological construct and establishing its validity proceeds as follows:

1. Develop a set of tasks or items based on a rational analysis of the construct.
2. Derive testable predictions regarding the relationship between the construct and other variables; for example, if the test measures anxiety, we should expect to find some relationship between test scores and clinical ratings of anxiety level, and so on.
3. Conduct empirical studies of these theoretical predictions.
4. Eliminate items or tasks that operate contrary to theory (or revise the theory) and proceed again with steps two and three.

To determine whether an instrument possesses construct validity, one should be fully aware of the theory underlying the instrument. Observable behaviors are identified from the theoretical construct and defined and described in the instrument. Finally, statistical analyses are conducted, demonstrating that persons possessing the construct to a greater degree score differently on the instrument than those possessing the construct to a lesser degree. Going back to the tactile defensiveness construct described by

Royeen (1985), it may be seen that in addition to content validity, the specification of the domain of tactile defensiveness permitted her to provide evidence of construct validity for anyone developing a test or rating scale that uses these descriptors.

If a reader is interested in establishing construct validity of an instrument, further readings are suggested: Lord and Novick (1967), Campbell and Fiske (1959), or other references listed at the end of this chapter.

Reliability. Reliability is an estimate of the capacity of an instrument to measure the same thing every time it is used, that is, to consistently assess the value that the instrument is purported to measure. Reliability is generally considered in two categories: internal consistency and stability.

Internal consistency refers to the ability of the instrument to measure a dimension consistently, whereas stability refers to the capability of the instrument to measure the dimension every time the instrument is used. To fully grasp the concept of reliability, one has to consider that any measurement is a sample. Even in the physical realm, this is an important concept. Just as in measuring the height and weight of a person, each measurement will vary slightly each time. In measurement of psychological concepts there are many dimensions to the sample.

A behavior or psychological construct is being measured at a single point in time. The behavior or construct may vary depending on many factors influencing the subject from whom we are obtaining the assessment. In giving a test to the person, the person taking the test may vary in his mental abilities from hour to hour and from day to day. However, these are variances within a narrow band, and the accuracy of this sample of behavior may be estimated.

Furthermore, only a portion of whatever domain the instrument is designed to measure is being sampled. For example, if it were an IQ test, one could not hope to measure all of the dimensions of intelligence; therefore, appropriate components are sampled. Similarly, one cannot measure all aspects of occupational performance, but only a sample thereof. Even within those various components of intelligence or occupational performance that can be sampled, attention can be paid to only a portion of that component. If the component happens to be activities of daily living, one cannot hope to measure the entire range of activities. Therefore, a few sample items of activities of daily living are constructed to represent the entire component.

If the instrument is an observation scale, not only is a small sample of the subject's behavior for a short period of time being observed, only components of certain behaviors can be observed. In addition, the raters' behavior has now also been introduced. The rater can only grasp a certain number of elements of behavior, and will selectively focus on those that are determined to be appropriate.

Reliability therefore refers to how faithfully the sample represents the universe selected to be measured. This is operationally represented by how consistently one observes or assesses the elements of the sample, and therefore how consistently that behavior is being measured within the sampling limits. Reliability is directly related to validity. The foregoing discussion of sampling would apply to the concept of validity as well as the concept of reliability. Furthermore, unless an instrument measures the same thing every time, it cannot measure what it purports to measure; unless an instrument is reliable it cannot be valid.

There are two statistics to represent the faithfulness with which the sample is represented: the reliability coefficient and the standard error of measurement. A discussion of the reliability coefficient, both internal consistency and stability, will be followed by a discussion of the standard error of measurement.

Internal Consistency. Internal consistency concerns the sample within the instrument. It examines how consistently sampled behavior is assessed over a limited period of time, and how consistently the instrument assesses that behavior across the elements being measured. For those instruments that are not self-reporting, for example, a rating scale, internal consistency is an indication of how consistently the observer assesses the various sampled behaviors.

One observation, either by an observer or by a single test item, is a sample of behavior, but there is no way of assessing how consistently that behavior appears or how consistently it is measured. If two items measure the same construct or element of behavior, a comparison can be made of the two to see if they consistently measure that subject's behavior. For the most part, the more observations made, the greater the likelihood that the observed behavior is not merely a random incident and the greater the researcher's confidence that the instrument is internally consistent.

In assessing a particular behavior for the purpose of diagnosing or prescribing certain treatment, internal consistency of the observation is vitally important. One must know that the observation is reliable, that is, that it is not a random observation but that the behavior observed occurs with some regularity. One must know that adequate evidence of that behavior is sampled by the instrument to specify and identify the behavior.

Stability. If internal consistency deals with the adequacy of the measurement of a behavior at any given time, stability deals with the ability of that instrument to assess the same behavior repeatedly.

Stability is a somewhat different concept than internal consistency in that it is concerned with the consistency with which a behavior occurs as opposed to assurance that it has been adequately assessed. Whereas internal consistency is important in determining an adequate sample, stability is important in determining that a given behavior is repeatedly assessed. The repetitions may be over a period of time, over a number of subjects, across a number of raters or judges, or they may be over a number of treatments.

Stability usually is thought of as being measured over time. If a pretest were given and then a treatment introduced and an assessment made of the same behavior subsequent to the treatment, an instrument would be needed that would yield reliability in terms of stability across time. Such stability is necessary to assess that same behavior in the same manner with the same subject before and after treatment. Typically, schools give a test in the fall and again in the spring. They must know that the test is stable, that is, that it measures the same thing in the fall as it measured in the spring; even though they expect a different score in the spring because supposedly the students have learned during the intervening period of time. Similarly, a subject may have a particular disorder; the disorder is diagnosed, treatment prescribed, and therapy is applied. To assess that disorder and to see whether the therapy has reduced the dysfunctional effects of the disorder an instrument is needed that is stable across time.

If a number of persons appear to have the same disorder, and one is interested in whether the same treatment is beneficial to all persons, it might be of interest to measure that disorder across all of the subjects. The stability of interest in this instance is that the instrument measures the same thing across all subjects.

On the other hand, one may have a group of people and not know whether they have the same disorder. A number of raters might be asked to complete a checklist of behaviors on all subjects. At the end of this rating it is important to know that each rater consistently observed the same disorders among the same subjects. This instance refers to stability across raters as opposed to stability over time.

Lastly, one may be concerned with a variety of treatments for the same disorder. To assess the occupational dysfunction for a number of subjects prior to treatment, administer different treatments to different subjects and then reassess the occupational dysfunction to determine which treatment was most effective. Here, one is interested in stability across treatments; that is, that the instrument could pick up changes in behavior occurring as a result of each of the treatments or therapies.

While reliability may be referred to differently, there is almost no instance where types of reliability, internal consistency and stability, would not be important. Because internal consistency refers specifically to the ability of an instrument to assure an adequate sample within the instrument, internal consistency is always necessary. Because virtually any time a behavior is assessed, it will be assessed over time, over subjects, over raters, or across treatments, it is vital to know the stability of the instrument as well as the internal consistency.

Measurement of Labile Variables

Occupational and physical therapists as well as others in clinical practice often deal with behaviors or dysfunctions that are labile. How can one measure a phenomenon that is always changing and highly unstable? What can be done with a behavior that may be observed today, but almost certainly will not observed again with any regularity. Examples of such labile functions are attention and arousal, and tactile defensiveness.

There are methods for dealing with such variables, but it must be realized that neither concept, reliability, nor validity is an absolute. In each instance, these are characteristics that require application of judgment. Informed judgment will consider phenomena that are by nature labile and attempt to deal with such variables in a manner where the classical definition of reliability is less important. Failing to find alternative methods of dealing with such labile variables, the task of assessing the reliability of measurements of labile behaviors is possible but requires painstaking care.

Initially, it must be recognized that stability of the instrument is being sought, as opposed to stability of the behavior. By definition, labile behaviors or dysfunctions are not stable. An instrument to measure such variables must be stable. To assess the reliability, that is stability, of such an instrument, there is no alternative to repeated measures. The most appropriate methodology is generalizability, as discussed below, which involves an analysis of variance model (ANOVA). While regression is closely related to analysis of variance and can certainly be used, it becomes an awkward procedure. Repeated measures ANOVA is available in most statistical packages and will not be presented here. The interested reader should be aware that it requires multiple assessments of the same subjects at different times. For further discussion, see *Statistical Package for the Social Sciences* (Hull and Nie, 1977) or a statistical text.

Methods of Estimating Reliability

Reliability may be estimated by calculating a correlation coefficient or by computing an analysis of variance (ANOVA). Correlation is the most common method and has been responsible for establishing the correlation coefficient as the standard measure of reliability. Correlation will yield either a Pearson "r" coefficient of correlation, a Spearman "Rho" coefficient of correlation, or a Contingency Coefficient.

Despite the general term of correlation coefficient, there are several procedures, each of which may be appropriate under certain circumstances. Four of these will be discussed briefly.

Further discussion of these and other measures of reliability may be found in the references listed at the end of this chapter, such as Brown (1983), Ebel (1979), or Mehrens and Lehmann (1978).

Test-Retest

The simplest measure of reliability is to give the same test a second time to the same set of examinees. Correlation of the two sets of scores will yield a reliability coefficient estimating the stability of the test. There are several objections to this approach of estimating reliability. These objections include: a) the fact that the second administration of the same test items is not independent of the first; b) that the two administrations of the same set of items fail to consider that the test is only a sample of the entire universe of information measured by the test; and c) that it is not really practical to give the exact same test twice to the same individuals. To overcome some of these criticisms, two other reliability estimates can be used.

Equivalent Forms

If two or more forms of a test are prepared in such a way that each is equivalent to the other in terms of content and difficulty, each examinee may be given each of the forms. A correlation coefficient calculated between the scores of each of the forms will produce an estimate of the reliability of the tests. There still may be some objections to being tested twice, merely to obtain reliability estimates of the examinations. However, the objections of using the same items and of limited sampling of the universe of possible items has been reduced.

Split Halves

It would seem logical that two 50-item tests could be combined and given as a 100-item test with the intention of establishing the reliability through the equivalent forms approach. From the 100-item test separate scores could be obtained for the two halves and correlated. This would be a special case of equivalent forms reliability. Of course there are some difficulties associated with this approach to estimating reliability. For example, each half of the test must be parallel, that is, of equal difficulty and homogeneous in content. Furthermore, because reliability of a test is related to the length, i.e., the number of items in the test, by using a split-half method of estimating, the reliability coefficient has been reduced by some amount. Further, because the reliability estimate is within the test itself, this is a measure of internal consistency rather than a measure of stability. To overcome the limitation of the reduction in length of the test by one-half, a formula was devised to estimate the reliability of the full length test. The formula, known as the Spearman-Brown formula, may be found in any measurement text, such as Brown (1983), Ebel (1979), Mehrens and Lehmann (1978), or Stanley and Hopkins (1972). Kuder and Richardson developed a series of formulae for estimating reliability in 1937, two of which are widely accepted today (Ebel, 1979). Formula 20 (known as KR-20) is applicable only if the test is scored by giving one point for a correct answer and zero points for an incorrect answer.

This formula requires calculation of the difficulty of each item (proportion of correct response). This quantity may be approximated if items do not vary widely in difficulty. An alternate method using information about the mean test score and the number of items in the test may be calculated from Kuder and Richardson's formula 21 (KR-21).

The formula KR-20 is a special case of a more general formula developed by Cronbach and known as Coefficient Alpha (Cronbach, 1951). Like KR-20, Coefficient Alpha requires item level variance estimates and is not generally feasible unless programmed on a computer. Most computerized statistical packages have coefficient alpha as a standard output, e.g., *Statistical Package for the Social Sciences* (Hull and Nie, 1977).

Any number of text books will provide more detailed information concerning the computation and limitations of the reliability estimates shown above. However, a more thorough understanding of the concepts and most likely a more useful procedure for estimating reliability can be obtained through Analysis of Variance procedure (ANOVA). The following discussion and the examples in Appendix A have been adapted from Thorndike (1982) and from Brennan, Jarjoura and Deaton (1980) but originated as "Generalizability Theory" described by Cronbach and others (1972).

Analysis of Variance Methods

Reliability Estimates and Variance Components

Reliability is classically defined in terms of variance of true score and error score. As previously mentioned, "true score" cannot be observed, but must be inferred from observations. The same can be said for error score. The inferences that legitimately can be made depend on the nature of the samples of the behavior observed. Earlier, it was said that error is the result of sampling a universe, and that attempts to measure, especially human behavior, involve sampling along many dimensions. Assigning a measurement to each of these dimensions will involve two elements; the first is the true component and the second is the error component of the observed score. Therefore, any score obtained is made up of a number of true score and error score components. Reliability is described as the ratio of true score to observed score (true plus error score), or more correctly the ratio of the variances of these scores.

Appendix A shows the step-by-step computation of the example given below. Following these steps may help the reseacher to understand the concepts of true score and error score redefinitions, even though such analyses are seldom, if ever, computed manually.

Assume that there are ten clients with similar disorders for whom therapy is to be provided. To know how beneficial the therapy is, a rating scale to record the clients' behavior is devised. To assure completely objective results, three therapists are recruited to observe the clients. The observations are to be recorded on an instrument made up of five items, each of which is scored 0 to 9. The question is whether this instrument is sufficiently reliable to be used regularly.

The data gathered will provide the raw material to compute a three-way analysis of variance, which will provide the information for estimating seven distinct components of variance. By examining these components of variance it is possible to analyze the instrument and not only calculate a reliability estimate (actually in this instance a coefficient of generalizability), but also to determine how to increase the reliability most profitably.

The three-way ANOVA will partition or identify the seven variance components. These variance components may be examined across:
- Persons being rated;
- Items on the rating scale;
- Raters doing the rating;
- Both persons and raters;
- Both persons and items;
- Both items and raters; and
- The entire spectrum of persons, items, and raters.

Computation of the coefficient of generalizability proceeds from first examining an estimate of true score and observed score variance. The best estimate of true score variance is the persons variance. If the instrument and raters measured perfectly, the only variance should be evidenced by the objects (persons) being observed (measured): the persons variance. The expected true variance is calculated from the variance components for persons, which is then divided by the expected observed variance to obtain the coefficient of generalizability. It might be stated that this is an estimate of the correlation between two sets of observations for a group of clients when each client is observed by three randomly selected raters using an instrument made up of five randomly selected items. Note the emphasis of randomness in these assumptions.

Because the size of the coefficient is dependent on the ratio of the expected true to the expected observed variance, an increased coefficient is dependent on reducing the denominator or the observed components. Because these variance components have been partitioned, they can be examined individually. If the item variance, for example, is large, the items are not very homogeneous. The options are to increase the number of items of similar type or revise the items to be more homogenous. It is possible to estimate the effect of increasing the number of items by recalculating the coefficient with an increase in "n" number of items. If the rater variance component is large, there are also some options. It may be that more raters are needed, or it may be that rater training is needed to increase the rater's homogeneity.

The advantages of the ANOVA procedures should be apparent. Not only is there greater flexibility in calculating the reliability, but also there is an opportunity to analyze the weaknesses of the instrument or procedures and consider options for improvement.

A word of caution is in order. In the example given here, all raters rated all persons, using all items. This is known as a fully crossed ANOVA. If not all raters rate all persons on all items, this is known as a nested ANOVA. Nested designs require some modification in calculating variance components. Thorndike (1982) or other measurement texts will provide more detail in using generalizability theory in a variety of situations.

Nonparametric Data

Nearly all of the above discussion has assumed certain specified character-istics of the data collected by the instruments. It has assumed that we have interval data and in most instances, a normal distribution. Much of the data collected by observation instruments, interview schedules, and question-naires are likely to be less than interval data. Data that are nominal, ordinal, or categorical cannot be analyzed using the same parametric methods as interval and ratio data; they need special types of procedures.

Contingency Coefficient

A useful method of establishing reliability of instruments used to collect nominal (categorical) or ordinal data may be the Contingency Coefficient, "C". This coefficient makes no assumptions about the underlying continuity, the order of the categories, or the shape of the distribution of these data.

"The Contingency Coefficient C is a measure of the extent of association or relation between two sets of attributes" (Seigel, 1956, p. 196). This method is also useful for examining validity issues with criterion-referenced measures.

To compute C, one establishes a contingency table and enters the observed frequencies for each cell. The expected frequencies are computed by deter-mining what frequencies would occur if there were no association or correla-tion between the two variables, which are the dimensions of the table. The larger the discrepancy between the observed and expected frequencies, the greater the degree of association between the two variables.

If one has data that may be more appropriate for calculating a contingency coefficient than for a parametric test such as Pearson r, consult Seigel (1956, pp.196-202).

Additional nonparametric or distribution-free statistics are available for estimating reliability. Many are available in computerized statistical packages such as *Statistical Package for the Social Sciences* (Hull and Nie, 1977).

Spearman Rank Correlation

Generally referred to as Rho, the symbol for this coefficient is either a capital "R" or the Greek letter ρ. It is of value when one wishes to make no assumptions about the distributional characteristics of a variable or when one's data are ordinal in nature. For example, if in response to a questionnaire or an observational scale one has a series of responses that are progressive (increase in value) but are not in the form of intervals (increase in some continuous or equal manner), a nonparametric technique of analysis is called for, as opposed to some parametric technique.

Another example of where ρ may be the most appropriate statistic is with a split-half group, as opposed to a split-half instrument. An earlier discussion mentioned a split-half method of establishing reliability. By dividing the items in the instrument in half, the homogeneity of the items was examined. It may be more desirable to split the individuals rather than the items. In such instances, it is assumed that the items are not homogeneous, but that persons are. This is a measure of stability across persons. If the items were to be used as cases and the individuals randomly assigned to one of two groups, a correlation would estimate how reliably the instrument measures across persons. Rho is most appropriate for this type of analysis.

Rho may be interpreted the same as a Pearson coefficient of correlation, i.e., the closer it approximates 1.0, the greater the association between the two variables, and the closer to 0.0, the less the association between the two variables.

Procedures for calculating ρ may be found in most statistical texts. A specific reference is made to Seigel (1956, pp.202- 213).

Kendall Coefficient of Concordance

In some cases, one may be interested in examining the reliability across more than two variables. Suppose that one is using a panel of judges to rate a phenomenon. Neither of the above two procedures is appropriate. Because no assumptions about the item data being continuous or interval are to be made, only that it is ordinal, a nonparametric technique should be used for estimating interjudge reliability.

In effect, an average "ρ" is desired, considering all possible paired correlations among the panel of judges. Seigel (1956) has shown that a relatively simple method of calculating an average of all possible pairings is through a method known as Kendall Coefficient of Concordance, "W". Values for W range only between 0.0 and +1.0, while ρ may range between − 1.0 and +1.0.

A formula for calculating average ρ using W is found in Seigel (1956, p.229), and is more nearly interpretable as a coefficient of correlation. Again, consult Seigel (1956) for use of this methodology.

Standard Error of Measurement

The concept of standard error of measurement is analgous to standard error of the mean or, in a general sense, standard deviation. It represents a probability band around the true score. It has been stated that the true score cannot be measured, only inferred, from the observed score and that the observed score is equal to the sum of the true score and error score. Because the error score can be inferred from the standard error of measurement, it is possible to estimate the true score.

Because the information available to work with is the observed score and the reliability coefficient, the standard error of measurement is usually calculated from these statistics. Given the standard deviation of a set of observed scores and the reliability coefficient of these scores, the standard error of measurement is obtained from the following expression:

$$SEM = S \sqrt{1-r}$$

where:

SEM = standard error of measurement,

   S = the standard deviation of the scores, and

   r = the reliability coefficient.

From the area of the normal curve it can be determined approximately how many individual true scores will lie between ± a given number of standard errors of measurement. For example, an elementary statistical text will show that approximately 95% of all observed scores will have true scores between ±2 SEM of the observed scores.

The size of the standard error in relation to the mean of the total scores provides some meaningful information about the reliability of the instrument. The larger the standard error, the greater the variability of the data and therefore the less reliable the instrument. Conversely, the smaller the standard error, the less variability in the data and the more reliable the instrument.

Criterion-Referenced Measures

Estimating reliability for criterion-referenced measures is as important as estimating reliability for classical instruments. Methods and types of reliability are similar, though conceived somewhat differently. Interpretation of reliability may be somewhat different, and the reader should be aware that not all approaches may be applied in the same manner. For example, a split-half reliability on a criterion-referenced test should not be performed across the entire test, but across only that portion that pertains to a given objective. The coefficient that one would expect from such highly homogeneous test items is much higher than one would expect from such a small number of items under classical testing definitions. Furthermore, validity is also conceived in a different manner, yet good norm-referenced instruments will also have clear objectives and domain specifications.

Usability

As was stated earlier, a good measurement instrument must be valid, reliable, and usable (practical). Decisions regarding selecting an instrument versus devising one and of determining the reliability and validity of an instrument have been discussed. Implications that the clinical setting may have on instrument selection and/or development will now be discussed.

Generalizing the Findings

The purpose of research may be descriptive, correlational, or experimental. To some extent the purpose of the research may impinge on the decisions about an instrument. If the research is descriptive or correlational, it is not intended to be presented as appropriate beyond the population from which the data were collected. That is to say it is not presented as generalizable to any group other than that particular group (or like groups) from whom the data were gathered. In such instances, validity of an instrument for gathering the data is important only to the extent of measuring those constructs or behaviors in the given situation. One could say that it is situation specific. On the other hand, if the research is experimental in nature, the instruments must have validity for the population to which the experimental results are intended to be generalized.

Clinical research is unique from research in general in two specific ways. It often deals with small numbers of subjects in practical settings and it is likely to have a particular theoretical orientation. To the extent that these generalizations are true, they have implications for instrument selection/development. Most statistics used to describe validity and reliability are based on large samples. In particular, parametric methods assume normal distributions, and normal distributions are the result of repeatedly sampling from the general population. Distribution-free statistical tests, on the other hand, permit more freedom in interpreting data.

Differing theoretical orientations require great care in selecting or modifying existing instruments. Obviously the theoretical underpinning of the instrument must be made explicit and must agree with the theoretical model supporting the existing project.

There may be a third purpose for clinical research in addition to the two cited above. Royeen (1986) suggests that instrumentation is a goal of research in occupational therapy: "Instrumentation is the window that allows us to view human behavior in an objective manner,"(Royeen, 1986, p.2). To develop commonly accepted operational definitions or instruments to describe and define clinical judgments is a worthwhile process within the discipline of occupational therapy.

Some Measurement Issues

Whenever one starts to measure human behavior one has to consider the effect on the person being observed. That person has a right to know what is happening and why. Research is not a sufficient reason to take a measurement of behavior. The issue of rights of subjects is important and sensitive. On the other hand, without research there would be no progress.

Instrument development requires detailed standardization efforts. Once you have assembled your items and reviewed and revised them, there remains the task of trying out the instrument. Tryout involves recruiting a norm group, administering the instrument, and analyzing the data collected. There are no shortcuts to this process; the larger the norm group and the more closely the norm group resembles the research population, the better instrument.

Estimating instrument stability is one of the more difficult tasks because of the need to obtain two measurements of the same persons. If the factors mentioned above all apply, the group must be relatively large (n = 30 is a good rule of thumb), must resemble the appropriate research population, and be willing to spend the time and effort necessary to complete the tasks. The more heterogeneous the group along the dimension of interest, the more likely you will be able to demonstrate reliability.

The issue of labile variables or behaviors was mentioned earlier. There is some question as to whether the academic model of validity and reliability are suitable for instrumentation in occupational therapy and other fields of clinical research. There is no substitute for informed judgment. There is no reason to believe that any behavior cannot be measured, but we may not know yet how to go about measuring it. One of the first areas of research might well be in terms of instrument development to measure labile behaviors encountered by therapists in the clinical setting.

References

American Psychological Association. (1985). *Standards for educational and psychological tests*. Washington, D.C.: American Psychological Association.

Brennan, R. L., Jarjoura, D. and Deaton, E. L. (1980).*ACT Technical Bulletin Number 36. Some issues concerning the estimation and interpretation of variance components in generalizability theory*. Iowa City: ACT.

Brown, F. G. (1983). *Principles of educational and psychological testing*. (3rd ed.). New York: Holt, Rinehart and Winston.

Buros, O. (Ed.). (1938, 1941, 1949, 1953, 1959, 1965, 1972, 1978). *Mental measurements yearbook* (1st - 8th ed.). Highland Park, NJ: Gryphon Press.

Buros, O. (1974). *Tests in print*. Highland Park, NJ: Gryphon Press.

Campbell, D. T. and Fiske, D. W. (1959). Convergent and discriminant validation by the multitrait-multimethod matrix. *Psychological Bulletin*, 56:81-105.

Cronbach, L. J. (1951). Coefficient alpha and the internal structure of tests. *Psychometrika*, 16:297-334.

Cronbach, L. J., Glaser, G. C., Nanda, H., and Rajaratnam, N.. (1972). *The dependability of behavioral measurements: Theory of generalizability for scores and profiles*. New York: John Wiley and Sons.

Ebel, R. L. (1979). *Essentials of educational measurement*. (3rd ed.). Englewood Cliffs, NJ: Prentice-Hall Inc.

Gould, S. J. (1981). *The mismeasure of man*. New York: W. W. Norton and Co.

Gilfoyle, E.M. (1986) *Professional directions: Management in action, Presidential Address*. American Journal of Occupational Therapy, 40(a), 593-596.

Glaser, B. G. and Strauss, A. I. (1967). *The discovery of grounded theory. Strategies for qualitative research.* Chicago: Aldine.

Harrison, H. and Kielhofner, G. (1986). Examining reliability and validity of the preschool play scale with handicapped children. *The American Journal of Occupational Therapy,* 40(3):167-173.

Hull, C. H. and Nie, N. H. (1977). *Statistical package for the social sciences.* (Release 8). New York: McGraw Hill Book Co.

Keyser, D. J. and Sweetland, R. C. (Eds.). (1985, 1986). *Test critiques.* Vols. III and IV. Kansas City, Missouri: Test Corporation of America.

Lord, F. M. and Novick, M. R. (1968). *Statistical theories of mental test scores.* Reading, Massachusetts: Addison-Wesley Publishing Company.

Mehrens, W. A. and Lehmann, I. J. (1978). *Measurement and evaluation in education and psychology.* (2nd ed.). New York: Holt, Rinehart and Winston.

Robinson, J. P. and Shaver, P. R. (1970). *Measures of social psychological attitudes.* Ann Arbor, Michigan: Institute for Social Research, The University of Michigan.

Royeen, C. B. (1985). Domain specifications of the construct tactile defensiveness. *The American Journal of Occupational Therapy,* 39(9):596-599.

Royeen, C. B. (1986). Instrumentation in occupational therapy. Paper presented at the Occupational Therapy for Maternal and Child Health, Research and Leadership Development, Santa Monica, California.

Siegel, S. (1956). *Nonparametric statistics for the behavioral sciences.* New York: McGraw-Hill Book Company, Inc.

Simon, A. and Boyer, E. G. (1974). *Mirrors for behavior III: Anthology of observation instruments.* Philadelphia: Communication Materials Center, Research for Better Schools.

Spradley, J. P. (1980). *Participant observation.* New York: Holt, Rinehart and Winston.

Stanley, J. C. and Hopkins, K. D. (1972). *Educational and psychological measurement and evaluation.* Englewood Cliffs, NJ: Prentice-Hall, Inc.

Thorndike, R. L. (1982). *Applied psychometrics.* Boston: Houghton Mifflin, Company.

Yin, R. K. (1984). *Case study research: Design and methods.* Beverly Hills, California: Sage Publications.

CHAPTER 4

THE ROLE OF EXPLORATORY DATA ANALYSIS IN CLINICAL RESEARCH

Charlotte Brasic Royeen
Leigh Geiger

Chapter Overview

This chapter begins with an introduction to exploratory data analysis. The definition and purpose of exploratory data analyses are explained, as well as the differences between exploratory data analysis and confirmatory data analysis. Resources for use in exploratory data analysis are identified. Subsequently, procedures for hand calculation of two exploratory data analysis procedures, a stem-and-leaf and a boxplot, are presented. Finally, interpretation guidelines for exploratory data analysis are put forth.

An Introduction to Exploratory Data Analysis

In an article in the foundation section of the *American Journal of Occupational Therapy*, Maralynne D. Mitcham delineates the relationship between the process of research and the practice of a clinically based profession: occupational therapy (Mitcham, 1986). Within her delineation of the processes, a key point is the similarity regarding problem solving in research and occupational therapy. There is, however, another key point or dimension that is similar between the two processes: data analysis. For example, just as one conducts evaluation to learn more about a client, one conducts data analysis to learn more about a data set.

Exploratory data analysis is a specialized type or form of data analysis, just as there are specialized forms or types of evaluations in any field of clinical practice. Screening tests for identifying the characteristics of data sets are collectively known as procedures for exploratory data analysis (Hoaglin, Mosteller, and Tukey, 1981; Kotz and Johnson, 1982; Tukey, 1977). These procedures were developed primarily by John W. Tukey (1977). As the term implies, exploratory data analysis is a preliminary step conducted to determine what the data reveal; the process is designed to uncover the distributional characteristics of the data (Kirk, 1982). Subsequent to the exploratory data analysis, confirmatory or inferential statistical procedures can be selected based on the findings of the exploratory analysis. If abnormalities are indeed revealed, certain assumptions underlying the use of parametric tests may be violated and a nonparametric or robust statistical procedure may be preferentially selected for inferential statistical analyses (Royeen and Seaver, 1986).

Hartwig and Dearing (1979) define exploratory data analysis as a state of mind or a way of thinking. Thus, it may be considered to be a mindset or frame of reference. Just as clinicians and service providers adopt any variety of conceptual models (such as sensory integration, neurodevelopmental treatment, or occupational behavior as frames of reference to guide treatment), a research investigator may similarly adopt exploratory data analysis as a frame of reference to guide data analysis. Furthermore, it is a frame of reference that connotes an open mind, allowing data to reveal patterns and characteristics to the investigator, rather than having the investigator operate on existing assumptions regarding the data.

Figure 4-1 is based on concepts presented in the *Encyclopedia of Statistics* (Kotz and Johnson, 1982) and elaborated herein regarding exploratory data analysis.

Figure 4-1 reveals the dynamic balance between exploratory data analysis (preliminary) and confirmatory data analysis (secondary). The primary intent of exploratory data analysis is to explore the data and determine what the data reveals, whereas the intent of confirmatory data analysis is to confirm or reject some hypothesis or comparable proposition. Thus, one is attempting to understand the data in exploratory data analysis, whereas one is attempting to evaluate some aspect of the data in confirmatory data analysis.

The method of obtaining information and interpreting the information about the data also differs in these two approaches. In exploratory data analysis one uses pattern recognition to understand the characteristics of the data; in confirmatory data analysis one uses significance testing based on probability theory to evaluate the data. However, it is most important that Figure 4-1 reveals the relationship between exploratory data analysis and confirmatory data analysis to be a dynamic balance, because most data analysis conducted by a research investigator would incorporate both types of data analysis and strike a balance between the two approaches.

To further illustrate the comparison of exploratory data analysis and confirmatory data analysis, a listing of types of questions associated with one versus the other is presented below in Figures 4-2 and 4-3, respectively.

Review of Figures 4-2 and 4-3 suggests a main difference between questions asked in exploratory data analysis and questions asked in confirmatory

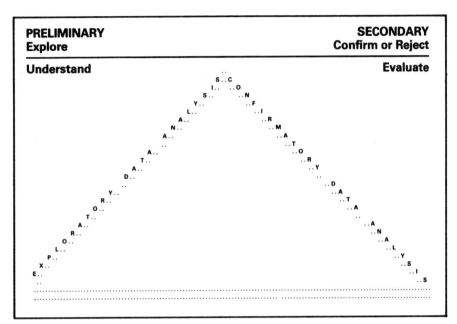

Figure 4-1. The Frames of Reference of Data Analysis.

data analysis. The former involves characteristics of data sets and the latter involves relationships between data sets or between a data set and some normative reference.

Historically, exploratory data analysis is relatively new in terms of a frame of reference. As previously stated, the collection of procedures as well as the attitude and approach subserving exploratory data analysis are attributed to John W. Tukey (*Encyclopedia of Statistics*, 1982). The collection of procedures known as "exploratory data analysis" may be characterized as primarily univariate. That is, the procedures analyze or pertain to only one data set for a given analysis. The most notable exception to this is the scatterplot or scattergram, which is a bivariate procedure involving the correlation of two variables. Recently, multivariate exploratory data analysis procedures have been developed (Freni-Titular, Law and Louv, 1984; Kleiner and Hartigan, 1981), but they are primarily in developmental stages and require programming capacity.

Exploratory data analysis procedures also are, to a large extent, visually oriented. They depend on pattern recognition that is visually conveyed. The stem and leaf graph and the boxplot are examples of such visually oriented exploratory data analytic procedures. The reader may recognize this as similar to visually oriented analysis procedures often employed in single subject research.

The purpose of exploratory data analysis is to learn about the characteristics of one or more variables prior to confirmatory data analysis (Hartwig and Dearing, 1979). The purpose of such exploration is to increase the appropriateness of the confirmatory data analytic procedure subsequently selected.

No.	Question
1.	In what range do most of the observations fall?
2.	Are any of the scores much higher or lower than the rest? If so, which individual observations are involved? Could these scores be invalid, inaccurately recorded or influenced by other variables?
3.	Is there enough difference between groups of responses to consider performing separate analyses for these groups?
4.	Are there any trends within or among age groups?
5.	Does the data appear to separate into specific groups?
6.	Are there any unexpectedly frequent scores?
7.	Approximately where are most of the values centered, or do there appear to be multiple centers?
8.	How widely are the scores spread?
9.	Which responses were given most frequently?
10.	What is the shape of the distribution? Describe the skewness and symmetry.
11.	Does the data collected from one location differ greatly from that collected in another location? If so, how?

Figure 4.2. Sample Questions in Exploratory Data Analysis

No.	Questions
1.	Does this statistical test demonstrate differences between proficient and non-proficient subjects?
2.	What is the best estimate of central tendency on Test X for the population of interest?
3.	Should funds be used to purchase Occupational Therapy Intervention Program A or Program B; i.e., which program was most effective?
4.	Is there a strong positive correlation between general intelligence and rehabilitation potential post cerebral vascular accident?
5.	With what level of confidence can it be stated that there is no difference between male and female scores on a test of fine motor skills?
6.	Is a high school boy's choice of leisure time activity related to his father's educational level?
7.	Which factors are the best predictors of success in an occupational therapy program for adults?
8.	Do the results of this study support the researcher's theory?

Figure 4.3. Sample Questions in Confirmatory Data Analysis

Thus, it is the purpose of exploratory data analysis to explore, without assumptions, what the data set reveals, just as a therapist explores, without assumptions, what a client reveals during an evaluation session.

The purpose of learning about data set(s) is to determine if assumptions underlying particular confirmatory data analytic procedures are met. Many confirmatory data analytic procedures are predicated on assuming certain things about the data sets. Without meeting those assumptions one potentially has the result of "garbage in, garbage out" (Chambers, Cleveland,

Kleiner & Tukey, 1983, p. 192) regarding a confirmatory data analysis. Therefore, when employing exploratory data analytic procedures one is analyzing distributional characteristics of data sets to determine if there are problems that can effect the alpha or level of significance (p-value) used in confirmatory data analysis testing (Wainer, 1986). The particular distributional characteristics most often analyzed in exploratory data analytic procedures are symmetry, skewness, and equality of spread of the data.

Currently, exploratory data analytic procedures are extensively used in the field of statistics. However, they are rarely employed in applied disciplinary research in clinical or in service professions. This appears to result more from a lack of orientation to and knowledge of exploratory data analytic procedures than for any other reason. In many clinically or service based professions such as occupational therapy, variables of interest are just now being identified and investigated in systematic and comprehensive research investigations. Thus, there is all the more reason to employ exploratory data analysis in the specification, delineation, and investigation of variables of interest in occupational therapy research specifically and in clinical research generally. Walburg, Strykowski, and Rovai (1984) argue that many variables in biology, criminology, economics, geography, psychology, and sociology are skewed, i.e., non-normally distributed. This lends support to the notion that as clinically based professions such as occupational and physical therapy begin specification of variables of interest to the field, exploratory data analysis be systematically conducted to determine whether skewness characterizes some of the variables of interest, as it appears to do in many other disciplines.

The systematic and comprehensive exploratory data analysis of variables of interest in clinical research seems even more logical if one considers that, in almost every case, it is the non-normal or dysfunctional manifestation of the variable of interest in which clinical researchers are most interested. It does not seem prudent to assume that the manifestation measurement of such subsets or variations of variables will be normally distributed.

To illustrate, consider the variable post-rotary nystagmus. For the most part, unless one is doing normative work, it is the children displaying hypoactive (too little) and hyperactive (too much) duration of post-rotary nystagmus in which a clinical researcher is most interested when considering sensory integrative theory and practice. Thus, according to theoretical reference, the research investigator is interested in the systematic extremes of a variable. Systematic extremes of a variable, or those whose variance is limited by parameters of theoretical interest, may not be normally distributed. Only by compilation of data from exploratory data analysis during such investigations can distributional characteristics be determined.

Thus, exploratory data analysis, in addition to serving to set the stage for the most appropriate confirmatory data analytic technique, can also serve to help the clinical investigator clarify and understand variables, subsets, or variations thereof, which are of interest to the investigator's discipline. For example, the discipline of occupational therapy has just begun to identify the variables of interest, let alone ascertain their characteristics and nature; exploratory data analysis is one additional way to do so.

As previously stated, exploratory data analysis is a process similar to that employed by a clinician when screening a client. Data sets can be screened to explore their characteristics prior to inferential data analysis in the same way that the functioning of clients can be screened prior to full evaluation and/or treatment.

Why should one be concerned with abnormalities in data sets? Earlier, it was explained that assumptions about data sets underlie many procedures in confirmatory data analysis, and that abnormalities in a data set could compromise those assumptions. A clinical example or analogy will serve as an illustration. It is difficult to execute a proper treatment program if one is not aware of all areas of non-normality characterizing a client. Similarly, it is difficult, if not impossible, to execute an appropriate data analysis a) without knowing whether a given data set is abnormal in some way, and b) without understanding the nature of the abnormality (i.e., skewness, outliers, etc.). Just as knowledge about a client can increase the effectiveness of treatment, knowledge about data set(s) can increase the effectiveness of confirmatory data analysis.

Given the usefulness of exploratory data analysis procedures in clinical research, there are numerous resources for the procedures. Procedures for exploratory data analysis are available on most statistical packages such as the Statistical Package for the Social Sciences (SPSSx) (Nie, Hull, Jenkins, Stein-beamer and Bent, 1975) and the Statistical Analysis System (SAS) (User's Guide, 1982). However, not all clinical researchers have access to these statistical packages. Moreover, many of the data sets that occupational therapy researchers compile are so small that computer analysis is not necessary. In such cases, procedures can be executed by hand. The next section of this chapter addresses execution of exploratory data analysis procedures.

System	Description
Purpose	Summary representation of most commonly used characteristics of the distribution including extremes, range, median, mean and quartiles.
Main Frame Computer Package	SPSS-X; Computes the minimum, maximum, and range and displays extreme values. SAS; Calculates maximum, minimum, range, quartiles and the values of Q3-Q1.
Micro Computer Package	SPSS-PC (V.1.0); Computes the minimum, maximum and range and displays extreme values. PC-SAS (V.6.0); Calculates minimum, maximum, range, quartiles and the value of Q3-Q1. STATPRO. (V.2.0); Displays a minimum, maximum and range. EDA (Vellerman, 1981). Designed specifically for EDA techniques.
Hand Calculation	Tukey (1977); Complete description provided.

Figure 4.4   EDA: Number Summaries

System	Description
Purpose	Graphic representation of the separation of data into groups, symmetry of the distribution, frequent and infrequent values, centering and range of the data.
Mainframe Computer Package	SPSS-X Does not provide stem and leaf graphic representation but performs preparatory work for stem and leaf by sorting data by value or frequency for any variables; displays histogram or bar chart.
	SAS Sort data and displays bar charts with symbols for categorical data or numbers for numerical data; can produce side by side bar charts; displays block charts for multiple comparisons.
Micro Computer Package	SPSS-PC (V1.0) See SPSS-X above.
	PC-SAS (V6.0) See SAS above.
	EDA Provides a variety of stem and leaf displays.
Hand Calculation	Tukey (1977)

Figure 4.5. Stem and Leaf Displays.

Stem	Description
Purpose	Graphic representation of calculations from number summaries, including range, identification of extreme points, quartiles, median, trimean and other calculations.
Main Computer Package	SPSS-X Provides graphics representation; displays extreme values, quartiles, means and medians.
	SAS Provides graphics representation
Micro Computer Package	SPSS-PC (V1.0) See SPSS-X above.
	PC-SAS (V6.0) See SAS above.
	EDA Executes boxplots.
Hand Calculation	Tukey (1977). This chapter. Also Vellerman & Hoaglin (1981).

Figure 4.6. Boxplots or Box and Whisker Plots.

Execution of Exploratory Data Analysis

This section of the chapter presents common exploratory data analysis (EDA) procedures that could be useful to clinical researchers. A series of figures (Figures 4-4, 4-5, 4-6, and 4-7) are provided that identify the EDA procedure, define its purpose, and suggest possible sources for execution of the procedure. These figures are not assumed to be comprehensive, but rather to present the most readily available resources regarding exploratory data analysis procedures.

Hand Computation of EDA Procedures

In this section of the chapter, certain procedures have been selected for presentation as procedures that can be hand calculated. Most exploratory

Stem	Description
Purpose	Determine whether underlying distribution approximates a normal curve
Mainframe Computer Package	SPSS-X Computes test statistic.
Micro Computer Package	PC-SAS Computes test statistic for normality; if the sample size is <2000 the Shapiro Wilks list is used; otherwise the Kolomogorov test is appropriate. Statpro Provides normality curves for testing statistical assumptions.
Hand Calculation	Lilliefors Test (Conover, 1980; Dallal & Wilkinson, 1986)

Figure 4.7   EDA: Tests of Normality

data analysis procedures are relatively elementary and they are not considered to require sophisticated mathematical or statistical backgrounds (Hartwig and Dearing, 1979). The two sets of procedures presented are the stem-and-leaf and the boxplot.

Stem and Leaf

The stem-and-leaf diagram is used to display the magnitude and spread of a data set. It is basically a vertical barchart that uses the actual data rather than graphic symbols to form the length of each bar.

Consider the following scores obtained from the administration of a gross motor skill evaluation to a group of 24, 14-year old boys:

5 3 2 8 6 9 5 3 7 4 9 8
8 1 4 8 4 7 8 2 8 8 7 3

These scores could be represented in a simple one-digit stem-and-leaf diagram, as shown in Figure 4-8. Note that each line is a stem that may contain one or more data values of leaves.

Uses of Stem-and-Leaf Diagrams. Figure 4-8 provides an effective picture of the mode, the minimum and maximum values, and the overall distribution. Specifically, Tukey (1977, p.19) notes five descriptive measures generally obtained from the stem and leaf.
1. The separation of data into groups.
2. Unsymmetric trailing off of minimum and/or maximum data values.
3. Unexpectedly "popular" or "unpopular" values.
4. The approximate centering of values.
5. The width of the spreading of values.

The stem-and-leaf diagram also provides some opportunity for controlling data accuracy. The optional frequency count in parentheses in the right column provides the opportunity to check against sample size to see that data has not been inadvertently omitted or added. Extreme or other "suspicious"

0		(0)
1	1	(1)
2	22	(2)
3	333	(3)
4	444	(3)
5	55	(2)
6	6	(1)
7	777	(3)
8	8888888	(7)
9	99	(2)
		(24) Check

Figure 4.8. Basic Stem and Leaf Diagram

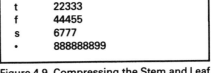

*	1
t	22333
f	44455
s	6777
•	888888899

Figure 4.9. Compressing the Stem and Leaf Diagram Using Multiples of Two

values also will be readily detected. Correction of data tabulation errors before extensive analysis is begun will avoid costly errors. This point cannot be overemphasized!

An additional benefit of the stem-and-leaf diagram is the opportunity it provides the researcher to develop a "feel for the data." The act of recording each data point encourages the exploratory thought process.

Stem and Leaf Techniques The basic stem-and-leaf diagram shown in Figure 4-8 above may be adapted to display a wide variety of data. The basic example included only single digit numbers; however, multiple digit values may be re-expressed and represented, as shown in Figure 4- 9. Categorical information and multiple data sets also may be explored through the techniques discussed below.

Compressing the Stem-and-Leaf Display. The data from the gross motor skills test may be compressed to represent scores in multiples of 2 (see Figure 4-9), in multiples of 5 (see Figure 4- 10) or in any other grouping that best serves the data. Data expressed in multiples of 2 is often referred to as a five-stem display, while multiples of 5 form a two-stem display. Note that Figure 4-10 is the most efficient in graphically illustrating the centering of higher concentration of scores in the 5 to 9 bracket. It effectively demonstrates that the median will fall between a score of 5 and 6.

Tukey (1977) suggests the convention, used above, of representing 0 and 1 by "*", 2 and 3 by "t", 4 and 5 by "f", 6 and 7 by "s", 8 and 9 ".". In the two-stem display shown in Figure 4-10, the "*" is used to represent values 0 through 4 and the "." to represent 5 through 9.

Stem-and-Leaf With Re-Expressed Data. The stem-and-leaf displays discussed thus far have been based on a unit of 1 point; however, data may be re-expressed in terms of any unit. Some typical units include percentages, logarithms, negative numbers, $100, .001, weeks, grade levels, etc. In the stem-and-leaf diagram shown in Figure 4-11, SAT scores of students enrolled in an occupational therapy program are represented as multiples of 100. The same data are then expressed in units of 1. Note that asterisks are used in the stem to represent place value.

Stem-and-Leaf Displays of Categorical Data. Although the examples thus far

```
*        122333444
•        556777888888899
```

Figure 4.10. Compressing the Stem and Leaf
Diagram Using Multiples of Five

Original Data:
412, 750, 664, 350, 476, 508, 600, 435,
378, 596, 640, 535, 550, 624, 550

UNIT = 100 UNIT = 1

```
3    xx       3**   50, 78
4    xxx      4**   12, 35, 76
5    xxxxx    5**   08, 35, 50, 50, 96
6    xxxx     6**   00, 24, 40, 64
7    x        7*    50
```

Figure 4.11. Stem and Leaf Displays with
Varying Units

Student Majors		LD Seniors-Major Field
Biology	Bi	'75 Bi ChGeEd EdEd Fl Ps
Business	Bu	'76 BuBu EdEd Fl HsHs Ps
Chemistry	Ch	'77 BuBuBuDpEdHsPhSpSp
Data Process.	Dp	'78 BuBuBuDpDpGeHsHs Ps Ps Ps
Education	Ed	'79 BuBuDpDpPs PsSp
Foreign Lang.	Fl	'80 BuBuBuDpDpDpDpEd Ps Ps Ps
Geology	Ge	'81 BuBuBuBuDpDpDpDpDpDp Fl Hs
History	Hs	'82 BuBuDpDpDpDpDpEd Fl PsSp
Philosophy	Ph	
Psychology	Ps	
Speech/Drama	Sp	

Figure 4.12   Stem and Leaf Display of Categorical Data

have been limited to continuous level data, the technique works equally well
with categorical data. In the following example a researcher compared the
majors selected by learning disabled college seniors during an eight-year
period at a major university. Figure 4-12 displays the codes used to represent
the students' majors and the resulting stem-and-leaf display.

This technique is effective in showing trends over time. The growing
popularity of business and data processing fields, for example, is clearly
illustrated in Figure 4-12.

Displaying Multiple Data Sets. Two data sets may be compared in a back-to-
back stem-and-leaf display. When raw values vary greatly between the two
sets, the data could be re-expressed as logarithms, square roots, or reciprocals
to minimize the spread of values necessary to represent the data. One
additional benefit of re-expression is to make patterns more symmetrical and
thus easier to describe. Figure 4-13 compares the scores on a gross motor skill
test for learning disabled and regular education students. Note the use of
labels for the extreme data points. In this case the labels identify students' last
names.

Example 4-1. For this example, teachers are used. Regular and special
education teachers in a suburban school district were asked to record their

LD STUDENTS				REGULAR EDUCATION STUDENTS
Smythe	0	0	0	
Blake, Rogin	11	1	1	Warner
	2222	2	22	
	3333	3	333	
	4444	4	444	
	55	5	55	
	66	6	6	
	7	7	777	
	888	8	8888888	
Warner	9	9	99	Nelson, Mastau

Figure 4.13   Stem and Leaf Display of Multiple Data Sets

total years of teaching experience, including present and past positions. In this example the researcher has not formulated any hypotheses; he or she is interested in exploring the data for descriptive rather than confirmatory evidence. In this exploratory phase all findings are of interest.

Subsequently, the data collected for 167 regular education and 67 special education teachers are shown in Table 4-1.

These data will be explored in this example through the following stem-and-leaf techniques:

1. Five-stem pattern;
2. Two-stem pattern;
3. Re-expressed as roots in a back-to-back display; and
4. Re-expressed as roots in a back-to-back compressed display.

The stem-and-leaf displays using the five-stem pattern, as seen in Figure 4-14, is probably the most useful for providing exploratory information.

Many "clues" are revealed in this diagram:

1. Regular education teachers (RT) tend to have more experience than special education teachers (ST). .
2. A greater proportion of ST were first-year teachers.
3. Values for both groups trail off unsymmetrically toward the higher values.
4. For RT, there is some clustering around popular values. This is particularly true for the values of 5, 8 to 10, and 20 years. The high frequency of these responses 5, 10, and 20 may have been caused by teachers rounding out, rather than giving the exact number of years of experience. (This is an example of information that is more likely to be obtained from intimate contact with the data; it might be lost in a computer data analysis that would only average the data.)
5. For ST the configuration is almost equal for all values up to 14, followed by the trailing noted above.
6. For RT, there is a dramatic "drop off" of values after 25 years.
7. For ST, values decline, although less sharply after 17 years. There is a tendency toward separation of the values into 2 groups; i.e., from 1 to 17 years and from 20 to 29 years with an apparent break for 18 to 19 years.

Table 4.1. Number of Years Teaching by Group						
Regular Education Teachers n=167					Special Education Teachers n=67	
20	21	11	10	19	5	16
13	10	15	12	24	15	6
11	7	32	9	8	13	7
11	18	15	8	7	10	5
6	3	10	7	19	3	21
9	31	14	4	7	1	27
19	16	11	11	21	6	2
7	4	25	13	18	8	4
9	8	22	5	5	6	12
10	6	4	19	20	3	4
13	5	10	8	27	2	3
20	3	8	12	8	2	23
10	13	9	10	8	3	11
12	2	15	17	1	10	6
12	10	5	15	9	1	3
16	8	1	13	10	10	20
9	12	1	20	15	9	13
40	20	10	10	11	21	11
22	14	4	25	8	12	25
1	12	13	7	3	12	17
18	18	13	35	11	9	2
13	15	25	21	17	2	17
5	14	5	28	24	29	1
5	20	5	21	37	22	1
19	16	1	9	8	10	5
3	25	10	20	8	13	4
23	24	9	7	5	1	16
8	2	8	9	4	9	13
5	3	11	22	6	14	7
3	21	8	22	9	8	12
7	28	17	18	12	12	11
2	22	13	20		12	7
2	25	5	9		6	5
20	25	20	12		8	

8. For RT the population of the values 8 and 9 years is emphasized. The values 6 and 7 are unexpectedly less popular.

9. For ST, the popularity of values 2 to 3 and 12 to 13 is emphasized.

Further attempts to utilize stem and leaf techniques are less effective. Compression of the data in a two-stem pattern, as shown in Figure 4-15, resulted in values being too crowded together to note separation, trailing, or popular values.

Because all of the numbers are positive and have some spread between values, it may be useful to re-express them as roots, logarithms, or negative reciprocals. Experimentation with each of these methods reveals that re-expression as square roots will bring the values a little closer together for

Regular Education Teachers	Special Education Teachers
0 * 11111	0 * 11111
t 2222333333	t 2222233333
f 4444455555555555	f 4445555
s 66677777777	s 66666777
• 88888888888888899999999999	• 888999
1 * 00000000000011111111	1 * 0000111
t 22222222333333333	t 2222223333
f 444555555	f 45
s 666777	s 6677
• 8888899999	•
2 * 0000000000011111	2 * 011
t 222223	t 23
f 44455555	f 5
s 7	s 7
• 88	• 9
3 * 1	
t 2	
f 5	
s 7	
•	
4 * 0	

Figure 4.14. Five Stem Pattern of a Stem and Leaf Display

Regular Education Teachers

0 * 11111222233333344444
• 55555566677777777888888888888888899999999999
1 * 000000000000111111112222222233333333334444
• 55555566677788888899999
2 * 0000000000011111222223444
• 55555788
3 * 12
• 57
4 * 0
•

Special Education Teachers

0 * 111112222233333444
• 5555566666777888999
1 * 000011122222233334
• 56677
2 * 01123
• 579
3 *
•

Figure 4.15 Squeezed Stem and Leaf Display

further examination. This concept is shown in Figure 4-16, which presents a back-to-back, five-stem display of the raw data for both groups re-expressed as roots.

In addition to bringing the values closer together for the observation of symmetrical displays, this visual presentation is also useful in providing the most efficient comparison of the two groups. In this exhibit, the configuration for the ST is relatively stable, almost rectangular, except for the trailing of values after 41. For RT, however, the pattern is similar to a series of triangles or pyramids with several sets of popular values (22, 28, 32 to 33, 36 to 37 and 44 to 45) at the bases. As in the other stem-and-leaf displays, the trailing of values for both groups remains relatively equal. The squeezed stem- and-leaf for square roots, which is presented in Figure 4-17, provides little new information.

There is, therefore, no need for further compression. This completes the section on stem-and-leaf diagrams. The calculation of a boxplot will now be presented.

Boxplot or Box-and-Whisker Plot

The boxplot is sometimes referred to as a box-and-whisker plot (Tukey, 1977). The boxplot is a graphical representation based on the quartiles of a

Regular Education Teachers		Special Education Teachers
00000	1 *	00000
	t	
4444	f	44444
777777	s	77777
	•	
00000	2 *	000
22222222222	t	2222
444	f	44444
66666666	s	666
88888888888888	•	888
0000000000	3 *	000
333333333222222222222	t	2222333
55555555	f	55555
777666666666	s	66667
99999	•	9
111000	4 *	0011
22222	t	
5555555544444	f	5
7777766666	s	667
9998	•	8
00000	5 *	0
332	t	2
	f	4
76	s	
9	•	
1	6 *	
3	t	

(# years as roots; unit = .1)

Figure 4.16   Reexpression Using Roots: 5 Stem Pattern

Regular Education Teachers		Special Education Teachers
444400000	1 *	0000044444
777777	•	77777
4442222222222200000	2 *	000222244444
888888888888866666666	•	666888
33333333222222222222200000000000	3 *	0002222333
99999777666666666655555555	•	55555666679
4444422222111000	4 *	0011
999877777666666555555555	•	56678
33200000	5 *	024
976	•	
31	6 *	
(# years as roots; unit = .1)		

Figure 4.17   Reexpression using Roots: Squeezed Stem and Leaf

distribution with emphasis placed on the tails or noncentral portions of the distribution (Koopman, 1981). By considering the calculations for the boxplot (to compute the quartile values) as well as the boxplot itself, one can evaluate the following distributional characteristics in a given data set (Hoaglin, Mosteller, and Tukey, 1981):

- Location (the center and range of a distribution),
- Skewness (assymetry of a distribution).
- Tail length (distance between extreme value and central portions), and
- Outliers (data values outside of the normal probability range).

The procedure for calculating a boxplot will be described. A worksheet for executing a boxplot will be presented, as well as methods for graphic presentation.

General Procedures for Execution of a Boxplot. The following data set will be used for illustrative purposes:

$$15 \quad 25 \quad 22 \quad 21 \quad 20 \quad 14 \quad 17 \quad 26 \quad 29$$

Step 1. Align all values of the data set in ascending order as follows:

$$14 \quad 15 \quad 17 \quad 20 \quad 21 \quad 22 \quad 25 \quad 26 \quad 29$$

Then, rank order the values.

Rank	(1)	(2)	(3)	(4)	(5)	(6)	(7)	(8)	(9)
	14	15	17	20	21	22	25	26	29

Step 2. Calculate the mean as well as the median position. The mean is caculated by summing all values and dividing by total number of data points as follows:

$$14 + 15 + 17 + 20 + 21 + 22 + 25 + 26 + 29 = 189$$
$$\text{Mean} = 189/9 = 21$$

The median is calculated by adding 1 to the total number of data points and dividing by 2 $[(n+1) \div 2]$ to identify the median position:

median = (9+1)/2 = 5th position

In this case, the fifth position in rank order has a value of 21; thus, the median is 21. The median is considered to be the second quartile (Q2).

Calculation of the first and third quartiles is next using the following equation:

(Median position + 1)/2 = quartile location
(5 + 1)/2 = 3rd position

(Note that if the median position was calculated to have a decimal, for example if it was 5.3, the decimal would be dropped and the resulting "truncated median position" would be substituted into the equation.)

The first quartile location (Q1) is counted up from the smallest data value. In this case, one would count up three positions from the smallest data value (14) to the one in the third position (17). Thus, Q1 is 17. Similarly, the third quartile location (Q3) is identified by counting down three positions from the largest data value. One would count down from the largest (29) to the third from largest (25). Thus, Q3 is 25.

The interquartile range (IQR) is computed by subtracting the value corresponding to Q1 from the value corresponding to Q3.

IQR = Q3 − Q1
IQR = 25 − 17 = 8

The scale factor is calculated by multiplying IQR by 1.5 (McGill, Tukey, and Larson, 1978).

IQR × 1.5 = scale factor
8 × 1.5 = 12

Step 4. Compute the lower fence (f1) value by subtracting the scale factor from the value for Q1.

Q1 − scale factor = f1
17 − 12 = 5

Compute the upper fence (fu) value by adding the scale factor to the value for Q3.

Q3 + scale factor = fu
25 + 12 = 37

Compute the outer, lower fence (FL) value by subtracting two times the scale factor from the value for Q1.

Q1 − (2 × scale factor) = FL
17 − (2 × 12) = −7

Compute the outer, upper fence (FU) value by adding two times the scale factor to the value of Q3.

$$Q3 + (2 \times \text{scale}) = FU$$
$$25 + (2 \times 12) = 49$$

Step 5. The boxplot chart presented in Figure 4-18 would then be filled in using the values calculated. Refer to Figure 4- 19 while reading through this section.

First, the calculated values for fl and fu would be inserted (1st). Second, the nearest adjacent values of the data set not going lower than the value of fl and not exceeding the value of fu would be inserted (2nd). Third, one would determine if any data values are outliers by seeing if any are less than fl or more than fu and record them (3rd). If there are none, designate so. Fourth, record the values for FL and FU (4th). Fifth and finally, determine if any values in the data set are less than FL or exceed FU (5th). Record the data values or, if there are none, identify so (5th).

Boxplot Graph. The following steps can be followed to execute a boxplot graph. Note, however, this is but one proposed format for a boxplot graph.

Data Set _____

Date Values _____

Ascending Order _____

Rank Order _____

Mean = _____

Median Position (n+1)/2 = _____

Median Value (Q2) = _____

Quartile location =
    (truncated median position +1)/2 = _____ position
    Value of Q1 = _____
    Value of Q3 = _____
    IQR = (Q3 − Q1) = _____

Scale Factor = 1.5 × IQR _____
    Lower fence (fl) = Q1 − scale = _____
    Upper fence (fu) = Q3 + scale = _____
    Outer, lower fence (FL) = Q1 − (2 × scale) = _____
    Outer, upper fence (FU) = Q3 + (2 × scale) = _____

Boxplot Chart (fill in values)

	_____	
	_____	
Nearest Adjacent Value	_____	Nearest Adjacent Value
fl	_____	fu
Mild Outlier	_____	Mild Outlier
FL	_____	FU
Extreme Outlier	_____	Extreme Outlier

Figure 4.18 Boxplot Worksheet (Calculate Values)

(2nd)	Nearest Adjacent Value	14	29	Nearest Adjacent Value
(1st)	fl	5	37	fu
(3rd)	Mild Outlier	none	none	Mild Outlier
(4th)	FL	−7	49	FU
(5th)	Extreme Outlier	none	none	Extreme Outlier

Figure 4.19. Boxplot Chart with Illustrative Data Set

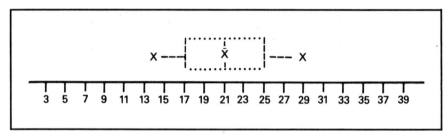

Figure 4-20. Boxplot Graph of Illustrative Data.

There are many variations of the boxplot graph and there is no absolute standardized convention for execution.

Plot quartile Q1, Q2 (the median) and Q3 with vertical lines.

Plot the mean with an "x" embedded within an open circle, or with an "x" with a bar across the top.

Plot adjacent values (lower and upper values closest to but not exceeding the upper and lower fences, respectively) with an "x" and draw the tails.

Plot mild outliers. These are observations falling between a) the lower fence (fl) and the outer, lower fence (FL) and b) the upper fence (fu) and the outer, upper fence (FU). If present, plot them with an open circle. In this case there are none.

Plot extreme outliers, that is, observations less than the outer, lower fence (FL) or exceeding the outer, upper fence (FU) with a blackened circle. In this case there are none.

Figure 4-20 presents a boxplot graph of data used in the illustrative example.

Boxplot Analysis. Visual inspection of a boxplot graph consists of investigating the following questions regarding the data set.

1. Is the distribution lacking in symmetry?
2. Is the distribution skewed as revealed by extremely long tails and a discrepancy between the median and the mean?
3. Are there mild or extreme outliners?

For this particular data set, the boxplot reveals no abnormalities in the data set.

Table 4-2 presents data on another sample boxplot. Based on data pre-

Table 4.2.
Sample Boxplot Calculation

Data Set	Age variable for learning disabled boys n = 9
Data Values	93, 82, 114, 92, 80, 82, 79, 75, 92
Ascending Order	75, 79, 80, 82, 82, 92, 92, 93, 114
Rank Order	1 2 3 4 5 6 7 8 9

Mean = 87.667
Median Position $(n+1)/2$ = 5
Median Value (Q2) = 82

Quartile location = (truncated median position +1)/2 = 3rd position
   Value of Q1 = 80
   Value of Q3 = 92
   IQR = (Q3 − Q1) = 12

Scale Factor = $1.5 \times$ IQR = 18
   lower fence (f1) = Q1 − scale = 62
   upper fence (fu) = Q3 + scale = 110
   outer, lower fence (FL) = Q1 − $(2 \times$ scale) = 44
   outer, upper fence (FU) = Q3 + $(2 \times$ scale) = 128

Boxplot Chart.

Nearest Adjacent			Nearest Adjacent
Value	75 _____ 93		Value
f1	62 _____ 110		fu
Mild Outlier	none _____ 114		Mild Outlier
FL	44 _____ 128		FU
Extreme Outlier	none _____ none		Extreme Outlier

sented in Table 4-2, an example boxplot graph is presented in Figure 4-21.

For this particular data set, the boxplot reveals that the distribution is skewed and has one mild outlier. Thus, it would be appropriate to consider the effect the outlier has on the inferential data analysis, and consider whether the assumption(s) underlying the use of a parametric statistical procedure would be violated because of irregularities in the data set. A worksheet presenting guidelines for interpreting the results of exploratory data analysis is presented in Figure 4-22.

Summary

Earlier in this chapter it was stated that results of exploratory data analysis can influence choice of confirmatory or inferential statistical tests. Hartwig and Dearing state, "Application of exploratory data analysis techniques will largely determine types of other techniques which a data analyst can use to

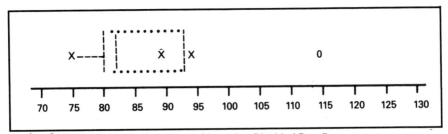

Figure 4.21 Boxplot of Data Set "Ages of Learning Disabled Boys"

I. Analysis of characteristics of the data set.
  A. What is the size of the data set?
    1.1 If the data set or subset thereof has a sample size of five or more, that data set or subset thereof will be subjected to exploratory data analysis.
    1.2 If the data set or subset thereof has a sample size of less than five, exploratory data analysis cannot be conducted.

II. What is the shape of the data set?
  A. What are the results of the boxplot?
  B. What are the results of the stem-and-leaf plot?
  C. Is the distribution symmetric?
  D. Is the distribution skewed (Walburg, Stykowski, & Hung, 1984) (This would be evaluated if computer analysis of skewness was conducted).
    1.1 Is it mildly skewed (.5 − .99)?
    1.2 Is it moderately skewed (1.0 − 1.99)?
    1.3 Is it profoundly skewed (2.0 >)?
  E. Are there long tails present?

III. Is the distribution normal?
  A. What are the percentage of outliers as revealed by the boxplot?
    1.1 Hartwig and Dearing (1979) suggest that if five percent or more of the data points are outliers, the distribution is not normal.
  B. What are the results of the goodness of fit test?

IV. What is the range of the data?
  A. Are there gaps?
  B. Are there excessive repeated values?
  C. Are there outliers?

V. What are conclusions about this data set?

Figure 4-22. Guidelines for interpreting EDA

examine a given set of data" (Hartwig and Dearing, 1979, p.5). That is to say, characteristics of data set(s) become manifest during exploratory data analysis, and thus influence choice of inferential techniques. However, it is rare that the choice is clear cut and that only one inferential technique is appropriate. Tukey explained that it is unusual for a given data set to clearly reveal a single best way to proceed for inferential data analysis.

Thus, one may consider a variety of options to enact based on the results of exploratory data analysis. The advantages and disadvantages of any one inferential statistical procedure should be identified and evaluated before proceeding. Selection of confirmatory or inferential data analytic techniques are further discussed in the next chapter of this book.

References

Chambers, J. M., Cleveland, W. S., Kleiner, B., and Tukey, J. W. (1983). *Graphical methods for data analysis*. Belmont, California: Wadsworth International Co.

Conover, W. J. (1980). *Nonparametric statistics*. New York: John Wiley and Sons.

Dallal, G. E., and Wilkinson, L. (1986). An analytic approximation to the distribution of the Lilliefor's test statistic for normality. *The American Statistician*, 40(4), 294-298.

Freni-Titulaer, L. W. J., and Louv, W. C. (1984). Comparisons of some graphical methods for exploratory multivariate data analysis. *The American Statistician*, 38(3), 184-188.

Hartwig, D and Dearing, E.F. (1979). *Exploratory data analyses*. Beverly Hills: Sage Publications.

Hoaglin, D. C., Mosteller, F., and Tukey, J. W. (1981). *Understanding robust and exploratory data analysis*. New York: Wiley and Sons.

Imhof, M., and Hewett, S. *State - Pro*. New York: Penton Software, Inc.

Kirk, R. E. (1982). *Experimental design* (2nd ed.). Belmont, CA: Wadsworth Publishing Co.

Kleiner, B., and Hartigan, J. A. (1981). Representing points in many dimensions by trees and castles. *Journal of the American Statistical Association*, 76, 260-269.

Koopman, L. H. (1981). *An introduction to contemporary statistics*. Boston, MA: Duxbury Press.

Kotz, S., and Johnson, N. L. (Eds.). (1982). *Encyclopedia of statistics*. Vol. 2. New York: Wiley and Sons.

Mitcham, M. D. (1986). Integrating research competencies into basic professional education. *American Journal of Occupational Therapy*, 40(ll), 10-11.

McGill, R., Tukey, J. W., and Larson, N. A. *American Statistician*, Variations of Boxplots 32(1)12-22.

Nie, N. H., Hull, C. H., Jenkins, J. G., Steinbeamer, K. and Bent, D. H. (1975). *Statistical package for the social sciences*. New York: McGraw-Hill.

Norusis, M. (1984). *SPSS - PC*. Chicago: SPSS Inc. *PC-SAS*.(1985). Cary, North Carolina: SAS Institute.

Royeen, C. B., and Seaver, W. L. (1986). Promise in nonparametrics. *American Journal of Occupational Therapy*, 40(3), 191-193.

Tukey, J. W. (1977). *Exploratory data analysis*. Reading, Massachusetts: Addison-Wesley Publishing Co.

Vellerman, P. (1981). *Exploratory data analysis*. Iowa City, Iowa: Author.

Vellerman, P., and Hoaglin, D. C. (1981). *Application, basics and computing of exploratory data analysis*. Boston: Duxbury Press.

Wainer, H. (1986). Can a test be too reliable? *Journal of Educational Measurement*, 23(2), 171-173.

Walberg, H. J., Strykowski, B. F., Rovai, E., and Hung, S. S. (1984). Exceptional performances. *Review of Educational Research*, 54(1), 87-112.

CHAPTER 5

PROVISIONAL GUIDELINES FOR THE PROCESS OF DATA ANALYSIS IN CLINICAL RESEARCH

Charlotte Brasic Royeen

Chapter Overview

The purpose of this chapter is to provide a "blueprint" or plan for the process of data analysis in clinical research. This process of data analysis involves more than simply selecting a test for descriptive or inferential statistics; it includes verification and exploration prior to selecting an inferential or confirmatory test statistic. The entire conceptual process underlying data analysis will be identified and described.

Introduction

Planning for data analysis in clinical research is similar to treatment planning in clinical practice. Mitcham (1986) has identified aspects of the similarities of the two processes considering the field of occupational therapy research and occupational therapy under the common factor of solution planning. Another way to consider the similarity of the two processes is that in clinical intervention one specifies a plan of action for treatment, just as one specifies a plan of action for data analysis in clinical research. However, in both cases the plan of action is subject to change. To illustrate, a treatment plan for a client may be modified, suspended, or radically altered if a client presents new and different needs subsequent to initial evaluation. Similarly, a plan for data analysis may be altered if results of exploratory data analysis reveal outliers, severe non-normality, or other such problems.

For example, one's plan of action for data analysis may consist of testing the differences regarding a particular variable between two groups using an independent t-test. Exploratory data analysis, however, may reveal extreme non-normality in both groups to be compared, such that the Mann Whitney Wilcoxon test would be preferred and the data analysis plan changed accordingly. Or, a one-way analysis of variance may be planned for use in another research plan, but exploratory data analysis reveals that the variable of interest in each group is not distributed normally. The data analysis plan may then be adjusted to substitute the Kruskal-Wallis nonparametric test.

It is probable that any data analysis plan is provisional, depending on the results of exploratory data analysis. However, in spite of the provisional nature of any data analysis plan, this chapter will provide guidelines of what might be delineated and how to proceed with data analysis in clinical research.

Guidelines for Data Analysis

Guidelines for data analysis may be considered as tentative rules. Reed defines rules as propositions that "...contain information about how to interact successfully with the environment to achieve certain ends" (1984, p.130). The "rules" or guidelines presented herein contain information about how to interact successfully with data to achieve valid results from analysis of that data.

Guidelines for data analysis are varied in the research literature, depending on the framework an author uses to specify data analysis decision rules. One example is a recent publication in the *American Journal of Occupational Therapy* by Mann (1986). Mann approached the problem of selecting data analysis procedures from a conceptual viewpoint based on indexing or categorizing the variables under investigation. In another publication with a slightly different orientation to selection of data analysis procedures, Soper (1985) dichotomizes aspects of selection of data analysis procedures into those for measured variables (mean, variance) and those for categorical variables (frequency, proportion, and association).

Unique to the particular set of guidelines presented in this chapter are: a) the sequential nature of data analysis delineated as a step-by-step process; b) the emphasis on data verification; and c) the assumption of exploratory data analysis as a step in the process. When should these proposed guidelines be used? Ideally, they can serve as a reference or a model when planning an investigation to sequence the steps of data analysis and then during as well as after execution of data analysis. However, they also may be employed during preliminary data collection, which may be the case with a pilot study or data collected during the first phase of an investigation. (Note: It is recommended to analyze preliminary data collected during the first phase of any study to identify possible problems.) These guidelines also may be used when data

Step	Procedure
1.	Review research issue(s)
2.	Review research design
3.	Identify possible procedures for confirmatory data analysis
4.	Data verification
5.	Exploratory data analysis
6.	Selection of confirmatory data analytic procedure, execution and evaluation of remaining assumptions
7.	Delineation of interpretation criteria

Figure 5-1. Overview of the steps in the process of data analysis

collection is completed. Finally, it should be noted that these guidelines consist of one approach and can be used in conjunction with other approaches.

Figure 5-1 presents an overview of the steps in the process of data analysis. Each of the steps identified in Figure 5-1 will be discussed in turn. Collectively, these steps constitute guidelines for data analysis in clinical research.

Step 1. Review of Research Issues

Step 1 of the process is the review of research issue(s). Before valid data analysis can be executed, the very nature of how the data relates to the research issue should be re-evaluated and considered. That is, the investigator should verify that indeed, the data to be analyzed will relate to or address the research issue(s) under investigation. The following are examples of the types of questions to be posed during this step of the data analysis process.

- What are the research question(s) in the investigation, and how are they related to the research issue?
- Has the data already been collected or must it be collected to answer the research question(s)?
- How many questions are being addressed with a given data set?

Corresponding to the research questions driving this investigation are the hypotheses or propositions that relate to the research questions. Asking too many questions and having too many hypotheses for a given data set is a common problem in data analysis, and the result is overinterpretation and over "testing" of the data. Given the data set to be analyzed, are there sufficient data points to validly address the research question(s)? Or, are there too many research questions and corresponding hypotheses given the size of the data set?

To illustrate, if one has a data set consisting of two groups with ten in each group, it may not be reasonable to have four research questions and four corresponding tests of confirmatory statistics given the small sample size. Rather, in this case it would be prudent to put the research questions in order of priority and only address two of them, i.e., test for the first two ranked in order of importance.

If one finds that, indeed, too many questions are being asked of a given data set, a process of elimination must be executed. Such a common sense viewpoint of number of confirmatory data analysis procedures per data set is related to the statistical concept of power analysis and experimental error rate. For, increasing the number of statistical tests calculated per experiment increases the risk of falsely rejecting the null hypothesis, i.e., increasing the experimental error rate (Silverstein, 1986). Thus, there must be a determination of how many research questions and corresponding hypotheses can be executed judiciously considering a particular data set. Consequently, research questions should be arranged in order of importance, and only the questions that the data can validly address should be executed.

Given the completion of Step 1 of data analysis, Step 2 consists of review of the research design.

Step 2. Review of the Research Design

The research design employed is to be verified and the plan for the research or how the research was actually executed is to be mapped out graphically and verified. It may be helpful to determine into which of the following categories of research (Soper, 1986) the investigation can be placed:

- Experimental
- Quasi-experimental
- Qualitative
- Descriptive
- Ex Post Facto

Given an understanding of the design employed, two components of the research should then be verified for data analysis. First, confirmation of the number of groups in the study should be completed. To do so, review the criteria for group definition, and review how the subjects within the group(s) were obtained. Types of questions to ask are:

- Was random sampling employed?
- Were matched pairs used?
- Were the matched pairs randomly sampled?
- Was purposive sampling employed that would have implications for generalizability of the results of the data analysis?

Similarly, variables should be verified. The investigator may wish to reaffirm the following:

- What are the independent variables?
- What are the dependent variables?
- Are there any confounding variables, that is, are there unanticipated and therefore uncontrolled variables that can effect the validity of the study?

Finally, the level of measurement of the variables of interest must be confirmed and reviewed. Questions to consider may be those specified as follows:

- Does the data reflect the presumed level of measurement?
- Due to ceiling effects of tests or other related phenomenon, are there "flukes" resulting in restricted ranges, etc., that may change the judged level at which variables are measured?

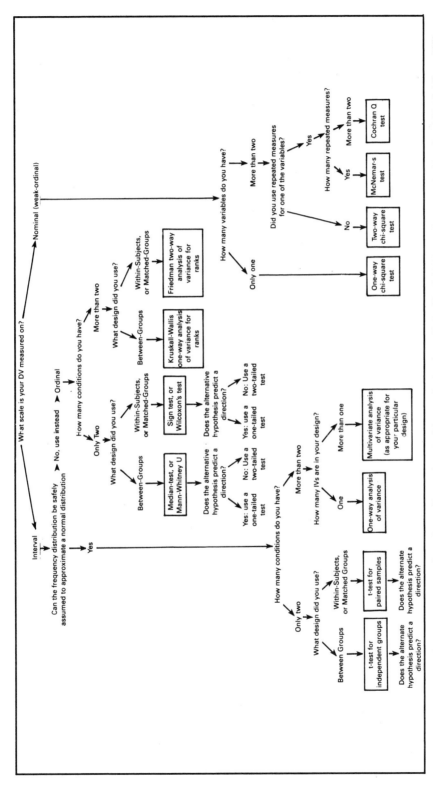

Figure 5-2. Decision tree for choosing a statistical test. (Reproduced with permission from Holly Skodol Wilson, *Research in Nursing*, 1985 Addison- Wilson Publishing Co., Inc.)

Situation	Parametric Method	Nonparametric Method	References
One-sample location one sample	t test	Sign Test or Wilcoxon Signed Rank Test	Gibbons JD: *Nonparametric Methods for Quantitative Analysis.* New York: Holt, Rinehart and Winston, 1976
paired sample	t test	Sign Test or Wilcoxon Signed Rank Test	Gibbons JD: *Nonparametric Methods for Quantitative Analysis.* New York: Holt, Rinehart and Winston, 1976.
Two-sample location common dispersion	pooled t test	Mann Whitney Wilcoxon	Daniel WW: *Applied Nonparametric Statistics.* Boston, MA: Houghton, Mifflin, 1978.
uncommon dispersion	Behrens-Fisher t test or Welch's t test	Wilcoxon test for the generalized Behrens-Fisher problem or a modification of Mood's median test	Potthoff RF: Use of the Wilcoxon statistic for a generalized Behrens-Fisher problem. *Annals of Mathematical Statistics* 34:1196-1599, 1963 Fligner MA, Rust SW: A modification of Mood's median test for the generalized Behren-Fisher problem. *Biometrika* 69:221-226, 1982.
Location for several independent samples	F test (one-factor ANOVA)	Kruskal-Wallis* or Jonckheere test	Gibbons JD: *Nonparametric Methods for Quantitative Analysis.* New York: Holt, Rinehart and Winston, 1976. Hollander M, Wolfe DA: *Nonparametric Statistical Methods.* New York: Wiley, 1973.
Location for several related samples	F test	Friedman test*	Hollander M, Wolfe DA: *Nonparametric Statistical Methods.* New York: Wiley, 1973.

Situation	Parametric test	Nonparametric test	References
Two-sample test for dispersion	F test	Ansari-Bradley test	Hollander M, Wolfe DA: *Nonparametric Statistical Methods.* New York: Wiley, 1973.
		Mood test	Daniel WW: *Applied Nonparametric Statistics.* Boston: Houghton, Mifflin, 1978.
		Moses test	Hollander M, Wolfe DA: *Nonparametric Statistical Methods.* New York: Wiley, 1973.
		Miller jacknife test	Hollander M, Wolfe DA: *Nonparametric Statistical Methods.* New York: Wiley, 1973.
Independence of bivariate observations	Pearson Correlation	Kendall's tau	Gibbons JD: *Nonparametric Methods for Quantitative Analysis.* New York: Rinehart and Winston, 1976.
Regression one independent variable	simple linear regression	Thiel's method	Daniel WW: *Applied Nonparametric Statistics.* Boston: Houghton, Mifflin, 1978. Hollander M, Wolfe DA: *Nonparametric Statistical Methods.* New York: Wiley, 1973.
more than one independent variable	multiple linear regression	Generalized Thiel-type methods to the multivariate case	Hussain SS, Sprent T: Nonparametric regression. *Journal of the Royal Statistical Society (Series A), 146:*182-191, 1983
Two or more factor designs with concern for testing main effects and interactions	ANOVA	General linear models based on ranks	Hettmansberger TP, McKean JW: Statistical inference based upon ranks. *Psychometrika,* 43:69-79, 1978. Pirie WR, Rarch HL: Simulated efficiencies of tests and estimators from general linear models analysis based on ranks: The two-way layout with interaction. *Journal of Statistical Computation and Simulation, 20:* 197-204, 1984.

Figure 5.3: Parametric and Equivalent Nonparametric Statistical Procedures Identified by Situation. (Reproduced with permission from C.B. Royeen and W.L. Seaver, 1986, The *American Journal of Occupational Therapy*)

*There are multiple comparison procedures for the nonparametric tests, just as for the parametric equivalents.

Name of Procedure	Description of Procedure	Purpose of Procedure
Analysis of Covariance	A combination of analysis of variance and regression that tests the significance of group means after first adjusting scores of the DV to eliminate effects of covariance	If an experimental design is not possible and you want to adjust or control statistically for differences between treatment groups
Canonical Correlation	A test that analyzes the relationship of a set of IVs with a set of DVs	Answers the same questions that a multiple regression does except here you have multiple DVs as well
Discriminant Analysis	An alternative to multiple regression when the criterion variable (DV) is at the nominal rather than interval level of measurement.	Used to predict membership in a category or group based on measure of the IVs
Factor Analysis	A statistical means for condensing or combining many variables into smaller numbers that are interrelated	Used to reduce a large set of variables into a smaller set of unified concepts
Multivariate Analysis of Variance	A test that does for ANOVA what canonical correlation does for multiple regression. Extends ANOVA to two or more DVs	Lets you answer ANOVA questions when you have multiple DVs
Multiple Regression	A way of making predictions by understanding the effects of two or IVs on a DV. Also called multiple correlation	When the DV is interval level data you have two or more IVs and you want to know how much the IVs correlate with the DV
Path Analysis	A method of untangling the relative contributions of various IVs to the variance in a DV	To determine which of a number of IVs is the most influential predictor
Stepwise Multiple Regression	A method in which all potential predictors can be considered simultaneously to see which combination has the greatest predictive power.	When you have many IVs and want to know which set is most powerful in predicting the DV

Figure 5.4 Multivariate (Advanced) Statistical Procedures (Adapted and reproduced with permission from Holly Skodol Wilson: *Research in Nursing*, 1985, Addison-Wesley Publishing Co., Inc.)

Step 3. Identification of Procedures for Confirmatory Data Analysis

The third step in guidelines for data analysis is the identification of possible procedures to be used in the confirmatory data analysis. For example, if one is interested in determining the relationship between one variable and another, a correlational analysis may be selected. Or, if one wishes to investigate if performance on a task can be predicted by a perceptual motor measure, a regression analysis may be selected. Reference charts to assist in the identification of data analytic procedures are provided in Figures 5-2, 5-3, and 5-4.

Figure 5-2 is a flow chart mapping out decision lines for the process of selecting a confirmatory data analytic technique. To use Figure 5-2, one would start with verification of the level of measurement of the dependent variable. For example, if the level of measurement is verified to be interval, then the flow chart leads to the next question in sequence: Does the frequency distribution of the variable approximate a normal one? The results of the exploratory data analysis would assist in answering this question. One would subsequently follow one of the two arrows based on either preliminary assumptions about the data set or findings of exploratory data analysis. The decision making process would then continue to follow the arrows and decision points.

A slightly different, but not contradictory approach to gathering information on statistical procedures to be employed is presented in Figure 5-3.

Figure 5-3 presents parametric and equivalent nonparametric statistical procedures organized around the research situation to be analyzed, i.e., number of groups or process to be investigated. For example, if one desired information on two sets of observations regarding whether or not the two sets were dependent, Figure 5-3 reveals that the Pearson Product Moment Correlation could be an appropriate parametric procedure, whereas the Kendall's τ could be the nonparametric procedure.

The last figure presented in this section, Figure 5-4, presents summaries of advanced statistical procedures that may be appropriate for use.

Figure 5-4 presents summary information on multivariate statistical procedures regarding what the procedure is and when it is used. Additional references and sources would be necessary for final selection of any of these multivariate procedures.

Based on review of Figures 5-2, 5-3, and 5-4, the reader can at least form an idea about one or two statistical procedures that may be used appropriately for confirmatory data analysis for a given situation. After such identification, the reader is encouraged to pursue additional references and resources and to consult with colleagues and statistical/methodological experts as a method of verifying or refining choice of confirmatory data analytic procedure.

Whatever confirmatory data analytic procedure is tentatively identified for use, two considerations are essential. First, one should identify the assumptions underlying use of the confirmatory data analytic technique. Second, one should develop an understanding of the confirmatory or inferential statistical procedure both in terms of the concepts underlying the statistic and calculation procedures related to the procedure (independent of whether or not one will execute the procedure by hand or computer).

Step 4. Data Verification

The fourth guideline for data analysis is data verification. This is a most crucial step in data analysis and is often overlooked or skipped with resulting difficulties. A sad, but true, story serves to illustrate the importance of this step.

A colleague working on her doctoral degree gave all of her dissertation research to a consultant and paid 500 dollars for an analysis of covariance to be conducted. The consultant executed the analysis of covariance, but did not perform data verification. When the results were given to the dissertation student, she was informed the results were "nonsignificant." However, on review of this colleague's materials, it was discovered that all the data had been coded into the computer improperly, and that the resulting confirmatory data analysis was invalid. The colleague had, in fact, a "significant" result using analysis of covariance, but only when the data was properly coded into the computer. Thus, lack of data verification at the initial step resulted in the colleague spending 500 dollars for a bogus data analysis and experiencing considerable frustration, as well as a two-month delay in data analysis. All of these adverse conditions could have been avoided with data verification.

Thus, it is apparent that it is absolutely crucial to verify data prior to any sort of statistical analysis. It is a crucial step often skipped by novice and seasoned researcher alike. Data verification is essential to confirm the validity of the data in terms of recording, coding, and storing. Data verification also allows for the identification of missing data and determination of any systematic bias in terms of the missing data. Simply stated, data verification is a common sense way to evaluate the raw data.

A second component of data verification is computation of descriptive statistics on the data set(s). Depending on the type of variable(s) under study, one would calculate selected descriptive statistics on each variable by group as identified in Figure 5-5.

At this point in data analysis information from descriptive analysis could

Level of Measurement	Procedure
Nominal	Mode
	Frequency
Ordinal	Median
	Range
	Frequency
Ratio	Mean
Interval	Mean
	Mode
	Range (min, max)
	Standard Deviation

Figure 5-5. Procedures for descriptive statistics.

be valuable in deciding how to handle any missing data. Essentially, an investigator in clinical research has five options regarding missing data (Barokas, 1986). These options are not mutually exclusive and may be used in some combination. These options are specified as follows.

Options for Dealing with Missing Data. First, the investigator can "follow up" cases having missing data. It may be possible to acquire the data identified as missing unless such an action is limited by the research plan if, for example, all post-tests must occur at the same time or cost of follow-up is too exorbitant. Some degree of missing data may be recovered in this manner.

Second, depending on the nature and degree of missing data, it may be appropriate to qualitatively estimate the differences that may exist in missing cases or items. In this way, one can estimate, using logical reasoning, whether missing data has an effect on results and interpretation of the analysis.

Third, cases having too many missing data points may be eliminated from the analyses. Many "canned" computer programs do this automatically by executing either case-wise or pair-wise deletion of data.

Fourth, the mean or median score may be substituted or inputed for the missing data point.

Fifth and finally, regression procedures may be used to predict the value of the missing data.

Options three through five are probably the most extensively employed options in clinical research. The reader is referred elsewhere for more detailed explanations on how to handle missing data (Frane, 1976; Madow, Olkin and Rubin, 1983).

Step 5. Exploratory Data Analysis

Subsequent to data verification is the step of exploratory data analysis. Because this is addressed substantially in the preceding chapter on exploratory data analysis, the reader is referred to that chapter for detailed information.

Step 6. Selection and Execution of Confirmatory Data Analysis Procedure and Evaluation of Remaining Assumptions

It should be noted that the conduct of exploratory data analysis does not assure evaluation of all assumptions underlying certain confirmatory statistical procedures. Therefore, once the confirmatory data analysis procedure has been tentatively selected, testing any remaining untested assumptions is the next step in data analysis. To illustrate, many parametric data analysis procedures have assumptions that would not be evaluated during exploratory data analysis. For example, if one conducted regression analysis it would be appropriate at this point to test the normality of the distribution of the residuals. Or, if one was planning to use a t-test with pooled variances, it would be appropriate to test for homogeneity of variance between the two groups.

A discussion of the assumptions underlying use of the most commonly used confirmatory statistical procedures in the occupational therapy literature, Pearson Product Moment Correlation, t-test, ANCOVA, Chi square, regression and ANCOVA (Royeen, 1986), serves as the foundation for the next section of this chapter. This discussion section may serve as a reference for evaluation of assumptions underlying certain statistical tests during this phase of data analysis. It is probable that many of these same procedures are very common in other fields of clinical research such as physical therapy, audiology, etc.

Assumptions Underlying the Most Common Parametric Procedures in Occupational Therapy Research.

Assumptions of Pearson Product Moment Correlation. The assumptions of the Pearson Product Moment Correlation are specified as follows.
1. The underlying distribution is bivariate normal (Welkowitz, Ewen, and Cohen, 1971).
2. The relationship between the two variables is linear (Welkowitz, Ewen, Cohen, 1971).
3. The scale of measurement of the variables is interval or ratio level (Hinkle, Wiersma, and Jurs, 1979).

Generally, the Pearson r appears robust when sample size is large, that is, greater than 25 or 30 (Welkowitz, Ewen, and Cohen, 1971). However, if the relationship between variables is non-linear, r will likely be an underestimate of the relationship (Furfey, 1958). Moreover, Haldane (1949) states that r is robust to skewedness, but that it is not robust to kurtosis differences between distributions that may affect the precision of r. Thus, certain types of non-normality differentially influence the Pearson Product Moment Correlation.

Student's t-test (single sample, independent samples, and paired or matched samples). The assumptions underlying use of different forms of the t-test follow:
1. The variable(s) are distributed normally (Welkowitz, Ewen, and Cohen, 1971).
2. For the two-sample case, the variances of the two populations are equal (Welkowitz, Ewen, and Cohen, 1971).
3. There is random selection of the subjects (Hinkle, Wiersma, and Jurs, 1979).
4. There is interval or ratio level of measurement (Hinkle, Wiersma, and Jurs, 1979).

It often is assumed that one and two sample t-tests are robust and accurate due to the properties of the Central Limit Theorem (Pocock, 1982). For example, Welkowitz, Ewen, and Cohen (1971) maintain that the t-test is robust even "...if the assumption of normality is not met" (p. 141). Furthermore, they maintain that the assumption of equality of variance (for the two-sample case) is also irrelevant if the sample sizes are equal. However, it is reported that the test is non-robust if one sample is 1.5 times larger than the other, and if the respective variances are unequal (Welkowitz, Ewen, and Cohen, 1971). The issue of robustness of the two-sample t-test becomes complex and highly situationally specific if one considers that Gans (1981) reports that the t-test is robust for equal samples even if variances are unequal, unless the distribution is skewed, but that the t-test may be compromised if sample sizes are unequal.

Furthermore, the failure of the Central Limit Theorem to assure accuracy of the t-test computed with samples as large as 500 has been documented (Pocock, 1982). Other researchers argue that the student t is invalid if the distribution is non-normal (Benjamin, 1983; Tikie and Singh, 1981), particularly if the tails are long and heavy (Blair, 1981; Gross, 1976) In spite of Boneau's findings (1962) to the contrary, many researchers say not to use the two-sample t-test for pooled variances if the variances are unequal (Ramsey, 1980; Seaver, 1977). It is evident that controversy exists regarding robustness of the t-test.

Analysis of Variance. The following are assumptions underlying use of ANOVA as specified by Hinkle, Wiersma, and Jurs (1979):

1. Observations are random and independent samples from a population.
2. Interval or ratio level of measurement is employed.
3. Samples are derived from normally distributed populations.
4. The variances of the populations are equal.

For the fixed effects model, Gardner (1975) maintains that the robustness of ANOVA to non-normality and heterogeneity of variance is well accepted, but does not exist under all conditions. Consistent with this, Minimum (1978) reports that ANOVA is robust to heterogeneity of variance only if the sample size is very large. However, Feir-Walsh and Toolhaker (1974) found that a one-factor ANOVA was not robust when the underlying distribution was not normal even if variances were homogeneous.

Bishop and Dudequicz (1978) report that unequal variance can seriously affect inferences about means, especially if the cell sizes are unequal. Somewhat similarly, as early as 1947, Geary maintained that a small departure from normality can seriously affect the ANOVA. In addition, for the random effects model, non-normality can be more serious and heterogeneity of variance can be detrimental even if sample sizes between groups are equal (Neter and Wasserman, 1974). Conflicting views are presented by Box (1953) and Boneau (1962), who report that ANOVA is robust to non-normality and heterogeneity of variance, while Hollington and Smith (1979) provide a highly situation specific description of the robustness of ANOVA.

Regression. The following are the assumptions underlying the use of regression analysis (Montgomery and Peck, 1982):

1. The errors are uncorrelated.
2. The errors are normally distributed.
3. There is a constant variance of the error term, and the error has a mean of zero.
4. There is a linear relationship between dependent and independent variables.

Analysis of Covariance. The assumptions for the analysis of covariance (ANCOVA) are presented as follows (Olejnik and Algina, 1985):

1. There is a linear relationship between pre and post scores.
2. There is homogeneity of regression slopes.
3. There is independence of post-test scores both between and within groups.

4. There is a normal distribution of post scores for the values of the covariate within each group.

5. Variances of all groups are equal.

Levey (1980) reports that if sample sizes are equal, ANCOVA is robust to dual violations of inequality of regression slopes and non-normality. Similarly, Olejnik and Algina (1985) finds ANCOVA robust to violations of either non-normality or heterogeneity of variances. Glass, Peckman, and Sanders (1972) reviewed the literature and concluded that ANCOVA is not seriously affected by non-normality.

However, in other cases, the ANCOVA has not been found to be robust. To illustrate, Antiquilah (1964) found ANCOVA affected by non-normality even in balanced designs. Burnett and Barr (1977) discourage use of the parametric ANCOVA when high within- treatment correlations exist; that is, if treatment outcomes depend on the pre-treatment condition, then Burnett and Barr (1977) discourage use of the parametric ANCOVA. Olejnik and Algina (1985) found that both non-normality and heteroscedasticity compromised robustness when sample sizes were small, and also when sample sizes were unequal (Olejnik and Algina, 1985).

Evaluation of any Remaining Assumptions. Subsequent to exploratory data analysis and based on information contained herein and in other places, one would decide whether or not certain assumptions were met underlying the use of the confirmatory statistical procedure. For those assumptions rejected as not having been met, one must decide: a) if the violation of the assumption is serious as revealed by literature review; and b) if a nonparametric or robust confirmatory data analysis procedure should be alternatively selected. Figure 5-3 can be referred to for consideration of nonparametric alternatives to parametric tests when assumptions underlying the parametric test have been violated.

Step 7. Delineation of Interpretation Criteria

The seventh and final guideline for data analysis is generation and specification of interpretation criteria for the results of data analysis.

The commonly accepted alpha level (.05) is just that: a commonly accepted, yet arbitrary, standard. According to Salsburg (1985), the use of .05 as a standard is not always necessary. How meaningful that standard is for clinical research can be questioned. An article by Salsburg eloquently presents an argument that lesser levels of significance are acceptable when clinical treatments are being considered (1985). Furthermore, other researchers propose the use of confidence intervals (a range of significance) versus single points (Feinstein, 1977). Confidence intervals and other alternatives are subsequently discussed in Chapter 8.

Another consideration for setting standards of interpretation of results is findings from previous research. What does previous literature in related areas present for interpretation of the significance of results? And, in addition to the statistical conclusions of any study, what are the substantive conclusions? The classic illustrative example is the case of the significance of a correlation. Given a large enough sample size, almost any two variables can

Date: _____

Research Investigation: _____

    a) Results of exploratory data analysis revealed: _____

_____

    b) Procedure identified for use (cite references): _____

_____

    c) Sample size considerations: _____

_____

    d) Other considerations: _____

_____

Assumptions underlying use of the procedure: _____

_____

_____

Have all of the assumptions been met? _____

_____

    Implications _____

What are the criteria for interpretation? _____

_____

_____

Figure 5-6. Worksheet for identification of statistical procedure to use in data analysis.

be found to have a statistically significant correlation, even if the correlation itself is very low. Thus, statistical significance and meaningful significance must both be considered in interpretation criteria of data analysis.

Figure 5-6 is provided as a worksheet for recordkeeping and thought processes underlying selection of confirmatory or inferential statistical procedures for data analysis.

Summary

The delineation of these seven steps as guidelines in data analysis for clinical research are process-oriented. That is, the steps identify the sequence of the process of conducting valid and rigorous data analysis. It is clear that this process, like almost all processes, is not absolute. That is, there is not any one correct way to proceed, and thus the guidelines are general and flexible and encourage the addition of other sources, guidelines, and expertise. For, just as treatment planning and execution is a process requiring judgment and problem solving, so too the process of data analysis requires judgment and problem solving.

References

Antiquilah, M. (1964). The robustness of the covariance analysis of a one-way classification. *Biometrika* 51:365-372.

Barokas, J. (1986). Retrospective on missing data. Unpublished manuscript.

Benjamin, Y. (1983). Is the t-test really conservative when the parent distribution is long tailed? *Journal of the American Statistical Association,* 78(383), 645-654.

Bishop, T. A., and Dudequicz, E. J. (1978). Exact sample analysis of variables with and without equality of variance: Test probabilities and tables. *Technometrics,* 20(4), 414- 430.

Blair, R. C. (1981). A reaction to "Consequences of failure to meet assumptions underlying fixed effects ANCOVA and ANCOVA." *Review of Educational Research,* 51(4), 499-507.

Boneau, C. A. (1962). A comparison of the power of the U and t tests. *Psychological Review,* 69, 246-256.

Box, G. E. P. (1953). Non-normality and tests of variance. *Biometrika,* 40, 318-335.

Daniel, W. W. (1978). *Applied nonparametric statistics.* Boston: Houghton, Mifflin Co.

Feinstein, A. R. (1977). *Clinical biostatistics.* St. Louis: C. V. Mosby, Co.

Burnett, T.D. and Barr, D.R. (1977). A nonparametric analogy of ANCOVA. *Educational & Psychological Measurement,* 37, 2:341- 348.

Feir-Walsh, B. J., and Toolhaker, L. E. (1974). An empirical comparison of the ANCOVA, F test, normal scores and Kruskal- Wallis test under violation of assumptions. *Educational and Psychological Research,* 34(4), 789-799.

Fleigner, M.A. and Rust, S.W. (1982). A modification of Mood's median test for the generalized Behren-Fisher Problem *Biometrika* 69:221-226.

Frane, J. W. (1976). Some simple procedure for handling missing data in multivariate analyses. *Psychometrika,* 41(3), 411- 415.

Furfey, P. H. (1958). Comment on "The needless assumption of normality in Pearson's r". *American Psychologist,* 13, 545- 546.

Gans, D. J. (1981). Use of a preliminary test in comparing 2 sample means. *Communication in Statistics: Simulation and Computation,* B10(2), 164-174.

Gardner, P. L. (1975). Scales and statistics. *Review of Educational Research,* 45(1), 43-57.

Geary, R. C. (1947). Testing for normality. *Biometrika,* 34, 209-242.

Gibbons, J. D. (1976). *Nonparametric methods for quantitative analyses.* New York: Holt, Rheinhart, and Winston.

Glass, G.V, Peckman P.D. and Sanders, J.R. (1972). Consequences of failure to meet assumptions underlying the fixed effects analysis of variance and covariance. *Review of Educational Research* 42(3) 237-287.

Gross, A. M. (1976). Confidence interval robustness with long tailed distributions. *Journal of the American Statistical Association,* 71, 409-416.

Haldane, J. B. S. (1949). A note on non-normal correlations. *Biometrika,* 36, 467-468.

Hettmansberger, T. P., and McKean, J. W. (1978). Statistical inference based on ranks. *Psychometrika,* 43, 69-79.

Hinkle, D. E., Wiersma, W., Jurs, S. G. (1979). *Applied statistics for the behavioral sciences.* Boston: Houghton Mifflin Co.

Hollander, M., and Wolfe, D. A. (1973). *Nonparametric methods.* New York: John Wiley and Sons.

Hollington, T. L., and Smith, D. J. (1979). Distribution of the normal score statistics for nonparametric 1-way ANCOVA. *Journal of the American Statistical Association,* 74(367), 715- 733.

Hussain, S. S., and Sprent, T. (1983). Nonparametric regression. *Journal of the Royal Statistical Society* (Series A), 146, 182-191.

Levy, K.J. (1980). A multiple comparison study of ANCOVA under violations of the assumptions of normality and equal regression slopes. *Educational & Psychological Measurement* 40(4) 835- 840.

Madow, W. G., Olkin, T., and Rubin, D. B. (Eds.). *Incomplete data in sample surveys. Vol. 2: Theories and bibliography.* New York: Academic Press.

Mann, W. C. (1986). The choice of an appropriate statistic: A non-mathematical approach. *American Journal of Occupational Therapy,* 40(10), 696-701.

Minimum, E. W. (1978). *Statistical reasoning in education and psychology* New York: J. W. and Sons.

Mitcham, M. D. (1986). Integrating research competencies into basic professional education. *American Journal of Occupational Therapy,* 40(11), 787-788.

Montgomery, D. C., and Peck, F. A. (1982). *Introduction to linear regression.* New York: John Wiley and Sons.

Neter, J., and Wasserman, W. (1974). *Applied linear statistical models.* Homewood, Illinois: R. D. Irwin, Inc.

Nie, N. H., Hull, C. H., Jenkins, J. G., et al. (1975). *Statistical package for the social sciences* (2nd ed.). New York: McGraw Hill.

Olejnik S.F. and Algina, R. (1985). A review of nonparametric alternatives to ANCOVA. *Evaluation Review* 9(1) 51-83.

Pirie, W. R., and Rarch, H. L. (1984). Similated efficiences of tests and estimators from general linear models based on ranks: The 2 way layout with interaction. *Journal of Statistical Computation and Simulation,* 20, 197-204.

Pocock, S. J. (1982). When not to rely on the Central Limit Theorem: An example from absenteeism data. *Communications in Statistics-Theory and Methods,* 11(19), 2169-2169.

Potthoff, R. F. (1963). Use of the Wilcoxon statistic for a generalized Behren-Fisher problem. *Annals of Mathematical Statistics,* 34, 1596-1599.

Ramsey, P. H. (1980). Exact type I error rates for robustness of students t test with and without equal variances. *Journal of Educational Statistics,* 5(4), 337-349.

Reed, K. L. (1984). *Models of practice in occupational therapy.* Baltimore: Williams and Wilkins.

Royeen, C. B. (1986). *An exploration of parametric versus nonparametric statistics in occupational therapy clinical research.* (University Microfilms International no. 86206590).

Royeen, C. B., and Seaver, W. J. (1986). Promise in nonparametrics. *American Journal of Occupational Therapy,* 40(3), 191-193.

Salsburg, D. S. (1985). The religion of statistics as practice in medical journals. *The American Statistician,* 39(3), 220- 223.

Seaver, W. J. (1977). The right test but the wrong occasion. *National Association of Business Teachers Educational Review,* Issue 4 pages 15-17 (Spring Edition).

Silverstein, A. B. (1986). Statistical power lost and statistical power regained: The bonferroni procedures in exploratory research. *Educational and Psychological Measurement,* 46(2), 303-308.

Soper, J. B. (1985). Helping students select the appropriate formula. *Teaching Statistics,* 5(1), 20-24.

Tikie, M. L., and Singth, M. (1981). Robust test for means when population variances are unequal. *Communication in Statistics: Theory and Methods,* A10(20), 2057-2071.

Welkowitz, J., Ewen, R. B., and Cohen, J. (1971). *Introductory statistics for the behavioral sciences.* New York: Academic Press.

Wilson, H. S. (1985). *Research in nursing.* New York: Addison-Wesley Publishing Co.

PART II

CHAPTER 6

COMPARISON OF PARAMETRIC VERSUS NONPARAMETRIC STATISTICAL PROCEDURES

Charlotte Brasic Royeen

Chapter Overview

The predominant use of parametric versus nonparametric statistics in clinical research is addressed in this chapter. The theoretical rationale and assumptions underlying the predominant use of parametric statistics is questioned and discussed. Subsequently, an investigation by Royeen (1986a) is described that empirically evaluated the use of parametric versus nonparametric statistical techniques within a single field of clinical research: occupational therapy. Finally, the implications of the investigation are discussed in terms of occupational therapy research specifically and clinical research in general.

Introduction

Data analysis procedures for clinical research are centered primarily on the use of parametric statistical procedures (Royeen, 1986a) based on a normal distribution model. That is, use of parametric procedures assumes many characteristics of the data set(s), one of which is that the data is from a normally distributed population. The assumption of a normal disribution is frequently justified using the Central Limit Theorem (Edgington, 1969), which states that when randomly sampled, any population with finite variance will yield sample means that approach normality. However, the appropriateness of the Central Limit Theorem for use with finite populations, as is often encountered in clinical research, is questionable.

To illustrate, Plane and Gordon (1982) state "...when sampling from a finite population, increased sample size will not always bring the sample mean closer to normality" (p.175). In fact, they found that sometimes the "...sampling distribution departs from normality as the sample size approaches the finite population" (p.175). Thus, assuming that the Central Limit Theorem applies to all samples may not be prudent and may lead to violation of one or more of the assumptions underlying use of commonly used parametric statistical tests.

Thus, the prevalent use of parametric procedures in clinical research may be questionable due to distributional characteristics of the data sets (Hill and Dixon, 1982). It is suggested by Lezak and Gray (1984) that "...the research data in clinical neuropsychology do not conform to the requirements for parametric statistical analysis" (p.101). Lezak and Gray cite three primary reasons why parametric procedures are problematic in clincial neuropsychology, which may apply to clinical research in general.

First, data sets in clinical neuropsychology are often fraught with outliers. Outliers are data points located beyond the central range of the data if, indeed, the data set was normally distributed. Second, because research studies are primarily clinically based, large samples are difficult to obtain due in part to the limited incidence of clients having certain types of specifically identified clinical dysfunction. Third, there is an excessive amount of empty cells due to the wide range of variability in behavioral dimensions, and that given an array of tests, not all subjects can perform all tests. Consequently, there are considerable missing data. The problems Lezak and Grey identify as characteristic of data sets in clinical neuropsychology may well apply to data sets in other fields of clinical research as well.

As a solution to these problems, Lezak and Gray propose the increased use of nonparametric statistical procedures in clinical research. McSweeney and Katz (1978) present an excellent summary of reasons for using nonparametric statistics:
1. Nonparametrics are assumption free;
2. The data may not be put into metric form appropriately, i.e., unordered qualitative variables;
3. The data may be rank-ordered;
4. The data may be from small samples;
5. There may be a non-normal distribution of the variables;
6. Heterogeneity of variance between groups may exist, and;
7. Outliers may be present.

Why are parametric tests so prevalent in clinial research literature if, indeed, nonparametric methods offer more valid procedures when assumptions for parametric statistics are violated? One reason relates to power. Given a comparison between an equivalent parametric and nonparametric test run under conditions of normality, a parametric test has greater power (Kaplan, 1986; Siegel, 1956). Therefore, it is often assumed that a parmetric test is better.

But how powerful is a parametric test when the assumptions upon which it is based are violated? Gibbons (1976) infers that when assumptions underlying parametric tests are violated, or if one cannot document that the assumptions underlying parametric statistics have been met, the concept of power is irrelevant because the tests may not be valid and the significance levels (p values) may not be accurate.

Another reason parametric statistics are more prevalent than nonparametric statistics involves the concept of robustness. Many parametric procedures, especially the F- and t-tests, are thought to be robust to violations of assumptions under certain conditions (Boneau, 1960, 1962; Box, 1953; Gardner, 1975; Minium, 1978). However, the claim of robustness to violations of assumptions appears to have been overgeneralized beyond highly specified situations (usually delineated from simulation studies) to nearly all real life situations and data sets. Thus, almost all violations of assumptions, often ill-defined, are tolerated in the name of robustness (Bradley, 1978; Singer, 1979). Furthermore, Bradley (1978) argues that there is no quantitative definition of robustness, and that it is therefore a subjective claim and highly variable in form as it is commonly used.

To study the possible effects of violated assumptions using parametric procedures, a study was conducted by Royeen (1986a). Within the clinical field of occupational therapy, parametric versus nonparametric procedures were studied using the case study process of investigation as outlined by Yin (1984). That is, actual data sets within published occupational therapy research served as units of analysis embedded within each "case" or published research.

The investigation specifically explored the following two research questions.

1. Were assumptions violated when parametric statistical procedures were used in occupational therapy research?
2. Did violations of the assumptions make a difference to the substantive meaning of the statistical analysis, i.e., how similar or different were the findings?

Description of the Research

A detailed description of the research can be found elsewhere. (Royeen, 1986a). To summarize, the occupational therapy literature from 1980 to 1984. was indexed according to statistical procedure employed within an article. Subsequently, the frequency count of all procedures were obtained, and the most commonly used procedures in the occupational therapy literature identified.

To appropriately limit the scope of the investigation reported herein, only univariate statistical procedures identified as the most commonly employed in occupational therapy literature were studied. Thus, the following univariate procedures were identified as the most common in the occupational therapy literature and served as the basis of the investigation: a) Independent t-test; b) Paired t-test; c) one-factor ANOVA; d) Pearson Product Moment Correlation; and e) Regression.

Since Minium (1978) stated that nonparametric procedures are most appropriate to use when the sample size is small, data sets from published occupational therapy research were identified as possible cases for the current investigation when: a) one of the previously mentioned parametric procedures was employed; and b) when the sample size was small (less than 50 subjects). Thus, a form of purposive sampling was employed according to theoretical rationale (Yin, 1984). Accordingly, four to five articles per statistical procedure were identified for possible use. Of those articles thus identified for each category of parametric procedure, the two with the smallest sample size were selected for possible use in the current study. Once such articles were identified, the authors were contacted by letter, followed by telephone contact.

In all, five authors could not be located and contacted. Only one author refused to participate in the study, and three authors were willing to participate but could not locate their data sets. In cases of duplicative data sets for one category of procedure, the data set with the smallest sample size was used.

One or more of the following procedures was conducted with each data set to test the assumptions underlying use of the respective parametric analysis. All tests were performed on SAS (Statistical Analysis System User's Guide, 1982) unless otherwise specified. The procedures used were:

1. Boxplots (Royeen, 1986b);
2. the Shapiro Wilks test or W statistic;
3. the F-test (to test for equality of variance in the two-sample situation);
4. the Barlett-Box F test of homogeneity of variance (used for three or more samples);
5. the Squared Ranks test (for distribution-free testing of variance of k groups) (Conover, 1980);
6. correlations of one variable with another; and,
7. scattergrams.

Note that the above procedures were used for univariate tests of normality. In the bivariate case (the Pearson Product Moment Correlation), procedures for testing bivariate normality were employed based on Filliben (1975).

If exploratory data analysis could not be conducted due to small sample size, certain assumptions about the data set were made. First, it was assumed that the Central Limit Theorem did not necessarily apply. And, because evidence suggests that extremely small samples often do not follow a normal distribution (Lezak and Gray, 1984), it was assumed that distributional characteristics of the data set were questionable with regard to normality.

Results and Discussion

Each of the parametric analyses were replicated. Subsequently, the results of the exploratory data analysis were used to determine the appropriate nonparametric statistic. The nonparametric statistic was selected based on the question that the original author posed, as well as guidelines presented in Royeen and Seaver (1986).

Table 6-1 presents the results of the individual cases in terms of a multiple

Table 6.1
Multiple Case Study Summary Table of Results of Parametric versus Nonparametric Statistics Using Data Sets from Occupational Therapy Literature

Parametric	Nonparametric	Conclusion
		Case One
Paired t-test	Sign Test	Meaningful difference in p values. The nonparametric p value was much larger and better reflected the degree of similarity between the data sets. Skewness, two mild outliers and marginal normality were found in the data set of difference scores.
		Case Two
Independent t-test Common Dispersion	Mann Whitney Wilcoxon	No meaningful or substantive differences in p values for either comparison. One data set was mildly, positively skewed.
Uncommon Dispersion	Modified Mood's Median Test	
		Case Three
One Factor ANOVA (Psychiatric)	F test on Ranks	No meaningful or substantive differences in p values. Data of one group was a non-normal. Data of one group was a non-normal, uniform distribution and homogeneity of variance was marginal.
One Factor ANOVA (Grade Point Average)	F test on Ranks	No substantive differences in p values. A meaningful difference was not present using set criteria but results were close to a meaningful difference. One group within the data sets was mildly, negatively skewed with one mild and one extreme outlier.
One Factor ANOVA (Physical Dysfunction	F test on Ranks	Substantive difference in p values. Reject null using nonparametric test, accept null using parametric test. One group within the data set was not normally distributed and heterogeneity of variance existed.

Table 6.1 *(continued)*

		Case Four
Pearson r	Kendall Tau	No substantive difference in p values. Meaningful difference with one set of paired variables. The same set of variables was not bivariate normal and had two bivariate outliers. The nonparametric p value is much less than the parametric p value.
	Normal Children (n = 15)	
Pearson r	Kendall Tau	Nine of the 14 correlations had substantive or meaningful (or both) differences in p values. In each instance the Kendall Tau was more conservative, yielding a larger p value. Univariate and bivariate abnormalities had been noted in all single and paired variables having p value differences. All of the nine cases of differences had bivariate outliers and lacked bivariate normality.
	Learning Disabled (n = 15)	

		Case Five
	Normal Boys	
Parametric Regression	Nonparametric Regression	No meaningful or substantive difference in p values for slope or overall equation. Variable age had one mild outlier. Residual analysis for the normal boys data set yielded one outlier for the parametric analysis and mild skewness for the nonparametric analysis.
	Normal Girls	
Parametric Regression	Nonparametric Regression	No meaningful or substantive difference in p values for slope or overall equation. Neither residual analysis yielded abnormalities
	Boys with Sensory Integrative Dysfunction	
Parametric Regression	Nonparametric Regression	No meaningful or substantive differences in p values for slope or overall equation. One variable had one mild outlier. The results of the residual analysis yielded no abnormalities.

Table 6.2
Analysis of Assumptions Underlying Parametric Test in Each Case

Case	Procedure	Was Underlying Assumption Met?
1	Paired t-test	No. Data of difference scores tested as marginally normal, had two mild outliers, and was mildly skewed.
2	Independent t-test	Yes, with a minor qualification. Data sets tested as normal but one data set was mildly, positively skewed.
3	One factor ANOVA	No. True interval or ratio level of measurement was not employed. Samples did not appear to be from a normally distributed population. Heterogeneity of variance existed.
4	Pearson r	No. Bivariate normality lacking in nine (normal subgroup), and thirteen (learning disabled subgroup) of the paired variables.
5	Regression	Yes.

case study. Table 6-1 reveals that in certain cases, and in certain instances within certain cases, there were clear differences in results between the parametric and the nonparametric statistics. However, in other cases there were no differences in results between the parametric and nonparametric statistics.

Research Question one focused on whether or not assumptions underlying the use of parametric statistics were met. Table 6-2 presents a summary analysis of assumptions underlying each case.

In only one case (regression analysis) were assumptions unequivocally met. In one case (independent t-test), assumptions were met with a minor qualification and in three cases assumptions clearly were not met. Thus, Research Question one can be answered that in three out of five cases, assumptions underlying use of parametric procedures were not met during a multiple-case investigation of small sample size data sets.

Therefore, the belief that there is no need to test for assumptions underlying use of a statistical procedure when using small data sets can be questioned due to the prevalence of violated assumptions with three of the five cases purposefully selected due to small sample size.

Research Question two addressed whether violations of the assumptions made a difference regarding the substantive results of the parametric analyses compared with the nonparametric analyses. Table 6-3 is presented as a summary of interpretations pertaining to Research Question two.

Table 6-3 reveals that in Cases one, three and four, the violated assumptions were indeed important. Furthermore, Table 6-3 reveals that the marginal normality and outliers in Case one apparently did affect the parametric test, and the outliers may have functioned like a "heavy tail," which compromised the robustness of the paired t-test, as indicated in the literature.

Table 6-4 presents a concise summary of these findings regarding differences found related to whether or not parametric assumptions were met.

Table 6.3
Parametric versus Nonparametric Findings for Individual Cases

Case	Procedure	Findings	Difference Defined
1	Paired t-test	Difference	Parametric p value is .5061. Nonparametric p value is .8146 to 1.0
2	Independent t-test	None	NA
3	ANOVA	Difference in one of three instances	Parametric p value is .0557. Nonparametric p value is .0297
4	Pearson r	One out of 14 is different for normal subgroup	Nonparametric p value is smaller than parametric (.09 vs. .24)
		9 out of 14 are different for learning disabled	Nonparametric p value is more conservative in every case
5	Regression	None	NA

Table 6.4
Summary of Assumptions Met Related to Differences Found By Case

Case	Procedure	Assumptions Met	Differences Found
1	Paired t-test	No	Yes
2	Independent t-test	Yes	No
3	One Factor ANOVA	No	Yes
4	Pearson r	No	Yes
5	Regression	Yes	No

Testing Assumptions

Table 6-4 reveals that in each of the two cases where parametric assumptions were met, no differences between parametric versus nonparametric procedures were found. And conversely, in each of the three cases where parametric assumptions were not met, differences between the parametric and nonparametric procedures were found. This finding indicates that if cases are considered as a whole, there is a 100% agreement between whether or not parametric assumptions were violated and whether or not differences were discovered regarding parametric versus nonparametric tests. This supports the notion that assumptions must be tested and selection of parametric or nonparametric data analysis procedures conducted accordingly.

Power and Nonparametric/Parametric Statistics

Further analysis regarding Research Question two, how similar or different are findings, is based on the concept of power. The use of parametric analysis in these five cases did not support the notion that when conditions underlying appropriate use of the parametric procedures are met, parametric tests are more powerful. Siegel (1956) and Fergusen (1976) had found parametric and nonparametric procedures to be within a 5% range of comparable efficiency or power. Two cases within this multiple case study were found to be within an 11% comparable efficiency or power range set by Gans (1984); the independent t-test (Case two) and regression with the subgroups normal girls, normal boys, and boys with sensory integrative dysfunction (Case three). For these cases, the nonparametric procedures appeared as powerful as the parametric procedure.

Results Based on Parametric Versus Nonparametric Statistics

Thus, the claims that nonparametric procedures throw out information (Ager and Jacobson, 1980) and that they lack power (Boneau, 1960) are questioned, because nonparametric procedures rendered equivalent findings to those from parametric procedures in these cases. In addition, David and Perez (1960) propose that the argument for using a nonparametric procedure is strengthened by knowing it will usually yield the same answer as a parametric test. The current multiple case lends support to this concept because, generally speaking, if assumptions were not violated, the nonparametric test performed comparably with the parametric test.

More Appropriate Versus More Powerful

In certain instances when assumptions were violated, the nonparametric test was, in fact, more powerful than the parametric test. This is consistant with Blair (1981), who stated that nonparametric tests can be more powerful when assumptions are violated. In the case of the physical dysfunction ANOVA (assumptions violated were normality and homogeneity of variance), the nonparametric p value was much smaller than the parametric value, suggesting the nonparametric test was more powerful to reject the null hypothesis in these circumstances. Use of the nonparametric test in this instance theoretically could have prevented a Type II error.

In another instance, use of the nonparametric test yielded a p value much closer to a level of significance than did the parametric procedure (Pearson r = .24, Kendall τ = .09) when bivariate normality was lacking and there were two bivariate outliers. Again, the nonparametric test appeared more "powerful" in this case.

However, use of parametric tests when assumptions were violated also appeared to lead to Type I errors, i.e., innappropriate findings of significance. Thus, in these cases the nonparametric tests appeared to be more appropriate, not less powerful. For example, this happened in the case of the Pearson r with the subgroup of learning disabled (Case four) for nine of the fourteen correlations.

Based on the findings regarding Type I and Type II errors, it may be most appropriate not to define nonparametric procedures as more or less power-ful related to parametric procedures, but as possibly more validly employed with greater confidence in the Type I or Type II error rate probability.

Interactions Among Violated Assumptions

Although not addressed by the research questions posited for the study, two issues based on the findings of Royeen (1986a) must be discussed: a) the interactions of violations of assumptions; and b) distributional characteristics of the variables studied in occupational therapy clinical research. Each of these will be discussed in turn.

Bradley (1978) noted that most simulation studies into robustness and effects of the violation of assumptions on parametric tests investigated the effects of single violations in isolation from each other. It is worth noting that in Royeen's investigation (1986a), authentic data sets were used and all viola-tions occurred in multiples of two or three. That is, it was never a single violation influencing the robustness of a particular test, but rather the combination of two or three violated assumptions. These preliminary find-ings may have implications for continued research into the robustness of procedures when dual or multiple violations of assumptions are introduced into computer-generated data sets for simulation studies. Furthermore, the concept of robustness, as generalized from simulation research to practice, may need re-evaluation in terms of the complexity of interactions between violated assumptions and the parametric tests, as occurs in actual practice.

Variable Distribution and the Central Limit Theorem

The distributional characteristics of the variables investigated by the stud-ies comprising this multiple case investigation are noteworthy regarding two dimensions: non-normality and outliers. In three of the five cases (paired t-test, one-factor ANOVA, and Pearson r), instances of univariate or bivariate non-normality were documented (Royeen, 1986a). These findings lend sup-port to the notion proposed by Pocock (1982) that the Central Limit Theorem may not apply in all sampling situations and that an automatic assumption of normality based on the Central Limit Theorem may not be prudent.

Variable Distribution and Outliers

Furthermore, in four of the five cases reported by Royeen (1986c) (paired t-test, one factor ANOVA, Pearson r, and regression), there were outliers either in the original data set, the derived data set, or calculated residuals. Lezak and Gray (1984) purport that data sets in clinical neuro-psychology are often fraught with outliers; it appears that, at least in these cases, the same is true for data sets in occupational therapy research. Given the prevalence of outliers, the issue of "why" is paramount. Often, outliers are considered to be "errors" in a data set. Comrey (1985) states: "These 'bad' observations can result from many different causes, e.g., errors in test scoring, recording, and/ or keypunching; errors in reading data into the computer, such as incorrect formatting, extra or missing cards or lines in the data deck or data set; computer errors; errors in observation or recording; deliberate falsification of responses by subjects for any one of a variety of reasons, and so on" (p.273).

Nonparametrics as a Solution

At this point, it is difficult to assess whether a) the prevalence of outliers is an artifact of small data sets such as employed in this multiple case investigation, or b) outliers represent valid manifestations of variables of interest in occupational therapy clinical research. However, the outlier problem is not unique to occupational therapy research. For example, Tupper and Rosenblood (1984) have discussed how characteristics of attribute variables can confound neurologic research. Recently, the problem of outliers and non-normality was raised by Mooijaart (1985) regarding factor analysis procedures. He stated that, regarding non-normality and factor analysis: "Unfortunately, there are few psychological theories about how variables are distributed. It seems reasonable to apply models in which weak distributional assumptions are made" (p.324).

Mooijaart's solution to the problem of non-normality and factor analysis seems reasonable to apply to clinical research. That is, until more investigation is done and a data base on distributional characteristics of variables of concern in research is developed, and unless variables under investigation are documented to be distributed normally, it appears prudent to apply data analysis procedures in which weak distributional assumptions are made, i.e., nonparametric procedures.

Enhancement of Methodologic Tradition in Clinical Research

In closing, it must be noted that the process of improving the quality and quantity of clinical research in general will not be accomplished by a singular approach along one dimension, i.e., parametric versus nonparametric procedures, or even the more prevalent debate regarding quantitative versus qualitative research. As an illustration, Baum, Boyle, and Edward (1984) state "The most difficult phase of clinical research is the design . . . phase" (p.267). In addition, it is the domain of research design/methods (of which parametric versus nonparametric procedures are just a part) which needs to be addressed.

In this vein, Box (1984) discusses the general importance of practice regarding development of statistical procedures. In clinical research, the relationship between practice, research design, and statistical procedures is crucial and underlies the future development of a tradition of research methods and practice unique to the disciplines in clinical research as well as more generally based service professions. The adequate development of such may be predicated upon fostering and generating research methods within the professions, which in turn may be predicated upon the level of training (bachelor's or master's and doctoral level) within the professions (Royeen,

1986c). For it is impossible to facilitate the growth of a tradition of methodology in clinical research without support for graduate level education in occupational therapy, physical therapy, speech and language therapy, etc., concerning research and research utilization.

References

Ager, C. L., and Jacobson, B. R. (1980). Pure versus practical application of research methods: The robustness of the t and F. (Letter to the Editor). *American Journal of Occupational Therapy*, 34(6), 406.

Baum, C. M., Boyle, M. A., and Edwards, D. F. (1984). Initiating occupational therapy clinical research. *American Journal of Occupational Therapy*, 38(4), 267-269.

Blair, R. C. (1981). A reaction to "Consequences of failure to meet assumptions underlying fixed effects analysis of variance and covariance." *Review of Educational Research*, 51(4), 499-507.

Boneau, C. A. (1960). The effects of violations of the assumptions underlying the t-test. *Psychological Bulletin*, 57(1), 49-64.

Boneau, C. A. (1962). A comparison of the power of the U and t tests. *Psychological Review*, 69, 246-256.

Box, G. E. P. (1984). The importance of practice in the development of statistics. *Technometrics*, 26(1), 1-8.

Box, G. E. P. (1953). Non-normality and tests of variance. *Biometrika*, 40, 318-335.

Bradley, J. V. (1978). Robustness? *British Journal of Mathematical and Statistical Psychology*, 31, 144-152.

Comrey, A. L. (1985). A method for removing outliers to improve factor analytic results. *Multivariate Behavioral Research*, 20(3), 273-280.

Conover, W. J. (1980). *Practical nonparametric statistics*. New York: Wiley and Sons.

David, H. A., and Perez, C. A. (1960). On comparing different tests of the same hypotheses. *Biometrika*, 47(3-4), 297-306.

Edgington, E. S. (1969). *Statistical inference: The distribution-free approach*. New York: McGraw Hill.

Ferguson, F. A. (1976). *Statistical analysis in psychology and education*. New York: McGraw Hill.

Filliben, J. J. (1975). The probability plot correlation test for normality. *Technometrics*, 17, 1.

Gans, D. J. (1984). The search for significance: Different tests on the same data. *Journal of Statistical Computer Simulation*, 19, 1-21.

Gardner, P. L. (1975). Scales and statistics. *Review of Educational Research*, 45(1), 43-57.

Gibbons, J. D. (1985). *Statistical inference*. New York: Marcel Decker, Inc.

Gibbons, J. D. (1976). *Nonparametric methods for quantitative analyses*. Columbus, Ohio: American Sciences Press, Inc.

Hill, M. A., and Dixon, W. J. (1982). Robustness in real life: A study of clinical laboratory data. *Biometrics*, 38, 377-386.

Kaplan, S. H. (1986). Asymptotic relative efficiency (Letter to the Editor). *American Journal of Occupational Therapy,* 40(6), 433.

Lezak, M. D., and Gray, D. K. (1984). Sampling problems and nonparametric solutions in clinical neuropsychological research. *Journal of Clinical Neuro-psychology,* 6(1), 101-109.

McSweeny, M., and Katz, M. (1978). Nonparametric statistics: Use and non-use. *Perceptual and Motor Skills,* 4(3), 1023-1032.

Minium, E. W. (1978). *Statistical reasoning in psychology and education.* New York: John Wiley and Sons.

Mooijaart, A. (1985). Factor analysis for non-normal variables. *Psychometrika,* 50(3), 323-342.

Plane, D. R., and Gordon, K. R. (1982). A simple proof of the nonapplicability of the Central Limit Theorem to finite populations. *American Statistician,* 36(3), 175-176.

Pocock, S. J. (1982). When not to rely on the Central Limit Theorem: An example from absenteesism data. *Communications in Statistics: Theory and Methods,* 11(19), 2169-2169.

Royeen, C. B. (1986a). *An exploration of parametric versus nonparametric statistics in occupational therapy clinical research.* (University Microfilms International, No. 8620659).

Royeen, C. B. (1986b). The boxplot: A screening test for research data. *American Journal of Occupational Therapy,* 40(8), 569-571.

Royeen, C. B. (1986c). Entry level education in occupational therapy. *American Journal of Occupational Therapy,* 40(6), 425-427.

Royeen, C. B., and Seaver, W. F. (1986). Promise in nonparametrics. *American Journal of Occupational Therapy,* 40(3), 191-193.

Siegel, S. (1956). *Nonparametric statistics for the behavioral sciences.* New York: McGraw Hill.

Singer, B. (1979). Distribution-free methods for nonparametric problems: A classified and selected bibliography. *British Journal of Mathematical and Statistical Psychology,* 32, 1-60.

Statistical analysis user's guide. (1982). Cary, North Carolina, SAS Institute

Tupper, D. E., and Rosenblood, L. K. (1984). Methodological commentary: Methodol gical considerations in the use of attribute variables in medical research. *Journal of Clinical Neurology,* 6, (4), 441-453.

Yin, R. K. (1984). *Case study research: Design methods.* Beverly Hills: Sage Publications.

CHAPTER 7

NONPARAMETRIC DATA ANALYSIS PROCEDURES FOR CLINICAL RESEARCH

William L. Seaver

Chapter Overview

This chapter examines nonparametric procedures that are most appropriate for clinical research in light of recent research trends in one clinical discipline: occupational therapy. Guidelines and decision trees are provided to assist the researcher in choosing the proper nonparametric statistical test for data analysis. Nonparametric techniques for one-sample location, two-sample location, three or more sample location, association, and regression are covered. The assumptions, hypotheses, procedures, large sample approximation, efficiencies, and an example are provided for each nonparametric test. In addition, interval estimates or multiple comparisons are given where appropriate. A key objective of this chapter is to put nonparametric techniques into the hands of today's researcher in a service profession.

Introduction

Many users of statistics in the field of clinical research do not realize that today the researcher may choose among several statistical methods: parametric, robust, and nonparametric. Each of these methods works best when certain conditions or assumptions are valid for a data set. For instance, when dealing with inferences about and interval estimation of means and variances, the assumption of normality is necessary. This means that the parent population of the random variables of interest is at least approximately normally distributed. Statisticians seem to agree that when working under those assumptions or under the conditions where the underlying parent population is known, continuous, and completely specified the appropriate statistical methods are called parametric.

However, there has been an increasing awareness that some of the most popular parametric statistical procedures (particularly those optimized for an underlying normal distribution) are extremely sensitive to minor deviations from the assumptions. As a result, robust procedures, which are insensitive to small deviations from the assumptions, have been proposed as a second choice. The primary concern of robust methods is with distributional robustness, particularly in light of skewness or longtailedness in a distribution because of outliers (Hoaglin, Mosteller, and Tukey, 1983). These unusual observations called outliers may distort means and certainly will inflate variances, creating confidence intervals wider than they should be and increasing the likelihood of accepting the null hypothesis in inference. Robust statistical methods may be used to mitigate this problem, although generally there is more effort involved.

The third choice open to the researcher interested in estimation and inference is in the area of nonparametrics or distribution- free methods. Strictly speaking, the term "nonparametrics" implies an estimation or inference statement that is not directly concerned with parameters, while "distribution-free" implies that the underlying distribution of the random variable from which the sample was drawn is either unknown or unspecified (i.e., all the parameters that determine the distribution are unknown). Thus, these two terms are not exactly synonymous, but we will use the two words interchangeably in this chapter. The use of nonparametric methods would seem to indicate that at least one of the following conditions exists:

1. The sample size is quite small.
2. The data are measured on a nominal or ordinal scale.
3. The data are an interval or ratio scale of measurement from a distribution that is either unknown (and thought to bear little resemblance to the normal) or unspecified.

In certain service oriented disciplines, such as occupational and physical therapy, these conditions arise quite frequently. For example, the distributional characteristics of most variables of interest in occupational and physical therapy are unknown.

Choice of Procedure

The primary advantage of nonparametric methods is that exact inferences and estimations can be formed when the standard parametric assumptions cannot be made or one or more of the three above-cited conditions exist. Practitioners, however, due to their training in statistics, generally remember that some parametric test procedures are not very sensitive to mild deviations from assumptions. These practitioners therefore generally use parametric methods. For instance, the univariate t-test is said to be robust to non-normality, mainly in the forms of slight skewness, which should have little effect on significance levels.

In light of these comments, by way of analogy, a word of warning is necessary: "A healthy or robust individual may ignore some of the requisites for good health (adequate sleep, diet, exercise) some of the time, but if too many requisites are ignored too often, even the healthiest person will suffer" (Madsen and Moeschberger, 1986, p.382).

Royeen and Seaver (1986) recently raised this issue in occupational therapy literature. If the underlying distribution is symmetric and "normal" in the middle but heavier in the tails than normal, then the t confidence intervals are too wide and thus too conservative (Benjamin, 1983). To counter this difficulty practitioners, who can take large samples, will invoke the Central Limit Theorem, because for a sufficiently large n the sampling distribution of the mean approaches normal, irrespective of the underlying parent population. If the parent population is symmetrical and relatively concentrated around the point of symmetry, the normal approximation and parametric methods will be good even for small sample sizes (Ott, 1984). On the other hand, if the parent population is highly skewed, many practitioners assume that the normal approximation and parametric methods are always adequate for n > 30. However, Pocock (1982) has shown that if the parent population is highly skewed, as it is for job absences, the n needed for invoking the Central Limit Theorem with valid levels of significance is greater than 500.

The previous comments on the robustness of some parametric procedures and invoking the Central Limit Theorem emphasize that today's researcher, regardless of discipline, cannot blindly choose statistical methodology, whether it be parametric or nonparametric. In addition, a choice between several statistical procedures for a given situation can be based on the criterion of efficiency, i.e., the ratio of sample sizes needed to achieve the same variance. Assuming that the methods based on the assumption of normality are 100% efficient and that one wants to compare two procedures for estimating central tendency or location of a distribution, the variances for each sampling distribution are needed to determine efficiency. For example, in estimating the mean of a normal population, the variances of the sampling distribution of the mean is $\sigma^2 \div n$. If one wanted to use the median instead, the variance for its sampling distribution is approximately $1.57 \sigma^2 \div n$. The ratio of the variance of the sampling distribution of the mean to that of the variance of the sampling distribution of the median under normal conditions is $1 \div 1.57$, or an efficiency of approximately 64%. Restated another way, the median based on a sample of size 100 or 50 gives just as reliable estimates of central tendency for a normal population as the mean based on a sample of 64 or 32, respectively.

However, if the assumption of normality is invalid, then this measurement of efficiency for the nonparametric test or estimate understates its value and is most likely inappropriate (Gibbons, 1985). In general, statisticians use asymptotic relative efficiency (ARE) to measure efficiency, because it is the " . . . limiting value of relative efficiency as sample size (n) increases without limit" (Mikulski, 1982, p.468).

Choosing the right statistical procedure, whether parametric or nonparametric, will depend on the consequences of the choice and the sample size of information available to the decision maker. Figure 7-1 summarizes these consequences.

Figure 7-1 illustrates that if a nonparametric approach is used when

	True State	
	Nonparametric Procedure Appropriate	Parametric Procedure Appropriate
Action		
Use Nonparametric	Correct Decision	Correct levels of significance but a loss of power
Use Parametric	Unknown or incorrect levels of significance	Correct Decision

Figure 7-1. Consequences of procedure choice.

parametric methods are appropriate the significance levels will be close, but there will be a loss of "power." By power, we mean that the probability of rejecting a null hypothesis (H_o) for a given value of some parameter corresponding to the alternate hypothesis (H_a) being true is less for the nonparametric than for the parametric procedure. If it can be assumed that the H_o that relates to the parametric procedure is appropriate, then to use nonparametric methods when parametrics is true is no great loss, because the significance levels should be close. However, if parametric procedures are used when nonparametrics are appropriate, then the levels of significance are incorrect or unknown and the power probably inappropriate, because it depends on the shape of the underlying distribution.

The practical implication of these thoughts are three-fold. First, if there is any doubt as to the appropriateness of the parametric assumptions being valid, use nonparametric methods. Secondly, because invalid or unknown levels of significance result from using parametric methods when nonparametric procedures are appropriate, it seems that a larger sample size of information from the theoretical and applied realms of a discipline would be necessary to make a correct choice of procedure. Thirdly, if a discipline has no prior knowledge of distributional assumptions or accumulation of statistical support for distribution form, then a clinical discipline such as occupational or physical therapy may consider an emphasis on nonparametric methods in research.

Classification of Nonparametric Procedures

While the previous section delineated the decision processes that the researcher must resolve in choosing nonparametric methods, this section highlights the different ways that nonparametric procedures can be classified. There are a multitude of nonparametric procedures, and often any one of several may be used in any given situation. Nonparametric methods, however, are somewhat specialized for specific tasks. An understanding of the classifications will enable the researcher to narrow the choice of the appropriate nonparametric procedure.

Most nonparametric techniques are relatively quick and easy to apply, although the theory behind the technique may be somewhat difficult. On the other hand, there are some nonparametric methods that have a slightly higher difficulty factor computationally; but the potential gains in asymptotic relative efficiency are worth the effort (Conover, 1980). Thus, the majority of nonparametric methods may be classified as quick and easy, and a minority as having intermediate difficulty in computation and understanding.

Nonparametric methods also can be classified according to the level of measurement for the variable: nominal, ordinal, interval, or ratio. Another means of classification may be by the type of nonparametric problem: a) location; b) dispersion; c) goodness of fit; d) dichotomous data; e) association; f) regression; g) randomness; and h) miscellaneous (Daniel, 1978; Gibbons, 1985; Hollander and Wolfe, 1973). Within these two classification systems most categories can be broken down by type and number of samples: a) one sample; b) two independent samples; c) three or more independent samples; d) two related samples; and e) three or more related samples (Daniel, 1978). Finally, within the problem classification system the nonparametric methods can be classified according to their parametric equivalent, as noted by Govindarajulu (1976) and Royeen and Seaver (1986).

Because very little information is lost in replacing variable values in the sample with their respective ranks, two illustrations of these classification schemes that use rank methods are given in Figures 7-2 and 7-3. If the level of measurement is at least ordinal, if the parent population of the variable is non-normal, and if the focus is on the problem of location, Figure 7-2 displays the rank procedures to be considered.

Given the above conditions, the appropriate nonparametric procedure is further narrowed by the number of samples and dependence or independence. On the other hand, if the scale of measurement is interval or ratio, and location for two samples is the interest, Figure 7-3 parallels the classification scheme of parametric and nonparametric (Seaver, 1977).

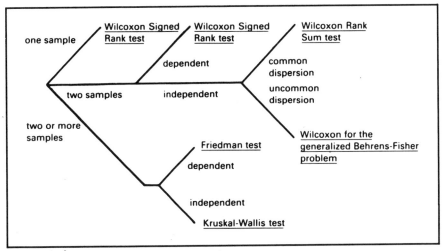

Figure 7-2. Nonparametric location alternatives.

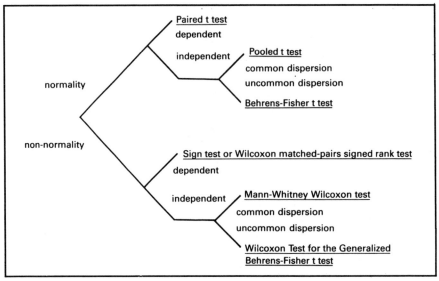

Figure 7-3. Parametric and nonparametric two-sample location alternatives.

A decision tree that focuses on all of the alternatives, no matter what level of variable measurement, could be constructed (Gibbons, 1985); but for brevity and simplicity, nonparametric methods that use ranks and that are used for the problems of location, association, and regression will be emphasized.

As reported in *Research Tradition in Occupational Therapy: Process, Philosophy and Status* in reviewing the occupational therapy literature from 1980 to 1984, Royeen (1986) found that 14% of the procedures were nonparametric, with location and association being the major concerns. In her tally of frequencies for parametric procedures, at least 64% of those procedures covered location, association, and regression. Thus, the methods discussed in the following sections will focus on nonparametric procedures most appropriate to occupational therapy research, but which may be applied to all fields of clinical research in light of recent trends (Royeen, 1988;1986).

Location for One Sample or Two Dependent Samples

If the underlying parent population is non-normal and the interest is in testing or estimating location for a one-sample problem or for two dependent samples (i.e., paired samples), the appropriate rank test from Figures 7-2 and 7-3 is the Wilcoxon signed rank procedure, the nonparametric analog of the parametric t and the paired t-tests, respectively (Wilcoxon, 1945). The dependent sample situation that is most likely would be checking for a median difference of zero for a treatment versus a control group of subjects.

Assumptions

1. A random sample of n independent observations or independent random pairs are taken.

2. The variable of interest, $d_i = X_i - Y_i$, for the paired situation or $d_i = X_i - M_o$ for the one-sample situation, comes from a continuous population that is symmetric about zero (where M_o is the hypothesized median).
3. The level of measurement is at least ordinal.

Hypotheses

1. H_o: $M = M_o$ H_o: $M \leq M_o$ H_o: $M \geq M_o$
   H_a: $M \neq M_o$ H_a: $M > M_o$ H_a: $M < M_o$

2. H_o: $M_d = 0$ H_o: $M_d \leq 0$ H_o: $M_d \geq 0$
   H_a: $M_d \neq 0$ H_a: $M_d > 0$ H_a: $M_d < 0$

The first set of hypotheses above deals with two- and one-tail tests for the median for one sample and the second set for a median difference (M_d) of zero. It is possible to modify the difference, d_i, for the paired samples if one expects, for instance, that the treatment is 2 units higher on the average than the control by computing the difference, $d_i = X_i - Y_i - M_o$ or $d_i = X_i - Y_i - 2$.

Procedure
1. Define the variable of interest, $d_i = X_i - Y_i - M_o$, where M_o can be zero.
2. Compute the absolute value of d_i, $|d_i|$, and rank (R_i) these absolute values from smallest to largest.
3. If there are ties in rank, use the average rank over those ties. For instance, if in a sample of ten the three largest absolute differences are tied (ranks 8, 9, 10), the average rank assigned to each is $(8+9+10) \div 3 = 9$. The exceptions to this rule are zero differences. The simplest approach is to ignore zero differences and reduce n accordingly; but there are other schemes (Pratt and Gibbons, 1981).
4. Return the sign of the difference in Step 1 that was removed in Step 2 to the ranks, R_i.
5. Find the sum of the positive ranks, ΣR_+, and the sum of the negative ranks, ΣR_-, ignoring the signs on the latter.
6. Compute the test statistic for the Wilcoxon signed rank test, T, which is equal to the minimum of ΣR_+ and ΣR_-.
7. Reject the H_o if the test statistic, T, is less than the critical value, T^*, from Appendix C.1 for a given sample size and level of significance. If zeros are ignored and ties are handled by the average rank procedure, the exact sampling distribution of T is no longer covered precisely by Appendix C.1. However, the effect of the nonzero ties is very insignificant in most cases (Gibbons, 1985).

Example A
Suppose a random sample of nine subjects was taken to see if there was a significant difference between the duration of nystagmus (a rhythmical back-and-forth eye movement that is an automatic response to spinning) under bright and dim light conditions at a 10% level of significance. Preliminary

analysis of the data shown in Table 7-1 would reveal normality of the observations for bright and dim light conditions with slight skewness left and right, respectively, and a strong positive association between bright and dim data values. However, the boxplot of the differences, d_i, shown in Figure 7-4 reveals skewness right with a mild outlier, a sample mean of 2.22, and a sample median of 1.00. Therefore, the assumption of normality is questionable.

If the interest of the researcher is still in checking for a difference in location or for a median difference of zero ($H_o:M_d = 0$), then the Wilcoxon signed rank test is a feasible choice.

The calculations are shown in Table 7-1. The Wilcoxon signed rank test statistic, $T = \min(\Sigma R_+, \Sigma R_-)$ or $T = \min(7.5, 37.5) = 7.5$.

In comparing the test statistic, $T = 7.5$, versus the critical value for $n = 9$, $\alpha = .10$, and for a 2-sided test given in Appendix C.1, critical value, $T^* = 8$, the conclusion is that there is a difference at this significance level. Using the p-value approach, the conclusion is the same with $.05 < p < .10$ (or exactly .086 using MINITAB [Ryan, Joiner and Ryan, 1985]). It is interesting to note that if the t-test for paired data had been used the p-value would have been .07. Thus, for this situation at a 10% level of significance, there is no substantive difference in conclusion for the nonparametric and parametric tests. The crucial advantage is that normality was not needed for the nonparametric test in light of the findings in Figure 7-4.

Table 7.1
Calculations of the Wilcoxon Signed Rank Statistic

Subject	Bright Light	Dim Light	d_1	[d_i]	Signed Rank of Negative	Positive
1	23	22	1	1		2.5
2	21	20	1	1		2.5
3	14	16	−2	2	5.0	
4	27	19	8	8		9.0
5	17	16	1	1		2.5
6	23	17	6	6		8.0
7	18	15	3	3		6.5
8	23	24	−1	1	2.5	
9	22	19	3	3		6.5

$\Sigma R_- = 7.5 \quad \Sigma R_+ = 37.5$

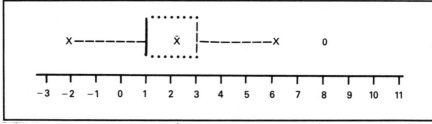

Figure 7-4. Boxplot of differences.

Large Sample Approximation

When n>25, the sampling distribution of T, defined earlier as the sum of ranks, is approximately distributed as a normal with:

$$\mu_T = \frac{n(n+1)}{4} \text{ and } \sigma_T^2 = \frac{n(n+1)(2n+1)}{24} \qquad \text{(1)}$$

Thus, for large sample sizes the statistic

$$Z = \frac{(T - \mu_T)}{\sigma_T} \qquad \text{(2)}$$

has approximately a standard normal distribution. There are adjustments for ties that can be incorporated into the formulae. Using Example A, μ_T=22.5, α_T=8.44, T=7.5, and Z=1.77, giving p-value of .077 (determined from Appendix C.2), which is very close to that for the small sample approach.

Efficiencies

The asymptotic relative efficiency (ARE) of the Wilcoxon signed ranks test versus the single sample t or paired t-test within the class of continuous, symmetric populations never falls below .864, implying that the Wilcoxon signed rank test can never be a bad choice under these conditions (Hodges and Lehman, 1956). If the d_i are normally distributed, the ARE is .955. If the d_i are distributed as a uniform or a double exponential, the AREs are 1.0 and 1.5, respectively.

Confidence Intervals

Assuming that the population is symmetric, it is possible to construct an interval estimate of the median or median difference for the nonparametric statistic just as described for the parametric statistic in chapter 8.

To do so will necessitate putting back all observations that had a zero difference and letting n refer to the original sample size. The procedure follows: 1) compute $n(n+1) \div 2$ averages of either $(X_i + X_j) \div 2$ or $(d_i + d_j) \div 2$ for all i and j, even i=j for the median or median difference, respectively; 2) sort these averages, called Walsh averages; 3) the median of the Walsh averages is the point estimate of the population median; and 4) with the desired degree of confidence and sample size n, the confidence interval end points are the kth smallest and kth largest Walsh averages, where for n>25,

$$K = .5 + \frac{n(n+1)}{4} - Z \left[\frac{n(n+1)(2n+1)}{24} \right]^{1/2} \qquad \text{(3)}$$

The Walsh averages of the differences are shown in Table 7-2. A 90% confidence for n=9 using equation (3) and Z=1.645 from Appendix C.2, gives k=9.11 or, rounding down to the closest integer for conservatism, k=9. The median position of $n(n+1) \div 2$ Walsh averages (i.e., 45) is 23, which

	-2	**-1**	**1**	**1**	**1**	**3**	**3**	**6**	**9**
Table 7.2									
Walsh Averages									
-2	-2.0	-1.5	-.5	-.5	-.5	.5	.5	2.0	3.5
-1		-1.0	0.0	0.0	0.0	1.0	1.0	2.5	4.0
1			1.0	1.0	1.0	2.0	2.0	3.5	5.0
1				1.0	1.0	2.0	2.0	3.5	5.0
1					1.0	2.0	2.0	3.5	5.0
3						3.0	3.0	4.5	6.0
3							3.0	4.5	6.0
6								6.0	7.5
9									9.0

corresponds to the sample median of 2.0. The ordering of the 9 smallest and 9 largest Walsh averages would be as follows:

$$-2.0 \quad -1.5 \quad -1.0 \quad -.5 \quad -.5 \quad -.5 \quad 0 \quad 0 \quad 0$$

and

$$4.5 \quad 4.5 \quad 4.5 \quad 4.5 \quad 5.5 \quad 5.5 \quad 6 \quad 7 \quad 8$$

Thus, the approximate 90% interval is written as $0 \leq M \leq 4.5$ and the 95% interval as $-.5 \leq M \leq 4.5$. There are faster ways to construct such interval estimates as well as small sample approaches (Daniel, 1978; Gibbons, 1985).

Location for Two Independent Samples

The Mann-Whitney-Wilcoxon or the Wilcoxon rank sum test is the nonparametric equivalent of the pooled t-test when the assumption of normality is inappropriate or invalid and there are no differences due to dispersion (Mann and Whitney, 1947; Wilcoxon, 1945; Figure 7-3). Without the restriction on dispersions, the significance level of this nonparametric test is not preserved (Hollander and Wolfe, 1973). There are possible modifications of this Wilcoxon rank sum test if there are dispersion differences, but the mathematics are much more complicated.

Assumptions
1. There are two independent random samples of size n and m.
2. The variable of interest is a continuous random variable (i.e., preferably no ties).
3. The two populations differ only with respect to location.

Hypotheses

$$H_o: M_x - M_y = \Delta_o \qquad H_o: M_x - M_y \geq \Delta_o \qquad H_o: M_x - M_y \leq \Delta_o$$
$$H_a: M_x - M_y \neq \Delta_o \qquad H_o: M_x - M_y < \Delta_o \qquad H_o: M_x - M_y > \Delta_o$$

The difference, Δ_o, could easily be zero if the concern is to test for equivalence of medians.

Procedure

1. Combine the two samples, X and Y, into one.
2. Rank the combined m+n observations in ascending order. Assign the tied values the average rank.
3. Find the sum of ranks for the X sample and the Y sample such that $T_x = \Sigma R_x$ and $T_y = \Sigma R_y$, respectively.
4. Let W be the test statistic for the Wilcoxon rank sum, the sum of ranks assigned to the sample of size m where m≤n.
5. For a specified level of significance, a specified m and n, and for a 1- or 2-tailed test, look up the critical value W_* (which will be either W_l or W_u) in Appendix C.3. If $W \geq W_u$ for $H_a : M_m > M_n$, then reject H_o. If $W \leq W_l$ for $H_a : M_m < M_n$, then reject H_o. If $W \geq W_u$ or $W \leq W_l$ and $H_a : M_m \neq M_n$, then reject H_o. In other words, W_l and W_u form the lower and upper boundaries for the test statistic W in terms of acceptance of the null hypothesis, H_o, for the one-tail or two-tail test.

Example B

Suppose that a random sample of six male athletes and another random sample of five female athletes was taken at a college to test for differences in location for pulse rates at $\alpha = .10$. The pulse rates were all measured prior to exercise.

Males	60	61	63	65	58	42
Females	66	59	70	67	65	

If boxplots were performed on males and then on females, they would not be normal because of the outliers in each: 42 and 59, respectively. If a researcher was ignorant of or ignored this information on distribution form and used the parametric-pooled t-test, the computed t-value would have been -1.77, with nine degrees of freedom and a p-value of .11. The conclusion at $\alpha = .10$ would have been no difference in means.

Using the more appropriate nonparametric test, the Wilcoxon rank sum test, the hypotheses are as follows:

$$H_o : M_{males} = M_{females} \qquad H_a : M_{males} \neq M_{females}$$

The two samples combined into one and ranked with the observations of the smaller sample size (females, m = 5) noted by F are shown below:

Pulse Rates	42	58	59	60	61	63	65	65	66	67	70
Ranks	1	2	3	4	5	6	7.5	7.5	9	10	11
			F				F		F	F	F

The test statistic W, the sum of ranks for the smaller sample, is $W = 3 + 7.5 + 9 + 10 + 11 = 40.5$. Using the tables in Appendix C.3 for m = 5, n = m+1 or 6, and $\alpha = .10$ for a two-sided test, the acceptance region is defined between 20 and 40. Because W = 40.5 is greater than $W_u = 40$, then reject the null and accept the alternate hypothesis, saying there is a difference in location for pulse rates. Using MINITAB, the exact p-value was .0679.

Large Sample Approximation

When either m or n is greater than 25, the sampling distribution of W is approximately normally distributed with the following mean and variance:

$$\mu_w = \frac{m(m+n+1)}{2} \text{ and } \sigma_w^2 = \frac{mn(m+n+1)}{12} \qquad (4)$$

For large samples, even when m or n are greater than 12, the Central Limit Theorem applies to W such that

$$Z = \frac{W - \mu_w}{\sigma_w} \qquad (5)$$

See Gibbons (1985) for corrections for continuity and ties that enhance the estimation of the p-value. For Example B, $\mu_w = 30$, $\sigma_w = (30)^{1/2}$, $W = 40.5$, $Z = 1.92$, and the p-value is .0548, which is close to the appropriate p-value for the small sample approach.

Efficiencies

The ARE of the Wilcoxon rank sum test versus the two-sample t-test is the same as that of the Wilcoxon signed-rank test versus the one-sample t (see previous section on the Wilcoxon signed rank test). If two populations differ only in location, the ARE is never lower than .864 (Hodges and Lehman, 1956). If the two populations tend to be normal, the ARE is .955; if they tend to be uniform, the ARE is 1.0; and if they tend to be double exponential (a symmetric but concentrated and heavy-tailed distribution), the ARE is 1.5 (Hollander and Wolfe, 1973).

Confidence Intervals

If the interval estimate using the pooled t at a 90% confidence were wrongly used for Example B, the interval boundaries for the average difference in means would have been from -14.7 to 0.2. The estimate of this shift in location can be done easily with the Wilcoxon rank sum test (Gibbons, 1985; Hollander and Wolfe, 1973). Once the observations in the X sample and the Y sample are placed in ascending order, the X_i along the rows of a table and the Y_j along the columns as shown in Table 7-3, the m by n differences, d_{ij}, can be computed.

We would arrange these differences from Table 7-3 in ascending order, as shown below:

```
-28  -25  -24  -23  -17  -12  -10   -9   -9   -8   -7   -7   -7   -6   -6
 -5   -5   -5   -4   -4   -3   -2   -2   -1   -1    0    1    2    4    6
```

The .5(mn+1) positional value of the ordered differences is the estimate of the median difference. In this case, .5(6 × 5 + 1) = 15.5 position and the estimate of the median difference is the average of the values in the 15th and 16th

			Males			
Females	42	58	60	61	63	65
59	− 17	− 1	1	2	4	6
65	− 23	− 7	− 5	− 4	− 2	0
66	− 24	− 8	− 6	− 5	− 3	− 1
67	− 25	− 9	− 7	− 6	− 4	− 2
70	− 28	− 12	− 10	− 9	− 7	− 5

Table 7.3
Differences (Males-Females)

positions, that is, -5.5. The confidence interval endpoints are the kth smallest and the kth largest of the differences, d_{ij}, where k can be approximated as follows with the normal distribution:

$$K = .5 + \left[\frac{mn}{2} \right] - Z \left[\frac{mn(m+n+1)}{12} \right]^{1/2} \quad \text{(6)}$$

For a 90% interval estimate, the standard normal Z-value is 1.645, which gives:

$$K = .5 + \frac{5 \cdot 6}{2} - 1.645 \left[\frac{5 \cdot 6 (5+6+1)}{12} \right]^{1/2} = 6.49$$

or approximately 6, rounding down. The sixth smallest difference is -12 and the sixth largest difference is -1. Thus, the approximate 90% confidence interval for the median difference in pulse rate between men and women is $-12 \leq M \leq -1$, which is narrower and more appropriate assumptionally than the pooled t interval estimate noted earlier. Because the interval does not contain zero, then it is obvious that the $H_o : M_x = M_y$ is not tenable at $\alpha = .10$. For more information on interval estimates, see Conover (1980), Daniel (1978), Gibbons (1985), and Hollander and Wolfe (1973).

Location for Two or More Independent Samples

The Kruskal-Wallis test is a generalization of the two sample problems in the previous section (Kruskal and Wallis, 1953; Kruskal, 1952). The Kruskal-Wallis procedure is the nonparametric equivalent to one-factor analysis of variance, where normality and common dispersion are crucial assumptions. One-factor analysis of variance is used to check for differences between means, where the focus for the Kruskal-Wallis procedure, which utilizes ranks, is on medians. The assumptions for the Kruskal-Wallis test are almost identical to those for the Wilcoxon rank sum test.

Assumptions
1. There are k independent random samples of sizes, $n_1, n_2, .. n_k$.

2. The variable of interest is continuous.
3. The level of measurement is at least ordinal.
4. The k populations are identical except for location for at least one of those populations.

Hypotheses

$$H_o: M_1 = M_2 = \ldots = M_k \qquad H_a: \text{At least one median } (M_j) \text{ is unequal}$$

Procedure

1. Rank all observations across k treatments in ascending order. If there are ties, assign the average rank as done in previous rank procedures.
2. Find the sum of ranks for reach treatment j and call it R_j.
3. The average rank for any one observation is $\bar{R} = (n+1) \div 2$. The average rank for any one of the k treatments is $\bar{R}_j = R_j \div n_j$.

Thus, the test statistic for location for two or more independent samples could be written as follows (Hollander and Wolfe, 1973):

$$H = \frac{12}{n(n+1)} \sum_{j=1}^{K} n_j (\bar{R}_j - \bar{R})^2 \qquad \qquad (7)$$

Equation (7) conceptually looks at the variability between the average treatment rank and the overall average rank ($\bar{R}$) for any one observation just as one-factor analysis of variance does for means. Equation (7) is generally rewritten in the following form for simplification:

$$H = \frac{12}{n(n+1)} \left[\sum_{j=1}^{K} \frac{R_j^2}{n_j} \right] - 3(n+1) \qquad \qquad (8)$$

4. This test statistic can be corrected for ties and is approximately distributed as a chi-square with k-1 degrees of freedom (see Appendix C.4) as long as $k \geq 3$ and each $n_j \geq 5$ (Daniel, 1978; Gibbons, 1985). There are exact tables for the situations where $k = 3$, each $n_j \leq 5$, and there are no ties (Iman, Quade and Alexander, 1975).
5. If H is greater than the appropriate chi-square value for k-1 degrees of freedom and for a specified level of significance in Appendix C.4, then reject the null hypothesis of equivalent medians; or instead, the p-value can be found and compared with the level of significance for a conclusion.

Example C

Suppose that an occupational therapy department has three personal computers with some differences in hardware and software. Because of budget constraints a service contract can be supported only for the one or two personal computers with the highest usage rate in hours per week. Test for a significant difference in median usage at $\alpha = .05$ and make a recommendation as to which computers should take a service contract. Random samples of five weeks were taken for PC-1 and PC-2, while a sample of six weeks for PC-3 was available.

PC-1		PC-2		PC-3	
Obs.	Rank	Obs.	Rank	Obs.	Rank
13	5	43	14	39	13
8	2	10	4	33	12
6	1	16	7.5	23	11
14	6	18	10	16	7.5
9	3	44	15	17	9
				46	16
Rj	17		50.5		68.5
nj	5		5		6
R̄j	3.4		10.5		14.42

Because the boxplots on the observations for each personal computer do not appear to be very normal, then the Kruskal-Wallis test seems appropriate. The hypotheses would be stated as follows:

H_o: $M_1 = M_2 = M_3$ or all three medians are equal

H_a: At least one median is different

The computation of the test statistic, H, using equation (8) yields:

$$H = \frac{12}{16 \cdot (16+1)} \left[\frac{17^2}{5} + \frac{50.5^2}{5} + \frac{68.5^2}{6} \right] - 3(16+1) = 8.55$$

At two degrees of freedom the p-value is $.01 < p < .025$ from Appendix C.4.

Because this p-value is less than the .05 level of significance, we reject the H_o and conclude that at least one median is different. however, the Kruskal-Wallis test does not specifically pinpoint which median is different. The resolution of this problem leads to the need for multiple comparison procedures.

Multiple Comparisons

In light of finding a difference among medians in Example C, the question still remains as to which median usage rates are different. Is the difference between M_1 and M_2, between M_2 and M_3, or between M_1 and M_3, because for this example all possible pairs would be of prime concern to the researcher (i.e., all possible pairs = $k(k-1) \div 2 = 3(2) \div 2 = 3$)?

A special statistical technique called multiple comparisons allows the researcher to simultaneously test all pairs of medians, selected comparisons as with a control group, or even linear combinations of median comparisons. If there were c independent comparisons, each with a significance level of α for comparison, the probability of declaring at least 1 significant difference as a result of chance is $\alpha_o = 1 - (1-\alpha)^c$, or about $c\alpha$ for small α (Daniel, 1978). This α_o is called the overall level of significance, or the experimental error rate. If $\alpha = .05$ and there were 3 independent comparisons, the overall level of significance, α_o, is equal to .1426, using $\alpha_o = 1 - (1-\alpha)^c$. The most common overall levels of significance chosen in practice are .10, .15, and .20. As the total number of comparisons increases, the chance of finding 1 false significant comparison also increase. Thus, it is not unusual to find an $\alpha_o = .25$ in such cases.

The multiple comparison procedure described here is easy, conservative, and versatile (Dunn, 1964). First, find the average ranks, $\bar{R}_j$, for each treatment. Second, calculate all $k(k-1) \div 2$ absolute differences for all pairs, k-1 absolute differences for a treatment versus a control, or selective absolute differences, $|\bar{R}_i - \bar{R}_j|$. Let c be the total number of comparisons. Third, choose an overall error rate, α_o, such that the α for comparison is reasonable (Gibbons, 1985). Finally, find the absolute differences, $|\bar{R}_i - \bar{R}_j|$, which satisfy the following inequality for a given α_o and c comparisons:

$$\left| \bar{R}_i - \bar{R}_j \right| \leq Z_{\alpha/2c} \left[\frac{n(n+1)}{12} \right]^{1/2} \times \left[\frac{1}{n_i} + \frac{1}{n_j} \right]^{1/2} \quad i \neq j \qquad (9)$$

Those absolute differences that satisfy equation (9) are not significantly different.

Using Example C, with an overall error rate of .10 and with an interest in all pairs (where c = 3), the approximate α for comparison is $\alpha_o \div 2c$, or $.10 \div (2 \times 3) = .01667$. Using $\alpha_o = 1 - (1 - \alpha)^c$ and solving for α for 2-tailed tests, we would get .0173. The standard normal Z-value is 2.13 with a .01667 probability in the tail. Table 7-4 shows the multiple comparison calculations with $\bar{R}_1 = 3.4$, $\bar{R}_2 = 10.5$, and $\bar{R}_3 = 14.42$ from Example C.

Because $|\bar{R}_1 - \bar{R}_2|$ is greater than 6.414 and $|\bar{R}_1 - \bar{R}_3|$ is greater than 6.141, then M_1 and M_2 are not equal and M_1 and M_3 are not equal. The end result is that PC-2 and PC-3 have a higher median usage rate than PC-1 and should receive the service contract, all other things being equal, such as cost and service availability. The multiple comparison revealed no difference in median usage rates for PC-2 and PC-3.

Efficiencies

The ARE of the Kruskal-Wallis test relative to the F test in one-factor analysis of variance is never less than .864 if the distribution functions have the identical shape but differ only in location. If the populations are normal the ARE is .955, which implies that little is lost in efficiency for small sample situations where normality is questionable or possible (Daniels, 1978).

Table 7-4			
Comparison	$\lvert \bar{R}_i - \bar{R}_j \rvert$	$Z_{\alpha/2c} \left[\dfrac{n(n+1)}{12} \right]^{1/2} \times \left[\dfrac{1}{n_i} + \dfrac{1}{n_j} \right]^{1/2}$		
PC-1 vs PC-3	(3.4 − 10.5)=7.1*	$2.13[16(17)/12]^{1/2}$	× $[1/5+1/5]^{1/2}=6.414$
PC-1 vs PC-2	(3.4 − 14.42)=11.02*	$2.13[16(17)/12]^{1/2}$	× $[1/5+1/6]^{1/2}=6.141$
PC-2 vs PC 3	(10.5 − 14.42)=3.92	$2.13[16(17)/12]^{1/2}$	× $[1/5+1/6]^{1/2}=6.141$

*These pairs are significant at an overall error rate of .10.

Finally, in randomized trials, in controlled clinical trials, and in therapeutical studies, where k populations may be under study for equal lengths of time and when the observations may be subject to arbitrary one-sided censorship, which can occur in clinical disciplines (possibly due to the subjects dying or moving away or the allocated time and budget elapsing prior to conclusion of the experiment or treatment), Schemper (1983) has developed a generalized Kruskal-Wallis test. Other modifications of the Kruskal-Wallis test that use either normal scores or expected normal scores greatly enhance the ARE to 1 or greater (Conover, 1980).

Independence of Bivariate Observations

Frequently, a researcher is interested in examining the existence of a possible association between two or three, at least ordinal variables. Anyone with previous exposure to statistics should recall the Pearson correlation coefficient ρ, a parametric measure of independence for two continuous variables. Unfortunately, most exposures to ρ minimize the importance of the following assumptions: a) X and Y are both random variables; b) X and Y are each normally distributed; c) the joint distribution of X and Y is a bivariate normal; and d) a linear association between X and Y is presumed. These tight distributional assumptions make the Pearson correlation coefficient suspect as an appropriate measure of independence when the samples are small and distribution characteristics are unknown. Many statistical practitioners like to assume that if X and Y are individually distributed as a normal, then bivariate normality holds; but only the converse is true (Johnson and Wichern, 1982). Checking for bivariate normality is of moderate mathematical difficulty and time consuming. The best alternative is to use a nonparametric measure that is free of distributional assumptions, which will provide a point estimate of the strength of the association or dependence, and which also will allow construction of an interval estimate.

In 1983, Kendall suggested a measure of correlation that is distribution-free and that is based on the degree of disarray between pairs of observations. Given pairs of variables (X_i, Y_i) and an increasing order of these pairs on X, the degree to which the corresponding Ys depart from this increasing order describes the weakness of the relationship between X and Y. The number of interchanges among the Ys to place them in the same increasing order of the Xs is the degree of disarray, i.e., "...the number of pairs among the n observations that are in inverse order" (Stuart, 1982, p.367). The minimum number of inversions, I, is zero; and the maximum number is $n(n-1) \div 2$, the number of distinct n pairs. The three examples subsequently provided show four pairs in increasing order on X with inversions of zero, six, and four, respectively.

I=0		I=6		I=4	
X	Y	X	Y	X	Y
1	2	1	5	1	3
2	3	2	4	2	5
3	4	3	3	3	4
4	5	4	2	4	2

If the inversions are at the minimum of zero, the positive agreement is reflected by a (+1). If the inversions are at the maximum, $n(n-1) \div 2$, the negative perfect agreement is measured by a (−1). Thus, Kendall's τ can be estimated as follows:

$$\hat{\tau} = 1 - \frac{2I}{n(n-1)/2} = 1 - \frac{4I}{n(n-1)} \qquad (10)$$

For the three examples above $\tau = 1$, −1, and −.33, respectively.

Stuart (1982) notes that if each inversion was weighted by the distance apart from the ranks in each pair, which for $I = 4$ above for the pairs (1,3), (2,5), (3,4), and (4,2) would give weights of 2, 3, 1, and 2, respectively, the resulting measure would be a weighted τ, exactly equivalent to the Spearman rank correlation. While it could be argued that the choice between Kendall's τ and Spearman's rank correlation is a matter of taste, the interval estimation procedures, the partial correlation possibilities, the lead-ins to non-parametric regression, and the distribution of τ approaching normal more quickly make Kendall's τ a preferable nonparametric measure of independence.

Assumptions
1. The data consist of a random sample of n individual pairs (X_i, Y_i) of observations, each of which comes from the same continuous population.
2. The level of measurement is at least ordinal.

Hypotheses

H_o: $\tau = 0$ (X and Y are independent)
H_a: $\tau \neq 0$ (X and Y are dependent or related)
H_o: $\tau \leq 0$
H_a: $\tau > 0$ (X and Y are positively related)
H_o: $\tau \geq 0$
H_a: $\tau < 0$ (X and Y are negatively related)

Procedure
1. Order the pairs by X in ascending order.
2. Count the number of inversions, I, for Y.
3. Compute $\hat{\tau}$ by equation 10.
4. Use either a table for Kendall's τ from Gibbons (1985) or Daniel (1978), which are valid for $n = 30$ and when there are no ties. For tied pairs or triplets and $n = 10$, exact tables do exist. However, because the distribution of τ has a mean of zero and a variance of

$$\sigma_{\hat{\tau}}^2 = \frac{2(2n+5)}{9n(n-1)} \qquad (11)$$

and tends to normality very quickly for $n = 10$, only the large sample approach shall be illustrated hereafter.

Example D

Suppose that a random sample of former adult patients treated for depression was taken to see if there was a positive relationship between their physical fitness level and a self concept test score. Given that $\alpha = .01$ and $n = 10$, and that the pairs are already ordered on the physical fitness score, test the appropriate hypothesis.

Adult	1	2	3	4	5	6	7	8	9	10
Fitness score	50	54	59	62	65	67	71	74	83	95
Concept Score	45	57	68	52	78	73	85	82	80	90
Inversions	0	0	0	2	0	1	0	1	2	0

Because the total number of inversions is six ($I = 2+1+1+2$), then $\hat\tau = .733$ by equation (10). Using the appropriate table from Gibbons (1985), the p-value would be .001. However, the large sample approach using equation (12),

$$Z = \frac{\hat\tau - 0}{\sigma_\tau} = \frac{\hat\tau - 0}{\left[\dfrac{2(2n+5)}{9n(n-1)}\right]^{1/2}} \tag{12}$$

yields a Z-value of

$$Z = \frac{.733 - 0}{\left[\dfrac{2(2 \cdot 10 + 5)}{9 \cdot 10(10 - 1)}\right]^{1/2}} = 2.95$$

The probability of $Z > 2.95$ from a standard normal table (Appendix C.2) is .0016, extremely close to the exact p-value. Thus, there is a positive relationship between physical fitness level and self-concept at $\alpha = .01$.

Efficiencies

The ARE of this Kendall procedure for testing for independence versus the t- test for Pearson's correlation coefficient under conditions of normality is .912. For a uniform or double exponential distribution, the AREs rise to 1.0 and 1.27, respectively (Hollander and Wolfe, 1973).

Confidence Intervals

The distribution-free, two-sided confidence interval for τ for a confidence coefficient of $1-\alpha$ is approximately (of course, $Z = Z_{\alpha/2}$),

$$\hat\tau \pm Z \left[\frac{2}{n(n-1)}\right] \hat\sigma \tag{13}$$

where

$$\hat\sigma = 4 \sum_{i=1}^{n} a_i^2 - 2 \sum_{i=1}^{n} a_i - \frac{2(2n-3)}{n(n-1)} \left[\sum_{i=1}^{n} a_i\right]^2 \tag{14}$$

and a_i equals the number of pairs that are in agreement in ordering (i.e., no inversions) with the pair (X_i, Y_i) and so on for $i = 1$ to n. Methodologically, $a_i = n - 1 - I_i$, or the sample size less one minus the number of inversions for that pair. Hollander and Wolfe (1973) and Daniel (1978) have good discussions of the how-tos of the a_i. Of course, all the approaches assume no ties.

The corresponding pairs and the number of pairs in agreement are shown below for Example E.

Pair	1	2	3	4	5	6	7	8	9	10
X_i	50	54	59	62	65	67	71	74	83	95
Y_i	45	57	68	52	78	73	85	82	80	90
a_i	9	9	9	7	9	8	9	8	7	9

The 95% confidence interval would yield the results below using equations (13) and (14):

$$.733 \pm 1.96 \left[\frac{2}{10(10-1)} \right] \cdot \left[4(712) - 2(84) - \frac{2(2 \cdot 10 - 3)(84)^2}{10(10-1)} \right]^{1/2} \quad \textbf{15)}$$

$$.733 \pm 1.96 \left[\frac{2}{90} \right] (14.4)^{1/2} = .733 \pm .165 \quad \textbf{(16)}$$

$$.568 < \tau < .898 \quad \textbf{(17)}$$

We would be 95% confident that τ is between .568 and .898, meaning that τ is not only different from zero, but also other values less than .568 and values greater than .898.

Nonparametric Regression

In many disciplines, regression analysis is one of the most widely used statistical methodologies. However, in parametric simple linear regression where β_o and β_1 are the unknown parameter values for the intercept and slope,

$$Y_i = \beta_o + \beta_1 X_i + \epsilon_i \qquad i = 1 \text{ to N} \quad \textbf{(18)}$$

there are several assumptions made about the random error terms, ϵ_i. It is assumed that these error terms are: a) normally distributed with a mean of zero and a variance of σ^2; b) have a constant variance; c) are not correlated with one another; and d) by implication produce normally distributed Ys because the value of the independent variable is a known constant (Montgomery and Peck, 1982). In addition, it also is assumed that the relationship between Y and X is linear or can be approximated by straight line. Outliers, small samples, and non-normality of the residuals (the error terms for the sample regression line) can easily invalidate the parametric approach. Depending on the purpose of the regression analysis, whether it be for description, inference, prediction, or any combination of the three, nonparametric regression is an excellent alternative for small sample sizes where outliers are present.

Assumptions

1. The basic model is $Y_i = \beta_o + \beta_1 X_i + \epsilon_i$, where β_o and β_1 are unknown parameters.
2. The ϵ_i are independent of one another.
3. The ϵ_i come from the same continuous population.
4. A random sample of n independent pairs is taken.
5. The regression of Y on X is linear.
6. The X_i are all distinct, i.e., no ties.

Slope and Intercept Estimation

Using Thiel's method (1950), which is discussed by Conover (1982), Daniel (1978), and Hollander and Wolfe (1973), the estimation process takes only three steps. First, compute all pair-wise slopes of which there are $n(n-1) \div 2$ possibilities and call these b_{ij},

$$b_{ij} = (Y_j - Y_i)/(X_j - X_i). \tag{19}$$

Secondly, the estimate of β_1 is the median of the b_{ij} or $b_1 = \text{median } [b_{ij}]$. The estimate of the intercept is the median of $Y_i - b_1 X_i$ or $b_o = \text{median } [Y_i - b_1 X_i]$. There are other ways to estimate these 2 parameters, but Thiel's procedure seems to be the simplest (Hussain and Sprent, 1983).

Example E

Suppose that a researcher wants to investigate the relationship between manual dexterity for the dominant hand versus the number of months of experience at a particular task. A random sample of seven adults who had been working X months at this task was given the Purdue Pegboard test for dexterity, Y. Describe the relationship between Y and X.

Months (X)	1.8	.2	2.0	1.0	.5	2.8	2.2
Dexterity Score (Y)	44	42	72	41	38	49	50

The scatter plot of the data in Figure 7-5 reveals a fairly linear relationship between Y and X, except for observation (2.0,72). If parametric simple linear regression had been performed on the data, the resulting model would have been as follows:

$$\hat{Y} = 38.440 + 6.374X \tag{20}$$

That is, for every additional month of experience, manual dexterity for the dominant hand goes up 6.374 points for this task. The t-test for the slope yielded $t = 1.41$, which had a p- value of $.20 < p < .50$.

Table 7-5 below shows the calculation of all pair-wise slopes. If all these slopes were sorted into ascending order, the median slope would be found in position 11, or $b_1 = 4.62$ (or 4.6154 to four significant digits). Using this

Table 7.5
Slope Calculations

X	X	1.8	.2	2.0	1.0	.5	2.8	2.2
	Y	44	42	72	41	38	49	50
1.8	44	—	1.25	140	3.75	4.62	5.0	15
.2	42		—	16.67	−1.25	−13.33	2.69	4.0
2.0	72			—	31	22.67	−28.75	−110
1.0	41				—	6.0	4.44	7.5
.5	38					—	4.78	7.06
2.8	49						—	−1.67
2.2	50							—

median slope b_1 to calculate the seven possible intercepts, $b_o =$ median $[Y_i - b_1 X_i]$, we get: 35.69, 41.08, 62.77, 36.38, 35.69, 36.08, and 39.85. Sorting these possible intercepts, the median intercept (position four) is 36.38. Thus, the nonparametric regression line is as follows:

$$\hat{Y} = 36.38 + 4.62X \tag{21}$$

Equation (21) above has a smaller intercept and slope than the parametric version in equation (20). The different lines are indicated on the scatter plot (Figure 7-5).

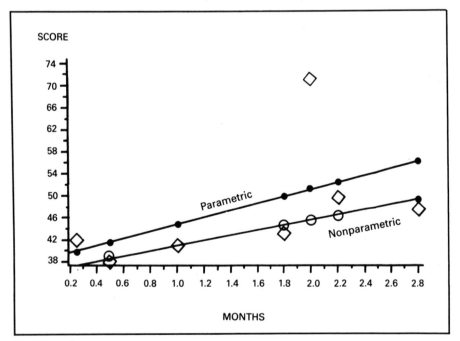

Figure 7-5. Scatter plot.

Testing the Slope

The test of the slope of the line for statistical significance (Thiel, 1950) is based on Kendall's τ using $(X_i, Y_i - \beta^*X_i)$ where β^* is the hypothesized value for the slope. The hypotheses could be two-sided where $H_o:\beta_1 = \beta^*$ and $H_a:\beta_1 = \beta^*$, or one-sided where the alternate could be either $H_a:\beta_1 \neq \beta^*$ or $H_a:\beta_1 > \beta^*$, whichever is appropriate.

The procedure for testing the slope is simplistic and five-fold: a) compute $Y_i - \beta^*X_i$ for each pair; b) order the pairs $(X_i, Y_i - \beta^*X_i)$ in increasing order by X_i; c) find the number of inversions, I; d) compute $\hat{\tau}$ according to equation (10): and e) lastly use the normal approximation approach of equation (12) to find the p-value if n is large enough, preferably 10 or more.

Testing the H_o: $\beta_1 = 0$ versus the H_a: $\beta_1 \neq 0$, computing the $Y_i - \beta^*X_i$ for each pair, and ordering the pairs by X_i, we get the following results:

X_i	.2	.5	1.0	1.8	2.0	2.2	2.8
$Y_i - \beta^*X_i$	42	38	41	44	72	50	49
I	0	1	1	0	0	1	2

The total number of inversions is five, and the estimate of τ is:

$$\hat{\tau} = 1 - \frac{4I}{n(n-1)} = 1 - \frac{4(5)}{7(6)} = .5238$$

Using the large sample approach of equation (12), we get

$$Z = \frac{.5238 - 0}{\left[\dfrac{2(2 \cdot 7 + 5)}{9 \cdot 7(7-1)}\right]^{1/2}} = 1.65$$

which has an approximate p-value of $2(.0495) = .099$ or an exact p-value of .1360 if the proper table had been used from Gibbons (1985). Thus the outlier, observation (2.0,72), has not only affected the coefficient size, but also its significance.

Confidence Interval for Slope

For the small sample approach on interval estimation, Hollander and Wolfe (1973) and Conover (1982) have clear discussions of procedures; but the focus in this section is on the large sample approach ($n \geq 10$). Once the $n(n-1) \div 2$ pair-wise slopes, b_{ij}, have been computed and placed in increasing order, then for a given α,

$$K = \left[\frac{n(n-1)}{2} - Z_{\alpha/2}\left[\frac{n(n-1)(2n+5)}{18}\right]^{1/2}\right] \div 2 \qquad \textbf{(22)}$$

is the position of the lower interval estimate and $(n(n-1) \div 2) - k + 1$ is the position of the upper interval estimate. Stated differently, the nonparametric interval estimate for β_1 is based on two order statistics.

Taking the b_{ij} from Table 7.5 for Example E and sorting them, we obtain the following sequence:

−110.00	−28.75	−13.33	−1.67	−1.25	1.25	2.69
3.75	4.00	4.44	4.62	4.78	5.00	6.00
7.06	7.50	15.00	16.67	22.67	31.00	140.00

To construct a 90% confidence interval with $Z = 1.645$, $n = 7$, then k in equation (22) equals 5 and $n(n-1) \div 2 - k + 1$ equals 17. The pair-wise slopes in positions 5 and 17 form the appropriate 90% interval estimate, $-1.25 < \beta_1 < 15.00$. This 90% confidence interval does contain zero so that at $\alpha = .10$, β_1 is not significantly different from zero.

Summary

There is much more that could be discussed regarding nonparametric methods, but this brief chapter has attempted to look at some of the best nonparametric procedures appropriate in clinical research for one-sample location, two-sample location, three or more sample location, association, and regression. In addition, there has been an emphasis on the less stringent assumptions of nonparametric methods along with the capability of constructing interval estimates or performing multiple comparisons as appropriate. There do exist nonparametric tests with ARE of 1 or greater that use normal scores or expected normal scores, but the reader is encouraged to study Conover (1982) for these tests. Nonparametric tests also exist for dispersion, trend, and goodness of fit, but these require more detailed explanation. All of the tests covered in this chapter can easily be done by hand or calculator.

Finally, it is hoped that Figures 7-1, 7-2, and 7-3 in conjunction with guidelines in Chapter 5 are helpful to the clinical researcher in choosing the appropriate statistical procedure or interval estimate and in understanding the importance of the assumptions prior to making the choice. When working with small data sets with unknown distribution forms, it is clear that there is "promise in nonparametrics" (Royeen and Seaver, 1986, p.191).

References

Benjamin, Y. (1983). Is the t test really conservative when the parent distribution is long-tailed? *Journal of the American Statistical Association, 78*, 930-936.

Conover, W. J. (1980). *Practical nonparametric statistics* (2nd ed.). New York: John Wiley and Sons.

Daniel, W. W. (1978). *Applied nonparametric statistics*. Boston: Houghton Mifflin Company.

Dunn, O. J. (1964). Multiple comparisons using rank scores. *Technometrics, 6*, 241-252.

Gibbons, J.D. (1982). Distribution-free methods. In S.Kotz and N.L. Johnson (Eds.). *Encyclopedia of statistical sciences*, vol. 2. New York: John Wiley and Sons, pp. 400-408.

Gibbons, J.D. (1985).*Nonparametric methods for quantitative analysis*(2nd ed.). Columbus, Ohio: American Sciences Press.

Govindarajulu, Z. (1976). A brief survey of nonparametric statistics. *Communications in Statistics-Theory and Methods*, A5(5), 429-453.

Hoaglin, D.C.,l Mostellar, F., and Tukey, J.W. (1983).*Understanding robust and exploratory data analysis*. New York: John Wiley and Sons.

Hodges, J.L., Jr., and Lehman, E.L. (1956). The efficiency of some nonparametric competitors of the t-test. *Annals of Mathematical Statistics*, 27,324-335.

Hollander, M. and Wolfe, D.A. (1973). *Nonparametric statistical methods.*New York: John Wiley and Sons.

Hussain, S.S. and Sprent, P. (1983). Nonparametric regression. *Journal of the Royal Statistical Society, Series A*,146, Part 2, 182-191.

Iman, R.L., Quade, D., and Alexander, D.A. (1975). Exact probability levels for the Kruskal-Wallis test. *Selected Tables in Mathematical Statistics*, 3, 329-384 (5.2, Appendix).

Johnson, R.A., and Wichern, D.W. (1982). *Applied multivariate statistical analysis.*Englewood Cliffs, New Jersey: Prentice- Hall.

Kendall, M.G. (1938). A new measure of rank correlation. *Biometrika*, 30, 81-93.

Kruskal, W.H. (1952). A nonparametric test for the several sample problem. *Annals of Mathematical Statistics* , 23, 525-540. Kruskal, W.H., and Wallis, W.A. (1953). Use of ranks in one-criterion variance analysis. *Journal of the American Statistical Association*, 47, 583-631. Addendum, 48(1953), 907-911.

Madsen, R.W. and Moeschberger, M.L. (1986). *Statistical concepts with applications to business and economics* (2nd ed.). Englewood Cliffs, New Jersey: Prentice Hall.

Mann, H.B. and Whitney, D.R. (1947). On a test of whether one of two random variables is stochastically larger than the other. *Annals of Mathematical Statistics*, 18, 50-60.

Mikulski, P. W. (1982). Efficiency, asymptotic relative (ARE) of estimation. In S. Kotz and N. L. Johnson (Eds.)., *Encyclopedia of statistical sciences*, vol. 2. New York: John Wiley and Sons, pp. 468-469.

Montgomery, D. C. and Peck, E. A. (1982). *Introduction to linear regression analysis*. New York: John Wiley and Sons.

Ott, L. (1984). *An introduction to statistical methods and data analysis* (2nd ed.). Boston: Duxbury Press.

Pocock, S. J. (1982). When not to rely on the Central Limit Theorem: An example from absenteeism data. *Communications in Statistics-Theory and Methods*, 11(19), 2169-2169.

Pratt, J. W. and Gibbons, J. D. (1981). *Concepts of nonparametric theory*. New York: Springer-Verlag.

Royeen, C. B. (1988). *Research Tradition in Occupational Therapy: Process, Philosophy and Status*, Thorofare, New Jersey: Slack Publishing Company.

Royeen, C. B. (1986). An exploration of parametric versus nonparametric statistics in occupational therapy clinical research. Doctoral dissertation, Virginia Polytechnic Institute and State University, Blacksburg, VA (University Microfilms International, Ann Arbor, MI: No. 8620659).

Royeen, C. B. and Seaver, W. L. (1986). Promise in nonparametrics. *The American Journal of Occupational Therapy*, 40(3),191-193.

Ryan, B. F., Joiner, B. L., and Ryan, T. A., Jr.(1985). *MINITAB: handbook* (2nd ed.). Boston: Duxbury Press.

Schemper, M. (1983). Generalized Kruskal-Wallis tests for comparing k samples subject to censoring. *Journal of South African Statistics*, 17, 1-11.

Seaver, W. L. (1977). The right test but the wrong occasion. *NABTE Review*, 4, 15-17.

Stuart, A. (1983). Kendall's tau. In S. Kotz and N. L. Johnson(Eds.)., *Encyclopedia of statistical sciences*. Vol 4. New York: John Wiley and Sons, pp. 367-368.

Thiel, H. (1950). A rank invariant method of linear and polynomial regression analysis I,II,III. *Proc. Kon. Nederl. Akad. Wetensch. A*, 53, 386-392, 521-525,1897-1912.

Wilcoxon, F. (1945). Individual comparisons by ranking methods. *Biometrics*, 1, 80-83.

CHAPTER 8

STATISTICAL SIGNIFICANCE TESTING: RATIONALE AND ALTERNATIVES IN CLINICAL RESEARCH

Kenneth J. Ottenbacher
Bette Bonder

Chapter Overview

This chapter describes the foundations of statistical significance testing and presents the traditional rationale for the use of significance testing in clinical research. Three adjuncts to statistical significance testing are described, and the argument is made that the application of supplemental procedures would improve the clinical relevance of research in occupational therapy as well as in other practice-based disciplines.

Researchers in occupational therapy, physical therapy, and other practice disciplines apply statistical significance testing as routine procedure to determine if a relationship or difference exists between variables of interest. Unfortunately, some of the quantitative procedures applied in clinical research have become what Mainland (1984) has labeled "statistical ritual." Several authorities have warned of the dangers involved in applying a statistical procedure, such as significance testing, while forgetting the statistical principles that allow an investigator to conclude that a particular result is beyond a chance event (Longnecker, 1982; Salsburg, 1985).

Foundations of Statistical Significance Testing

Conventional practices associated with statistical significance testing can be traced to the early work of Fisher (1925) and Neyman and Pearson (1933). The Fisherian approach specifies a null hypothesis with an effect size of zero and an "alternative" hypothesis where the effect size is not zero. Using the logic associated with this approach, a therapist might develop a null hypothesis that there is no statistically significant difference between two therapeutic interventions. The alternative hypothesis would state that there is a significant difference between the interventions.

Neyman and Pearson (1933) examined the problem of developing an optimal procedure for testing a null hypothesis against a family of alternatives. Their initial work examined the case of a single null against a single alternative. They showed that the probability of a Type I error increases as the probability of a Type II error decreases and vice versa. Neyman and Pearson (1933) recognized that we can never really know the alternative hypothesis; instead, we are forced to test the null against a family of alternatives. For example, if the null hypothesis is that the difference in mean change in range of motion between a treatment and control group is zero, we cannot propose as an alternative that the mean difference of range of motion is exactly 45°, but only that the mean difference for the family of alternative hypotheses is greater than zero.

The difference between the Fisherian approach and the Neyman-Pearson method is seen most clearly in the case of a directional alternative hypothesis. For the Fisherian school, only two-tailed tests are appropriate tests of the null hypothesis (no difference). One-tailed tests are possible only if it is assumed that the null hypothesis includes all effect sizes other than that specified by an alternative hypothesis. Neyman and Pearson (1933) attempted to identify effect sizes (family of alternative hypotheses) that were of interest and those that were not. Nonsignificant differences are considered trivial, rather than nonexistent in this framework.

Bakan (1966) has outlined the major differences in the two approaches. He notes that in the Fisherian inference model, the two alternatives from which the investigator selects on the basis of statistical significance tests, are "reject" and "inconclusive." As Fisher (1949) originally stated, "...the null hypothesis is never proved or established, but is possibly disproved in the course of experimentation" (p. 135). The choices available in the decision-theory approach (Neyman and Pearson, 1933) are "reject" and "support."

While the semantics may be confusing, the rhetoric that has evolved in the behavioral and social sciences is that a failure to reject a null hypothesis is not the same as support of it, or that support of the null hypothesis does not disprove the alternative, but merely fails to confirm it convincingly in that particular study. It is common to find the statement that the null hypothesis is never proven (Fisherian perspective) in the same text that explains that Type II errors are made when the null hypothesis is mistakenly supported or accepted. Regardless of the perspective, tests of statistical significance play a prominent role in the decision made relative to the null hypothesis.

The Significance of Significance

Tests of significance have evolved as the centerpiece of statistical inference in behavioral and social science research. Investigators often imply that there is some direct relationship between the statistical significance of a finding and its importance in the real world. Thus, it is common to find authors stating that a finding is "highly" significant or very significant, or reporting p-values to four or five decimal places, as if something of critical importance were contained in the several zeros preceding the final digit (Mainland, 1984). Most clinical investigators realize that statistical significance reveals nothing about real world importance. Nevertheless, the desire to have some basis for interpreting results seems so strong that inferential caution is dissolved in p-values.

Feinstein (1985a) recently commented on the negative effect an over-reliance on p-values can have on the interpretation of medical research literature. He notes that after the data are collected "...the investigator anxiously awaits the moment of crisis that occurs when the statistical calculations show whether the crucial value has emerged below or above the magic level, such as .05. A value of .04 is greeted with elated joy and .06 with bleak despair" (Feinstein, 1985a, p. 313).

The conceptualization of the .05 level of significance as a "probability cliff," with findings producing a level of ≤.05 considered statistically significant and findings associated with a level of >.05 not considered statistically significant places an unjustified importance on statistical evaluation that may interfere with accurate scientific inferences. For example, it can be demonstrated that a region of statistical uncertainty or indecision exists in null hypothesis testing where the results of significance tests are inadequate to either support or reject the null hypothesis. In the typical research investigation involving significance testing, the alternate distribution is established as a separate hypothesis. The alternative distribution may overlap with the null distribution. If alpha (α) is established as the area of the null distribution to the right of the unit deviate Z_α, then β is the area to the left of Z_α. Figure 8-1 is an

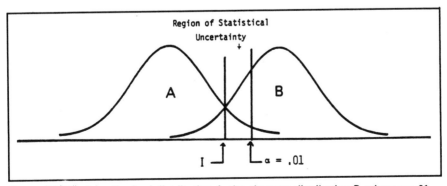

Figure 8-1. The hypothesized distribution A, the alternate distribution B, where $\alpha = .01$ and $\beta = .20$.

example of a hypothesis test in which A is the null distribution and B is the alternative distribution. The α for the null distribution (significance level) is set at .01. The alternate distribution is pictured as B. The β in distribution B is .20. The intersection of distribution A and B is labeled as I in Figure 8-1.

Figure 8-1 suggests that an investigator using the traditional decision rules associated with null hypothesis testing would conclude that all observations (test results) to the right of α would be members of the alternate (B) distribution, while all those to the left of α would be predicted to be members of the null (A) distribution. The region of uncertainty involves a sampling subspace between I and α where there are more B observations than A observations. The point here is that the conventional decision to support the null hypothesis that occurs when a calculated statistical value is obtained in the region of uncertainty is illogical from the standpoint of probability, because the investigator is betting that the observations that occur in the region of uncertainty are members of the null (A) distribution, when there are simply more observations from the alternative (B) distribution in this area. Using the information in Figure 8-1, a therapist investigating the effect of a particular treatment would identify results contained between a I and α as falling in the region of uncertainty (between $p = .01$ and $p = .20$). These results would be interpreted as an indication for additional investigation, rather than support for the null hypothesis.

It is generally acknowledged that clinical research results are unlikely to be considered statistically significant if the analysis fails to produce the traditionally accepted $p < .05$ for at least one outcome (Emerson and Colditz, 1983). Unfortunately, many readers equate statistical significance with practical or clinical significance and statistical nonsignificance with practical or clinical insignificance. This is a mistake. Lykken (1968) has correctly observed that "...statistical significance is perhaps the least important attribute of a good experiment. It is never a sufficient condition for claiming that a theory has been usefully corroborated, that a meaningful empirical fact has been established, or that an experimental report ought to be published" (p. 151).

The tendency of some clinical researchers to treat the .05 alpha level as a probability cliff, where a result associated with a p-value of .04 is treated as clinically important and a result with a p-value of .06 is judged as clinically nonsignificant, represents an unfortunate misinterpretation of significance testing. As a result of this common misinterpretation, research reports supporting the null hypothesis are treated qualitatively different from research reports failing to support the null hypothesis.

Statistical significance depends on several variables quite unrelated to the magnitude of any real world experimental effect. First, whether a finding is statistically significant depends on the alpha level that the investigator selects, which, by convention, is set at .05 or .01. The statistical significance of a finding is also a function of sample size, although the relationship of significance level to sample size is nonlinear, being in general a function of $\sqrt{N}$. Consequently, studies with large numbers of subjects tend to yield smaller p-values, all other variables being equal.

Statistical significance also depends on the power of the statistical evaluation and the precision with which the experiment is carried out. According to

Cohen (1977) "...the power of a statistical test of a null hypothesis is the probability that it will lead to the rejection of the null hypothesis, i.e., the probability that it will result in the conclusion that the phenomenon exists" (p. 4). Power is typically defined as $1 - beta$. Beta is the probability of making a Type II error. A Type II error occurs when a researcher (mistakenly) supports the null hypothesis when it should have been rejected.

When all other factors are kept constant, the larger the effect size, the smaller the p-value will be. The effect size refers to the degree to which the null hypothesis is false. Again, however, the relation between effect size and statistical significance is nonlinear, and it is unwarranted to draw inferences about the magnitude of an experimental effect from the statistical significance associated with it. For example, suppose a clinical researcher, White, reported a statistically significant result for treatment X using an appropriate design, only to have Black publish the results of a replication study indicating that no treatment effect existed. A closer look at both of their results might reveal the following:

White's study: $F = 4.88$ (df = 1,78, p<.05)

Black's study: $F = 1.12$ (df = 1,18, p<.30)

Further calculations reveal that the effect sizes (d – indexes) for the two studies are identical (i.e., $d = 2 \times \sqrt{F} \div \sqrt{df} = .50$). This finding suggests that the standardized mean difference (presumed treatment effect) is exactly the same in both studies, yet one reported a statistically significant result and the other a nonsignificant outcome. Further analysis reveals that the power of White's study is $>.70$, while the power of Black's study is $<.30$. In this example we know that the effect of the independent variable (treatment) is equal in both studies (i.e., $d = .50$), in spite of the difference in statistical outcomes. The discrepancy in this illustration is due to the difference in sample size. White employed a large sample ($N = 80$) that resulted in adequate power to test the hypothesis under consideration. Black, with a sample size of 20 and low power ($<.30$), did not report a statistically significant result despite the fact that the effect size (treatment effect) was the same in both studies. The low power in Black's study indicates the presence of a Type II error (supporting a false null hypothesis). Clearly, a strict reliance on statistical significance testing without consideration of other variables such as effect size, sample size, and power can lead to erroneous interpretation of research results.

The fact that statistical significance is a major determinant of publication practices is cause for considerable concern (Schulman, Kupst, and Suran, 1976). Research reports that produce statistically significant results (reject the null hypothesis) are much more likely to be published than are studies not reporting statistical significance. Atkinson, Furlong, and Wampold (1982) recently provided an example of the importance of statistical significance in publication practices. They asked 101 consulting editors from two well-known behavioral science journals to rate a research manuscript. All manuscripts were identical except that one-third reported statistically significant results, one-third reported results approaching statistical significance, and one-three reported statistically nonsignificant results. These investigators found that, all other things being equal, a research manuscript reporting a statistically significant result was three times more likely to be recommended for publication than was a manuscript reporting statistically nonsignificant findings. They concluded that "...the results of the present study confirm that outcomes found to approach traditionally accepted levels of statistical significance are essentially treated as statistically nonsignificant" (Atkinson, Furlong and Wampold, 1982, p. 192).

Supplements to Statistical Significance Testing

Given the limitations of significance testing, numerous supplements or alternatives have been advocated by various authorities. At one extreme, several authors have argued that researchers should abandon statistical significance testing and apply alternative methods of evaluation (Carver, 1978). The reality is, however, that significance testing is an established component of the research process and there are few indications that it will soon be abandoned by clinical investigators (Longnecker, 1982). Assuming that significance testing will remain an integral part of the way in which clinical researchers evaluate hypotheses, there are procedures that can be used as supplements to significance tests to help ensure the integrity of the statistical inferences that are made. Three of these supplements to significance testing are described below.

Confidence Intervals

Traditional evaluation of the null hypothesis relying on statistical significance testing uses an arbitrary point on a sliding scale of confidence. Gardner and Altman (1986) argue that the use of confidence intervals would produce a move away from a single-value estimate (i.e., p-value) to a range of values considered plausible for the population. The width of a confidence interval based on a sample statistic depends partly on its standard error; thus both the standard deviation and sample size are included in the computation.

The concept of confidence intervals is widely understood, if not widely employed, and many examples and illustrations exist in the clinical research literature (Berry, 1986). For example, confidence intervals for a difference between means are constructed using the t distribution assuming the data are approximately normally distributed with similar standard deviations. The procedure and formulae for computing a confidence interval for the difference between two means are given below.

$$S = \sqrt{\frac{(n_1 - 1) S_1 + (n_2 - 1) S_2}{n_1 + n_2 - 2}}$$

where S_1 and S_2 are standard deviations for the two groups under consideration and n_1 and n_2 the respective sample sizes. The above formula provides a "pooled" estimate of the standard deviation. This value, S, is then used to compute the standard error of the difference between the two sample means.

$$SE \text{ diff} = S \sqrt{\frac{1}{n_1} + \frac{1}{n_2}}$$

The confidence interval is then determined by:

$x_1 - x_2 - (t_{1-\alpha/2} \times \text{SE diff})$ to $x_1 - x_2 + (t_{1-\alpha/2} \times \text{SE diff})$ where x_1 and x_2 are the means for the two groups and $t_{1-\alpha/2}$ is taken from the t distribution with $(n_1 + n_2) - 2$ degrees of freedom.

An example may help clarify the concept of using confidence intervals to compare the difference between two means. Suppose two groups of subjects are being compared on the basis of their scores on an activity of daily living (ADL) task. The subjects are assigned to two groups with five individuals in the first group and seven in the second. The first group receives a program of ADL training administered by a therapist and the second group receives standard nursing care. The score on a standardized ADL evaluation is obtained at the end of four weeks of intervention. The question of interest is "Does the program of ADL training affect the performance of subjects on the ADL evaluation?" This question implies a null hypothesis and an alternate.

We will make the assumption that the population distribution scores are normal, and that the population variances are approximately equal. The significance level to reject the null hypothesis is set at .01. The test will be two-tailed and, therefore, the degrees of freedom will be $(n_1 + n_2) - 2$ or $(5+7) - 2 = 10$. The required t-value to reject the null hypothesis at the .01 level with 10 degrees of freedom is 3.17. Thus, a calculated t of 3.17 or greater is sufficient to reject the null hypothesis of no difference between the population means at the .01 level.

The data for the two groups are

$$
\begin{array}{ll}
n = 5 & n = 7 \\
\bar{x}_1 = 18 & \bar{x}_2 = 20 \\
S_1 = 6.00 & S_2 = 5.83
\end{array}
$$

Using the previous formulae we find that:

$$S = \sqrt{\frac{(5-1)\,6.00 + (7-1)\,5.83}{5 + 7 - 2}}$$

$$S = \sqrt{5.898}$$

$$S = 2.48$$

$$S_{\text{diff}} = 2.48\sqrt{\frac{1}{5} + \frac{1}{7}} =$$

$$S_{\text{diff}} = 1.45$$

Using the formula given above, the confidence intervals for the 99% limits are:

$$
\begin{array}{l}
18\text{-}20 - (3.17)\,(1.45) = -6.596 \\
18\text{-}20 + (3.17)\,(1.45) = +2.596
\end{array}
$$

Thus, the limits are -6.596 to $+2.596$. The probability is .99 or 99% that the true difference is covered by this interval.

Confidence intervals can be computed for a variety of sample statistics including the difference between means, proportions, and correlations (Berry, 1986; Feinstein, 1985b). Several clinical researchers have argued that confidence intervals "should become the standard method for presenting the statistical results of major findings" (Gardner and Altman, 1986, p. 748).

Region of Indecision

Ottenbacher (1984a) proposed a modification to the traditional approach of null hypothesis evaluation using statistical significance testing. This modification involves partitioning the continuum of confidence into three decision regions for any hypothesis that is to be statistically evaluated. The three regions are:

- *Region of Support*   where the test statistic can be considered to have supported the null hypothesis. This region is labeled as k.
- *Region of Rejection*   where the test statistic can be considered to have supported the rejection of the null hypothesis. This region is labeled K.
- *Region of Indecision*   where the test statistic is inadequate to either support or reject the null hypothesis. This region is labeled K'.

The region of indecision, which was conceptually introduced in a previous section of this chapter, always falls between the region of support (k) and the region of rejection (K). The region of indecision is defined by specifying, a prior, four parameters: a) sample size; b) effect size (determined from previous research, theory, or convention); c) the desired significance level (Type I error rate); and d) the desired power. Once the above parameters have been defined, all three regions (k, K, K') can be expressed in values of p. For example, given a conventional two group comparison with a total of 30 subjects (15 in each group), an expected effect size of .50, a significance level of .05, and a conventional power of $1-4\alpha$ or .80 and using Table 8-1, the region of support (k) would include all values of p>.16; the region of rejection (K) would include all values of p<.05; and the region of indecision (K') would include all values of p between p>.05 and p<.16.

Tables can be constructed containing values of K' for commonly used statistical tests. Following Cohen's (1977) recommendations of a 4:1 Type II to Type I error ratio, Table 8-1 was constructed specifying K' for varying sample sizes, varying effect sizes, and the traditional significance level p = .05 and Beta = .20 (Power = .80). Table 8-1 includes values of K' for a two group comparison (t-test). The region K' is found by specifying the expected effect size (top row) and the n per group. The tabled value is the largest value K' acceptable. For example, with an n of 45 and an effect size of .30, the tabled value of K' is .14. Thus, all values of p between .06 and .14 would be included in K' (the region of indecision) and would result in the decision to secure additional data. On the other hand, a calculated value resulting in a p>.14

Table 8.1
K' for t-test of $\bar{x}_1 = \bar{x}_2$ at K = .05 and power = .80 (one-tailed)

n	\multicolumn{10}{c}{Effect Size (d)}
	0.1	0.2	0.3	0.4	0.5	0.6	0.7	0.8	0.9	1.0
10	.76	.52	.40	.30	.22	.16	.10	.08	—	—
15	.68	.50	.36	.24	.16	.10	.06	—	—	—
20	.68	.48	.30	.20	.10	.06	—	—	—	—
25	.68	.44	.26	.14	.08	—	—	—	—	—
30	.66	.40	.24	.12	.06	—	—	—	—	—
35	.64	.38	.20	.10	—	—	—	—	—	—
40	.62	.36	.18	.08	—	—	—	—	—	—
45	.60	.32	.14	.06	—	—	—	—	—	—
50	.58	.30	.12	—	—	—	—	—	—	—
60	.56	.24	.10	—	—	—	—	—	—	—
70	.54	.24	.08	—	—	—	—	—	—	—
80	.50	.20	.06	—	—	—	—	—	—	—
90	.48	.18	—	—	—	—	—	—	—	—
100	.48	.16	—	—	—	—	—	—	—	—
125	.42	.12	—	—	—	—	—	—	—	—
150	.38	.08	—	—	—	—	—	—	—	—
175	.34	.06	—	—	—	—	—	—	—	—
200	.32	—	—	—	—	—	—	—	—	—

From: Ottenbacher, K. (1984) The significance of power and the power of significance: Recommendations for occupational therapy research. *Occupational Therapy Journal of Research*, 4, p. 46.

would fall in the region of support (k) and would indicate that the null hypothesis should be supported. The region of rejection (K) is interpreted in the traditional manner. It should be noted that the values for K' will vary for different alpha levels and levels of power. As stated previously, the entries in Table 8-1 were derived using the .05 significance level and a Beta of .20 as constants.

The region of indecision (K') was developed based on the premise that some findings that do not achieve statistical significance at the traditional level (.05 or .01) are worthy of continued investigation and should not be dismissed as clinically unimportant (Ottenbacher, 1982, 1984a). Often researchers note that their results "approach" statistical significance, or there is a "trend" in the anticipated direction, despite the failure to find statistical significance. Currently no formal criteria exist to evaluate such claims. If p = .06 is considered approaching significance, what about p = .09 or p = .11? What value of p should be considered convincing evidence in favor of the null hypothesis? The guidelines presented in Table 8-1 provide a more systematic method of interpretation for nonsignificant results. Assume for example that a therapist tests a control group of 20 subjects and an experimental group of 20 subjects on a vocational evaluation. A significance level of .05 is selected and power is established at .80. If the anticipated effect size is .40, then the region of rejection would be all values of p<.05, the region of indecision all values of p between p>.05 and p<.20, and the region of support, all values of p>.20

(See Table 8-1). This would suggest to the therapist that the interpretation of results between p>.05 and p<.20 is unclear and further investigation is warranted.

Effect Size Estimates

A third alternative or adjunct to statistical significance testing is the reporting of effect size estimates. Measures of effect size are increasingly being advocated as a supplement to/or replacement for traditional statistical significance testing (Ottenbacher, 1984b; Woolery, 1983).

Traditional statistical significance testing that compares an observed relation to the chance of no relation becomes less informative as evidence supporting a phenomenon accumulates. The question turns from "whether" to "how much" of an effect exists? Rothman (1978) has accurately observed that "...the p-value, which is the final common pathway for nearly all statistical tests, conveys no information about the extent to which two groups differ or two variables are associated" (p. 1362). Measures of effect size do convey this information. Cohen (1977) has presented formulae for computing effect size estimates from data provided by most commonly used statistical procedures, e.g., t-tests, F-tests, X^2, etc. For example, the effect size computed for the mean difference for two groups is the d-index. The d- index measures the difference between two means in terms of their common standard deviation units. If d = .20 then it means that $2 \div 10$ of a standard deviation separates the average subject in group one from the average subject in group two. The nondirectional standard version of the d-index can be computed directly from the means and standard deviation values or from the t-test results using the following formula:

$$d = \sqrt{\frac{2t}{df\ error}}$$

where t equals the value of a t-test, and df error is the degrees of freedom associated with the error term of the t-test. The d- index also can be computed for single degree of freedom F-tests. In such a case $\sqrt{F} = t$. An example of the d-index based on a two group comparison involving the F-test was provided earlier in this chapter.

Effect size estimates such as the d-index provide a standardized measure of treatment impact that directly conveys the degree or magnitude of effect produced by the independent variable. Cohen (1977) has presented several measures of "distribution overlap" to assist in the interpretation of effect size measures such as the d-index. These measures of distribution overlap make the assumption that the computed effect size for the mean difference between two groups or conditions is an estimate of the actual population mean difference. The most commonly reported measure of overlap for the d-index is called U_3. This measure tells what percentage of the population with the smaller mean is exceeded by 50% of the population with the larger mean. For example, the U_3 value for a d-index of .20 is 57.9. This value indicates that the average person in the group with the larger mean has a "score" greater than approximately 58% of the individuals in the lower meaned group. A table for converting the d-index to U_3 is presented by Cohen (1977, p. 22).

Several authorities in the behavioral and biomedical sciences have proposed that researchers report effect size measures to provide readers with an accurate indication of "how much" of a treatment effect is present (Carver, 1978; Feinstein, 1985b; Ottenbacher, 1986). The emphasis on reporting effect size measures has been particularly strong in clinical and applied fields, where the distinctions between effect sizes of practical or clinical significance and effect sizes of statistical significance are not easily made. For example, the Editor of the *Journal of Gerontology* stated that: "We are increasingly insistent that authors address the issue of effect magnitude, both in terms of the statistics reported and the discussion of the implications of the research. Any effect can be shown to be significant given sufficiently large sample sizes. The real question is whether or not the effect is important; measures of effect size help the researcher answer this question" (Storandt, 1983, p. 2).

Conclusions

The concern of many clinical researchers is not with the use of significance tests per se, but with a misinterpretation of the results. Specifically, there is the danger that p-values will be given more credibility and importance than they deserve. Bakan (1966) has observed that an overemphasis on the results of tests of significance "removes the burden of responsibility, the chance of being wrong, the necessity for making inductive inferences, from the shoulders of the investigator and places them on the tests of significance" (p. 430).

Feinstein (1985b) has accurately indicated that problems related to statistical significance testing can be dealt with in two ways: statistically or scientifically. No matter what statistical or technical supplement is adopted to reduce the potential misinterpretation of significance testing, a quantitative approach does not effectively address the larger issue of scientific inference. There is a continuing need in occupational therapy research for the concise formulation of hypotheses prior to the collection and analysis of data and to avoid the error of operationalizing scientific inference by equating it with statistical inference. Hypothesis testing is necessarily an empirical compromise between claiming too much and suggesting too little. Clinical researchers must prospectively define hypotheses as succinctly as possible, and interpret tests of significance in a manner consistent with their function as a quantitative tool.

References

Atkinson, D.F., Furlong, M.J., and Wampold, B.E. (1982). Statistical significance, reviewer evaluations, and the scientific process: Is there a (statistically) significant relationship. *Journal of Counseling Psychology, 29,* 189-194.

Bakan, D. (1966). The test of significance in psychological research. *Psychological Bulletin, 66,* 423-437.

Berry, G. (1986). Statistical significance and confidence intervals. *Medical Journal of Australia, 144,* 618-619.

Carver, R. (1978). The case against statistical significance testing. *Harvard*

Educational Review, 48, 378-399.

Cohen, J. (1977). *Statistical power analysis for the behavioral sciences.* (Rev. Ed.). New York: Academic Press.

Emerson, J.P., and Colditz, G.A. (1983). Use of statistical analysis in the *New England Journal of Medicine. New England Journal of Medicine.* 309, 709-714.

Feinstein, A.R. (1985a). Tempest in a p-pot. *Hypertension*, 7, 313-318.

Feinstein, A.R. (1985b). *Clinical epidemiology: The architecture of clinical research.* Philadelphia, Pennsylvania: W.B. Saunders.

Fisher, R.A. (1925). *Statistical methods for research workers.* Edinburgh, Scotland: Oliver and Boyd.

Fisher, R.A. (1949). *The design of experiments.* New York: Hafner.

Gardner, M.J., and Altman, D.G. (1986). Confidence intervals rather than p-values: Estimation rather than hypothesis testing. *British Medical Journal*, 292, 740-750.

Longnecker, D.E. (1982). Support versus illumination: Trends in Medical statistics. *Anesthesia*, 57, 73-74.

Lykken, D. (1968). Statistical significance in psychological research. *Psychological Bulletin,* 70, 151-159.

Mainland, D. (1984). Statistical ritual in clinical journals: Is there a cure? *British Medical Journal*, 288, 920-922.

Neyman, J., and Pearson, K.S. (1933). The testing of statistical hypothesis in relation to probabilities "a priori". *Proceedings of the Cambridge Philosophy Society*, 24, 492- 510.

Ottenbacher, K. (1986). Experiment-wise error rates in behavioral science research. *Journal of Applied Behavioral Science*, 22, 495-501.

Ottenbacher, K. (1984a). The significance of power and the power of significance. Recommendations for occupational therapy research. *Occupational Therapy Journal of Research*, 4, 38- 50.

Ottenbacher, K. (1984b). Measures of relationship strength in occupational therapy research. *Occupational Therapy Journal of Research*, 4, 271-285.

Ottenbacher, K. (1982). Statistical power and research in occupational therapy. *Occupational Therapy Journal of Research*, 2, 13-26.

Rothman, K. (1978). A show of confidence. *New England Journal of Medicine*, 299, 1362-1363.

Salsburg, D.S. (1985). The religion of statistics as practiced in medical journals. *American Statistician*, 39, 220-223.

Schulman, J.L., Kupst, M.I., and Suran, G.B. (1976). The worship of "p": Significant yet meaningless research results. *Bulletin of the Meninger Clinic*, 40, 134-143.

Storandt, M. (1983). Editorial: Significance does not equal importance. *Journal of Gerontology*, 38, 2.

Woolery, T.W. (1983). A comprehensive power-analytic investigation of research in medical education. *Journal of Medical Education*, 58, 710-715.

CHAPTER 9

DESIGN AND ANALYSIS OF REPEATED MEASURES DATA IN CLINICAL RESEARCH

Gabriella M. Belli

CHAPTER OVERVIEW

Repeated measures data can result from any study that involves measuring the same subjects repeatedly on some variable of interest. For example, this would be the case in a longitudinal study where the interest is either in determining optimal duration for clinical intervention or in assessing long-range effects of an intervention. Or, such data also may be a result of repeatedly measuring the same subjects under various treatment conditions. This chapter provides some general information about experimental studies and then details various types of repeated measures designs. The advantages and disadvantages of using different analysis techniques for repeated measures data are presented, concluding with a detailed description of a multivariate approach to analysis.

Introduction

In her Presidential Address, given April 22, 1986 at the 66th Annual Conference of the American Occupational Therapy Association, Elnora Gilfoyle stated: "We need research activity to permit notable scientific advancement and development of a system of theories . . ." (p. 594). She advocated an increase in funding for research activities and an effort to promote the profession of occupational therapy " . . . through the integration of research and practice" (p. 594). However, this goal is applicable to any clinically based service profession.

Before this worthwhile goal can be accomplished, one must first consider what kind of research should be promoted within different fields of clinical research. Considered in isolation, no single mode of research should be recommended over another. The main initial issue for any research development should always be the purpose of the research (i.e., what is to be determined, accomplished, or proved by this study). The purpose would then dictate an appropriate research method, as well as the variables that need to be considered. These, in turn, suggest appropriate strategies for design and analysis. The purpose of a study and its salient variables are concerns that the individual researcher or funding organization must determine. The purpose of this chapter is not to provide guidelines for this critical initial step, but to outline a design and analysis that often is the resulting second step in clinical research.

A variety of clinical research situations occur where it is useful to measure the same subjects repeatedly on the same dependent variable. Two general classes of such situations are: a) when subjects are measured over time; and b) when subjects are measured on the same variable under several different treatment conditions or levels of an independent factor. The first case is generally applicable due to the longitudinal nature of many clinical interventions, where changes over time are expected. While these changes may be examined using classical before-and-after treatment measurements, a more informative approach is to study changes over a complete time period that may span the course of a clinical intervention or may attempt to track carryover effects after termination of the intervention. An example of the second case, where repeated measurements are made under different conditions, may be a situation where specific motor functions for handicapped subjects are measured using first the right hand, then the left hand, and finally both hands. Here the same subjects are measured on some motor skill (the dependent variable) under three conditions.

Experimental designs where subjects are observed on two or more occasions are described by various terms; among these are: treatment by subjects (Lindquist, 1953), two-way mixed-model (Scheffé, 1959), Lindquist Type I and Type III designs (Huck, Cormier, and Bounds, 1974), design on the occasions (Bock, 1985), within-subject design (Keppel, 1982), randomized block and split plot factorial (Kirk, 1982). However, a common way to describe them is to refer to the repeated nature of the designs by calling them repeated measures designs. This will be the term used hereafter.

This chapter begins by providing some general background information for experimental research in general, leading up to repeated measures designs. Explicit examples of various simple repeated measures designs using occupational therapy examples are given, followed by an outline of the advantages, disadvantages, and major methods of analyzing repeated measures data. A detailed summary of one of these methods of analysis using a multivariate approach is presented and developed using examples of more complex repeated measures designs in clinical research. The final sections discuss the robustness of multivariate techniques and the use of computer statistical software to analyze such data.

Background For Experimental Research

Researchers may use a wide variety of experimental designs that allow them to assess the relative effects that different factors (the independent variables) have on observations (the dependent variables). These designs may involve one or more qualitative factors, where each factor consists of two or more levels (e.g., different treatments or groups that are being compared), and one or more quantitative dependent variables. For example, if five different intervention strategies for improving muscle response in post-cerebrovascular accident adults with hemiplegia are compared, the independent factor is therapy with five treatment levels. The dependent variable would be some numerical measure of muscle response. The term "treatment" is used here to describe a level of the experimental factor, not to describe any therapeutic treatment. To avoid confusion, the term treatment will be used only in this way. When referring to a therapeutic treatment, the terms "intervention" or "therapy" will be used.

Univariate Designs

In classical experimental research, the effect of manipulating one or more independent variables or factors on a single dependent variable is investigated. This involves testing the univariate null hypothesis about equal group means across levels of a given factor. The F-test is typically used in analysis of variance (ANOVA) in such cases. For further information on ANOVA, see Keppel (1982) or Kirk (1982).

For a one-factor study, the analysis may involve comparing groups of handicapped infants in neonatal intensive care who have been randomly assigned to one of three treatment conditions: infant bean bag, infant cuddle clinic, or infant prone board. A dependent variable used to assess differences across the three levels of the independent factor, or treatments, could be a measure of duration of crying. The null hypothesis is that there are no differences among the three treatment conditions in the duration of crying.

A second independent factor may be added to the design; for example, type of birth, with two levels: vaginal or caesarian. Now, in addition to the previous null hypothesis, two more nulls may be tested. One is for the second factor: there is no difference between babies born vaginally or by caesarian in the duration of crying. The other null states that there is no interaction between treatment conditions and type of birth. Notice a distinction between the two factors. Treatment condition is an active experimental variable, because subjects are randomly assigned to the different treatment levels. Type of birth, however, is a classification variable, where the experimenter has no control over placement of subjects. Both types of variables may be analyzed with ANOVA.

Multivariate Designs

There are two types of cases where more than one measure is taken on the same set of subjects. The first is where, under a given factorial design, subjects are measured on two or more different dependent variables. For example, in a one-factor study of different therapies to facilitate recovery after a disabling accident, two dependent measures might be: 1) the ability to dress independently, and 2) the speed at which one can dress independently.

Because multiple measures are taken on the same subjects, it is expected that the measures are interrelated within subjects. To illustrate, it is clear that competency in dressing and speed of dressing are, in some way, related. In such a situation, it is inappropriate to perform several ANOVAs, because this would inflate the overall probability level of the analyses and potentially lead to wrong conclusions. An analysis that takes into account the intercorrelations when several dependent measures are present is a multivariate analysis of variance (MANOVA) (for more detailed information see: Timm, 1975, Chapter 5; Lunneborg and Abbott, 1983, Chapters 11 and 12; and Bock, 1985, Chapter 5). In the given example, one would be examining competency of dressing and speed of dressing together to determine whether various therapy treatments (levels of the independent factor) were differentially effective on the pair of activities as a set. The null hypothesis would be that there are no differences among the therapies on both ability to dress and speed of dressing. As with ANOVA, other independent factors may be added to the design, with comparable additional hypotheses for the other factor(s) and their interactions.

Because the F-test is a univariate test statistic, it cannot be used to test hypotheses in multivariate situations. However, several multivariate generalizations of this test are available. Hotelling's T^2 statistic is used for one-sample tests of means and two-sample tests of mean differences (Anderson, 1958). In the former case, a researcher may be interested in testing the hypothesis that a single group of accident victims, after undergoing a particular form of therapy, have achieved some specified mean level on both ability to dress independently and speed of dressing. In the latter case, a Hotelling's T^2 test might be used to compare two groups of subjects who underwent two different therapies.

Four other common multivariate test statistics, used when there are more than two measures or more than two groups, are Roy's largest root, Hotelling-Lawley Trace, Pillai-Bartlett trace, and Wilks' likelihood ratio. Many statistical analysis packages provide one or more of these test statistics with their corresponding probability levels, or p-values. For most multivariate test statistics, formulae have been created to transform them to equivalent F-test values with corresponding probability levels. In some statistical packages, these F-test results are provided either instead of the multivariate values or with them.

Repeated Measures Designs

The second type of multiple measure situation is when the same dependent measure is repeatedly taken over the same subjects, previously stated as a repeated measures case. In the two distinct instances of repeated measures situations, the single dependent measure is taken as specified by a design on the measures, or occasions of testing. In the first case, this design may reflect the passage of time, with the same measures taken at equally spaced intervals;

for example, the same subjects may be tested on amount of recovery at weekly intervals for the duration of a clinical intervention to track progress or to determine optimal treatment time.

In the second case of a repeated measures situation, the design on the measures may represent a factorial structure, with the same measure taken after the same subjects are exposed to various treatment conditions. This may be used only when there is no possibility of carryover effects from one treatment level to another, and where it makes sense to use the same measure in each situation. For example, a therapist might test for muscle responses (the dependent measure) of the same group of post-cerebrovascular accident adults with hemiplegia under two methods of eliciting a reflex (either plain or reinforced head rotation) and under two methods of position (either supine or seated) (Warren, 1984). The dependent measure is therefore taken four times under a 2×2 design on the occasions of testing. In both cases, hypotheses are now stated in terms of the repeated factors.

To further clarify the distinction between a repeated measures situation and a typical multivariate situation, in the former case the multiple dependent scores are assumed to be in the same metric (i.e., having the same origin and unit), while in the latter or general multivariate case, the scores are on different metrics (i.e., having different origin and unit).

The design on the repeated measures may be the only factor in the study, thereby using a single group of subjects that are exposed to all levels of this repeated, or within-subjects factor. Additionally, there may be one or more between-subjects factors, creating multiple groups. In this case, the multiple groups may be formed as a result of some classification factor, or because they are placed in different treatment levels of some experimental factor. In both instances, each of the separate groups are measured repeatedly. With combinations of both between-subjects and within-subjects factors, hypotheses may be tested about differences among the groups, among the occasions, and about group-by-occasion interactions.

Assuming that some number of measures (say, p) are taken on subjects in some number of groups (say, k), the three overall null hypotheses may be stated as testing for: a) group effects of no differences among the k group mean vectors, where each vector consists of the group means for the p occasions; b) occasion effects of no differences among the p occasion mean vectors, where each vector consists of the occasion means for the k groups; and c) an interaction effect, which tests for no group-by-occasion interactions.

An example of a repeated measures design that incorporates both a design on the subjects and a design on the occasions in occupational therapy could be based on the previous example of dressing. Suppose a hospital wanted to know about recovery rates over time of dressing skills in adults who experienced spinal cord injuries. Assuming all other variables to be equal, the groups could consist of spinal cord-injured adults with three forms of injury: paraplegia, quadraplegia, and hemiplegia. In this case, assuming the same measure of dressing skills was taken at three one-month intervals, the null hypotheses may be stated as testing for: a) no difference in recovery of dressing skills among the paraplegic, quadriplegic, and hemiplegic groups;

Subjects (i)	Occasions (j)					
	1	2	.	.	.	p
1	Y1 (1)	Y1 (2)	.	.	.	Y1 (p)
2	Y2 (1)	Y2 (2)	.	.	.	Y2 (p)
.		.		.		.
.		.		.		.
.		.		.		.
N	YN (1)	YN (2)	.	.	.	YN (p)

Figure 9-1. Basic layout of an RM design with N subjects measured on p occasions, and where Yi(j) is the observation obtained from the ith subject on the jth occasion.

b) no differences in recovery of dressing skills over time; and c) no interaction between time and type of disability with respect to recovery of dressing skills. The group effects tests are usual MANOVA between-group tests (quadriplegic versus hemiplegic versus paraplegic), while the occasion tests are called within-group tests (time 1 versus time 2 versus time 3).

Single Sample, One-factor, Repeated Measures Designs

Although a repeated measures design may constitute designs on both subjects and occasions of testing, the simplest form of a repeated measures design is one that constitutes only a single group of subjects that are repeatedly measured under different levels of one factor. Because of its simplicity, this design will be detailed in this section, followed by a discussion of the advantages and disadvantages of repeated measures designs, the methods of analysis, and the necessary assumptions. Extensions will then be made to factorial designs on the occasions of testing, as well as on grouping structures for the subjects.

Design and Data Matrix

The basic layout of a repeated measures design is shown in Figure 9-1. The experimental units are called subjects, which are now considered to constitute a single group. The repeated measures are called occasions. These now involve a single factor with several levels indicating either different treatment conditions that constitute levels of that factor or measurements taken across time. An example will be given for each of these situations that will be referred to and expanded in subsequent sections.

Example 9-1. This example is of one group of 15 quadriplegic subjects who are used in an experiment to evaluate various wheelchair technologies with respect to their ease of mobility. Suppose the interest is in comparing three different types of activation devices: joystick, voice-activated, or light beam-activated. A numerical score based on some measure of ease of mobility of the wheelchair would be the dependent measure. The specific design is given in Figure 9-2.

Subjects	Wheelchair Activation Devices		
	Joystick (J)	Voice (V)	Light Beam (L)
1			
2			
.			
.			
.			
15			

Figure 9-2. One group of quadraplegic subjects repeatedly measured on ease of mobility under three levels of one factor representing three types of wheelchair activation devices.

Subjects	Measures over Time		
	Time 1 (T1)	Time 2 (T2)	Time 3 (T3)
1			
2			
.			
.			
.			
20			

Figure 9-3. One group of disabled subjects measured over three equally spaced time points on their ability to dress independently.

Example 9-2. For this example, assume that 20 subjects who suffered a disabling accident undergo a specific clinical intervention intended to facilitate their ability to care for themselves. The dependent variable selected to measure that ability is a numerical score that quantifies their ability to dress themselves. Measures are taken at the onset of treatment and at two more times at two-month intervals during the treatment. The specific design is given in Figure 9-3.

Advantages of Repeated Measures Designs

For any study designed to examine such phenomena as learning, practice effects, or retention rates over time, a repeated measures design is the most appropriate means of doing so. In such studies, interest is in describing the nature of the trend over time of some dependent variable that is being observed.

Even when the independent factor is not time, however, repeated measures designs have several advantages over completely randomized designs, where subjects are randomly assigned to different treatment groups. The main advantage is that the use of repeated measures allows for the control of subject heterogeneity, i.e., individual differences, by using subjects as their own controls (Keppel, 1982). This is particularly useful whenever between-subject variability may be large relative to treatment effects.

Consider a single factor design such as the experiment to examine different wheelchair technologies. This could be conducted as a typical three-group design, where quadraplegics are randomly assigned to one of the three types of wheelchairs. Although the subjects all suffer from quadraplegia, they may exhibit a range of peripheral movement. Therefore, their responses to the experimental treatments, i.e., levels of wheelchair technologies, may reflect variation attributable to these differences as well as to the experimental treatments.

This individual difference variability becomes part of the experimental error variance that is used as the denominator of the F-ratio, thereby decreasing the size of the F value and making it more difficult to reject the null hypothesis of no differences among wheelchair technologies, even if such differences exist. By selecting only one group of quadraplegics, instead of three, one still cannot claim that the only differences between the measures are due to wheelchair differences, because subjects do tend to vary across trials. However, because the variation within a subject would be less than the variation between subjects, there is a significant reduction in error variation due to individual differences. This produces a smaller error term, thereby providing a greater chance of finding significant differences if they do exist. Hence, the reduction in error due to the use of repeated measures represents a direct increase in the power of the statistical analysis to discern differences across treatment conditions.

Another advantage of using repeated measures designs concerns economy, because fewer subjects are required. This is particularly useful in clinical research, when obtaining an appropriate number of subjects of a particular type in order to randomly assign them to different treatment conditions may be problematic. Also, less time may be needed for each observation due to less detailed instruction needed for each subject.

Disadvantages of Repeated Measures Designs

The first disadvantage concerns the nature of repeatedly using the same subjects under different treatment conditions. There may be a practice effect, where subjects improve on the aspect that is being measured, causing a positive effect over the occasions of testing. Alternatively, there may be a negative effect produced by fatigue or boredom. The researcher must consider the task at hand and evaluate the potential for such occurrences or ways of overcoming them. For example, in any assessment of sensory functioning, practice effects should not be a problem. Fatigue or boredom may be eliminated by scheduling repeated trials on different days.

Assuming that practice effects may be a problem, one solution is to use a counterbalanced design. In such a design, each subject is presented with the treatment conditions in a different random order. So, for example, in the wheelchair experiment, there are six possible orders for testing subjects under the three wheelchair types. Using J for joystick, V for voice-activated, and L for light beam-activated, the possible ordered arrangements are: J-V-L, J-L-V, V-L-J, V-J-L, L-J-V, and L-V-J. Subjects would then be randomly placed in one of these six sequences. If there is no need to analyze the different sequences, the data may be recorded in the form given previously in Figure 9-2, and a one-factor repeated measures analysis may be performed. Or, this order may be taken into account and analyzed to determine if there were any differences attributable to the order of presentation. This is done through the use of a Latin square design, which is beyond the scope of this chapter (see Keppel, 1982, Chapter 18; Kirk, 1982, Chapter 6; or Edwards, 1985, Chapter 21).

A second potential disadvantage of repeated measures design is the possibility of specific carryover effects, which cannot be eliminated through counterbalanced designs. These occur whenever an administration of one treatment affects the subject's performance on a subsequent treatment. This would certainly be the case when treatments involved some form of learning or produced an amelioration of a condition being measured. To illustrate, consider a potential follow-up study to evaluate an adaptive seat developed by Anderson and Anderson (1986) to reduce extensor tone and diminish agitation in premature infants through proper positioning. This adaptive seat might be compared with various other positioning and seating devices. Here, a repeated measures design would not be appropriate. In such a case, if an infant were first placed in a very effective positioning device for a long enough period of time, this might sufficiently ameliorate the infant's condition. Then, this amelioration would carry over and affect subsequent measures taken after positioning the same infant in other devices. The only possibility is to use comparable groups of infants and to randomly assign them to the various devices being studied. Again returning to the wheelchair example, there should be no possibility of carryover effects in this situation, because a subject's ease of mobility is not improved subsequent to using any particular type of wheelchair.

In certain instances, it may be possible to overcome carryover effects by allowing enough time to pass between testing occasions so that effects of a prior treatment are extinguished. As stated previously, the researcher must determine whether such problems may exist, whether they could be overcome, or whether an alternative design is more appropriate.

The third disadvantage to repeated measures designs is statistical in nature and applies only to one type of analysis: a univariate approach. This concerns the rather restrictive nature of the assumptions under which a univariate analysis is valid. The following section on methods of analysis for repeated measures designs gives further information about this problem, as well as how it can be overcome through the use of a multivariate analysis.

Approaches To Repeated Measures Analysis

Two main approaches to analysis of repeated measures designs are a univariate approach, which uses a mixed-model design, or a multivariate approach. These will be detailed separately.

Univariate Approach

From a research perspective, if a study involves only one group of subjects measured repeatedly, the design consists of a single factor (i.e., the repeated measures dimension). However, from a univariate statistical analysis perspective, it consists of two factors, a fixed factor for the repeated measures dimension, and a random factor for the subjects. This is then analyzed using a two-way (subjects by occasions), mixed-model ANOVA (see Dayton, 1970, Chapter 7; Winer, 1971, Chapter 4; and Keppel, 1982, Chapters 16 and 17).

Recall that with a univariate analysis of variance, two different F-tests are possible, depending on whether factors are: a) fixed, i.e., when the levels of the independent variable(s) are set to specific categories of interest, or b) random, i.e., when the levels are a random sample from a domain of possible levels. For example, if four different intervention strategies were being considered because they were either the only four interventions possible for a given problem, or the only four interventions of specific interest to the researcher for whatever reason, the independent variable "intervention" would be fixed. On the other hand, if the four interventions chosen for inclusion in the study were randomly chosen from a larger range of possible treatments, then "intervention" would be a random factor. In the latter case, the purpose may be simply to document that there are different effects resulting from different interventions, with no immediate interest in the specific interventions selected. The nature of the factor is important because the F-ratio used in these two cases, while having the same numerator (mean square for treatment, which is a measure of variation between levels of the factor being tested), have different denominators (mean square error, which is a measure of the appropriate error variation for the test being performed).

A mixed-model design is one that incorporates both a fixed and a random factor. This is the case in a single group repeated measures design, where the subjects are considered a random factor and the occasions a fixed factor. This is appropriate because the levels of the repeated measures factor are generally of specific interest, while the individual subjects used in a study are not. They generally represent a random sample from a population to which results are to be generalized. Designs using one sample with one repeated measures factor result in only one observation per cell. Hence, there is no within-cell variation, and so the subjects by occasion interaction must be used as the error term for the F-test to test for differences across levels of the repeated measures factor.

When multiple independent groups are present, the data correspond to a split-plot design with subjects treated as a random factor, which is nested within groups (a fixed factor), and both are crossed with the occasions (also a fixed factor). Now the error term for a test of group effects is the variation among subjects, while the error term for both tests of occasion effects and of group by occasion interaction is the subject within group-by- occasion interaction term (see Dayton, 1970, Chapter 7; Winer, 1971, Chapter 7; and Keppel, 1982, Chapters 18 and 19).

Assumptions Underlying F-tests. Three assumptions are necessary for the parametric F-test to function properly (i.e., to produce correct decisions given a predetermined level of significance, which is typically set at .05).

These assumptions are that the observations are: a) independent and b) normally distributed with c) equal variances across levels of a factor. If a statistical test leads to conclusions similar to what would be expected if the assumptions were true, the test is said to be "robust" with respect to that violation. For fixed effects designs, the F-test has been shown to be fairly robust to violations of normality and, for designs with equal groups, to violations of equal variance (for a review see Glass, Peckham, and Sanders, 1972). These results do not apply to F-tests on random factors.

The assumption of independence is critical because non-independence of the observations is a serious threat, potentially causing actual significance levels to be quite different from the preset value. In a repeated measures case, observations across the repeated factor are not independent, because they are multiple measures taken on the same subjects. Therefore, the ANOVA test of interest, which is on the repeated measures factor, may not be valid.

Huynh and Feldt (1970) have demonstrated that a sufficient, but not necessary, condition for valid F-test results in repeated measures cases is that the matrix of variances and covariances among the repeated measures satisfies a statistical property known as "compound symmetry." This is the joint requirement for constant variances and covariances, which means that the variances for the measures must be equal to each other, as must be all the covariances. A covariance between two variables is equal to the product of the correlation between the variables and their standard deviations (i.e., the square roots of their variances). When variances are equal, the requirement that covariances be equal is equivalent to a requirement that correlations be equal. For instance, as applied to the previously given Example 9-2, where subjects are measured at three points in time, the first part of the compound symmetry assumption means that the variances of all the scores (i.e., over all subjects) at time 1 (T1) is the same as the variance of the scores at time 2 (T2) and time 3 (T3). The scores at each level of the repeated measures factor must have the same variance, σ^2, as represented by:

$$\sigma_1^2 = \sigma_2^2 = \sigma_3^2 = \sigma^2.$$

The second part of the assumption implies that the correlations between all pairs of scores across the time points are equal to the same value, r. With three measures, this would be represented by:

$$r_{12} = r_{13} = r_{23} = r.$$

Huynh and Feldt (1970) further demonstrated that a less restrictive assumption is required (i.e., both necessary and sufficient) for valid F-test results with repeated measures. This assumption, called "sphericity," states that the common covariance matrix for a set of orthonormalized variates must have equal variances and zero covariances or correlations. That is, the assumption must be met by a set of transformed variates and not the original variables. However, even this relaxed assumption is probably not met in practice by most designs having more that two repeated measures.

Studies conducted to evaluate the robustness of F-tests when sphericity is not met have indicated that such an analysis may yield a too liberal test for the within-subject, or repeated measures, factor (Box, 1954; Huynh and Feldt, 1980). This means that the Type I error is inflated, leading to too many false rejections of the null hypothesis of no differences across the levels of the repeated measures factor.

Disadvantages of the Univariate Approach. The first disadvantage relates to the likely violation of the above mentioned sphericity assumption. If this assumption is met, then the mixed-model analysis is more powerful than a multivariate analysis. But, as was indicated above, this assumption is not likely to be met with most repeated measures data. When measures are taken over time, a univariate analysis should not be considered. With measures taken over levels of an experimental factor, the variance-covariance matrix should be estimated from the observations and tested to determine if violation of sphericity is likely. Most computer packages for statistical analysis that perform multivariate analysis of variance include tests of this assumption.

A second disadvantage of the univariate approach relates to the need for the user to specify different error terms for the various tests of different hypotheses when an ANOVA analysis is used. While this is more cumbersome than difficult, model specification for the multivariate approach is much simpler. Also, a side benefit of performing a multivariate analysis with most computer packages is the automatic production of both multivariate and univariate results. These univariate results are identical to those achieved by using a univariate procedure, but when they are produced with a multivariate procedure they automatically use the appropriate error terms with no need for specification by the researcher.

A third disadvantage involves efficiency of computer execution. For a given data set, the univariate approach requires a considerably lengthier data matrix than the multivariate approach. For a univariate analysis of the data, the data matrix would need to have a variable for each factor (subjects and occasions in a one group design). For example, given a design with 50 subjects and six measures on each subject, the data matrix would consist of 300 lines that included three variables on each line: a subject identification number, a number from one to six indicating a particular measure, and the actual score for that subject on that measure. A multivariate analysis allows for a more compact data matrix, where only 50 lines of data would be needed. The data on each line would now include a subject identification number and the actual scores on the six measures, as represented in Figure 9-1.

Although not eliminating the second and third disadvantages, there are ways to overcome the first disadvantage and still use a univariate approach. These involve using a conservative F-test for the within-subject tests (see Box, 1954; Geisser and Greenhouse, 1958; and Greenhouse and Geisser, 1959). These tests make adjustments to the usual degrees of freedom for the F-tests. However, the researcher would generally need to make these adjustments by hand and use tables of F-distributions instead of using the computer output's p-value. At present, most analysis packages do not have the capability of making these adjustments. Thus, overcoming the disadvantages of a univariate approach can be problematic.

Multivariate Approach

The multivariate approach to the analysis of repeated measures designs is a modification of a MANOVA analysis that treats the repeated measures as separate dependent variables instead of as an independent factor. However, unlike a general MANOVA analysis, it allows for testing of within-subject differences, as well as for group-by-occasion interactions when multiple groups are used (see Timm, 1975; Bock, 1985).

Multivariate Assumptions. Three assumptions that mirror the univariate ones are required for a multivariate analysis to provide the correct probability levels. These are that the vector (or set) of multiple observations are: a) independent; b) multivariate normally distributed; and c) that the variance-covariance matrix of the dependent measures be equal across groups. Note that the third assumption does not apply in the one-group case. Because the measures are treated as dependent and not as an independent factor, there is no need to make the sphericity assumption about the form of the variance-covariance matrix, or to assume that the repeated measures are independent of each other. The independence assumption applies only to subjects or groups of subjects. This characteristic of a multivariate repeated measures analysis is important in considering occupational therapy research. In almost all instances where repeated measures would be used, these measures will be correlated. Therefore, a multivariate analysis that takes into account the correlated nature of the data is a useful tool for occupational therapy researchers.

Advantages of the Multivariate Approach. The primary advantage of this method of analysis is that all three of the disadvantages of using a univariate approach are eliminated by the multivariate approach. That is, the sphericity assumption and specification of error terms may be ignored, and the method is more efficient from a computer utilization perspective. Additionally, the production of both univariate and multivariate results, as well as tests of sphericity, from a single multivariate analysis allows the researcher to immediately determine if the assumption is tenable and then to select either the multivariate or the univariate portion of the output, as appropriate. Given the clear advantages of the multivariate approach, the next section of this chapter will present a detailed description of this method of analysis.

Multivariate Analysis of Repeated Measures

To demonstrate the underlying logic of a multivariate repeated measures (MANOVA of RM) analysis, the designs given previously in Example 9-1 and Example 9-2 will be used. From a multivariate perspective, in both examples the three measures are considered dependent variables. As such, no comparisons among them could be made under a general MANOVA analysis. However, in a repeated measures situation, comparisons across these measures not only make sense, but they typically are of major interest to the researcher.

Bock (1963) and Potthoff and Roy (1964) have suggested a variation of MANOVA that involves transforming the dependent variables to within-subject differences. These differences then constitute transformed variates, which are linear combinations of the original measures. A multivariate analysis can then proceed as usual, with the transformed scores replacing the original dependent measures in the analysis. To avoid confusion, the term "variable" will be used for the original measures and the term "variate" will be used for the new transformed scores.

The simplest way to conceptualize MANOVA of RM when only one group of subjects is measured repeatedly, say p times, is to consider it as an analysis of a new set of p variates. The first of these represents an average or constant term, which is generally ignored in single-group analyses. The remaining allowable p-1 variates reflect contrasts (or comparisons) between two or more of the original measures. A variety of contrasts are possible, and are formulated in such a way as to reflect the research questions of interest.

Pair-wise Contrasts

Consider comparing three wheelchair technologies, as in Example 9-1. Two contrasts of interest might be comparisons between the joystick and the voice-activated device and between the voice- activated device and the light beam-activated device. These are pair-wise contrasts, because differences are taken between successive pairs of scores (i.e., between the first and second measures and between the second and third measures). Using J for the joystick score, V for voice-activated score, and L for the light beam-activated score, these comparisons are represented as differences between the variables and result in the following two variates: 1) $J - V$ and 2) $V - L$.

Ignoring the constant contrast (because it is of no interest) the two remaining contrasts may be summarized by using the contrast coefficients and placing them in matrix form (i.e., a rectangular array of numbers). If we arrange this matrix, which will be denoted by C, so that the contrasts are in rows and the columns represent the original variables in their order of appearance in the design, the matrix would have the following form:

$$C = \begin{bmatrix} 1 & -1 & 0 \\ 0 & 1 & -1 \end{bmatrix}$$

Zeros are added where a particular repeated measure is not used in the contrast.

If the data are arranged in a matrix of dimension $N \times p$ (subjects by occasions), as represented in Figure 9-1, they may be transformed by post-multiplying the data matrix by the transpose (rows and columns are interchanged) of the contrast matrix C using matrix multiplication. The transpose matrix is denoted by C'. Although this multiplication would be carried out by a computer program, it is demonstrated here to provide an understanding of what the transformation does.

For simplicity, the transformation is demonstrated on the mean scores (over subjects) for the three wheelchair conditions. Letting Y. represent the set of these three means, with J., V., and L. representing the means on the three observations, the transformation is carried out using matrix multiplication.

$$Y.C' = [J. \ V. \ L.] \begin{bmatrix} 1 & 0 \\ -1 & 1 \\ 0 & -1 \end{bmatrix} = \begin{bmatrix} J.-V. \\ V.-L. \end{bmatrix} = Y.^*$$

To briefly describe what was done, matrix multiplication is performed in the following manner. Each value in the row of Y. is multiplied by a corresponding value in the first column of C'. These products are then added to produce the first element, or score, in the resulting Y.* vector. To illustrate the algebra: $(J.)(1) + (V.)(-1) + (L.)(0) = J. - V.$, which is a linear transformation of the original variables into a new variate representing a difference score. Likewise, each value in the row of Y. is multiplied by the corresponding value in the second column of C' and then added to produce the second variate. Most multivariate analysis textbooks provide a section on rudimentary elements of operating with matrices, including matrix multiplication. For a more detailed explanation of various aspects of matrix algebra useful for statistical work, see Searle (1982).

The null hypothesis that is tested in a multivariate analysis states that the vector of new variates, Y.*, is equal to a vector of zeros. This is comparable with the univariate hypothesis in a one-group situation, where one is testing the null hypothesis that the mean of the single dependent variable is equal to some specified value. What is tested now is that the means of the two variates together do not differ significantly from zero. If the hypothesis is not rejected, this would imply that $J. - V. = 0$ (i.e., that $J. = V.$) and that $V. - L. = 0$ (i.e., that $V. = L.$). This shows the pairs of means to be equal to each other in both comparisons. Assume that the hypothesis is rejected, and that the results show that these variates are greater than zero. This would then imply that $J.>V.$ and that $V.>L.$, which would not only specify that the means of the mobility scores differed, but would inform the researcher about how they differed. In this way, the research questions of interest would be answered.

Because the hypothesis being tested is multivariate, rejection implies that the set of variates are significantly different from zero. It is possible that one pair of means differ from each other and that the other pair do not. Separate tests of these two comparisons would be univariate in nature, because only one score (the difference between two means) is involved in each case. These univariate tests are provided after the multivariate test so that appropriate interpretation may be made.

Orthogonal Polynomial Contrasts

When measures on the occasions are taken at evenly spaced time points, the interest generally is in describing the trend, or profile, of the scores across time. Considering Example 9-2, the researcher may be interested in knowing if the disabled subjects improved their ability to dress themselves in a linear fashion, increasing steadily over time from the beginning of the occupational therapy intervention through its four-month duration. The transformation matrix C now consists of polynomial coefficients that transform the data into component scores such that each new variate represents a particular trend. For example, with $p=3$ time points, the new variates would consist of a constant, a linear, and a quadratic trend.

The exact specification of the values in the C matrix for time- ordered data depends on the number of time points. The specific values for orthogonal polynomial coefficients for up to ten measures may be found in Bock (1985). However, this is usually not necessary, because any computer analysis program that performs a MANOVA of RM analysis should provide options for specifying polynomial transformation on any number of time points. Therefore, the values for C in this example will not be given here. The same principles would apply here as in the previous example. The new variates are still linear combinations of the original variables. The only difference is that these new values do not represent specific comparisons between the original measures. Instead, they represent various trend components that may be present in the data.

As in the previous case where variables were transformed into pair-wise contrasts, the multivariate hypothesis considers all these trends as a set. If a test of this hypothesis is significant (i.e., has a p-value less than .05), then it is useful to examine the subsequent univariate tests of the trends separately. These are considered in reverse order, always beginning with the highest order trend. We hope to eliminate higher order trends (by finding them not significant) and end with the rejection of the null hypothesis for a simpler trend that is more easily described and interpreted. Suppose that, in this case with three measures, we do not reject the univariate null hypothesis for the quadratic trend, but do reject it for the linear trend. This implies that the data follows a linear trend, either increasing or decreasing across time. The means of the original variables should then be graphed for a pictorial representation of the trend.

If the univariate null hypothesis for the quadratic trend were rejected, it would imply that the data contains a curved component. The profile of the means, when graphed, could be somewhat of either a bell-shaped or a u-shaped curve. Assume a bell-shaped curve was evident. The interpretation is that scores increased from the first observation to the second, but then decreased from the second to the third. While this might not make sense in the present example, such a result could be useful in an extended time study to help determine optimal duration for an intervention.

Single Sample Designs with 2 Repeated Measures

Two examples will be considered. First, a variation of Example 9-1 where, instead of simply using three different wheelchair technologies, there is a structure on the levels so that one type of wheelchair has two distinct levels. Second, a case with two fully crossed repeated measures factors will be considered.

Example 9-3. In this example, the first factor is wheelchair technologies, with only two levels: joystick and light beam-activated chairs. The second factor is nested in one level of the first, and represents two types of joystick positions: horizontal or vertical. The design is given in Figure 9-4. The coefficients for a contrast matrix C have been included in the design to facilitate the discussion.

In this situation, a natural research interest would be first to compare the two types of technologies and then to compare the two forms within the

Subjects	Joystick (J)		Light Beam (L)
	Horizontal (H)	Vertical (V)	
1			
2			
.	1/2	1/2	−1
.	1	−1	0
.			
15			

Figure 9-4. One group of quadraplegic subjects repeatedly measured on ease of mobility under two levels of wheelchair activation devices, with two levels of position nested in the joystick level of factor one.

Subjects	Clockwise		Counter Clockwise	
	Accel.	Decel.	Accel.	Decel.
1				
2	1	1	−1	−1
.	1	−1	0	0
.	0	0	1	−1
.				
40				

Figure 9-5. One group of learning disabled children measured on eye movement under a 2 × 2 design on two repeated factors: direction and speed.

joystick technology. By applying the transformation matrix represented in the design, the first new variate would be $(H \div 2) + (V \div 2) - L$, which is equal to $([H+V] \div 2) - L$. The resulting score is therefore the average of the two original joystick scores minus the light beam score. The second variate would be $H - V$, a simple difference between the scores with the horizontal and vertical joystick positions. As before, after the multivariate null hypothesis is rejected, the researcher looks at the two univariate results to determine where and in what direction the differences lie.

Example 9-4. This example is based on a study of vestibular dysfunction in learning disabled (LD) children that was conducted by Polatajko (1985). As part of the study, 40 learning disabled children were tested using a dependent measure of eye movement, which was recorded under four treatment conditions that induced vestibular nystagmus. The procedure consisted of seating each child in the Stille Werner Rotation chair, rotating the child, and recording eye movements using Beckman's miniature electrodes placed near the eyes. Vestibular nystagmus was induced by first accelerating the child, and then decelerating. Both these conditions of speed were repeated twice under clockwise (CW) and counter-clockwise (CCW) rotation. Hence, the dependent measure (eye movement) was recorded under four treatment conditions, which reflect measures taken under CW acceleration, CW deceleration, CCW acceleration, and CCW deceleration. The design on the occasion therefore includes two factors: direction (with two levels, CW and CCW) and speed (with two levels, acceleration and deceleration). The design is given in Figure 9-5. Although several sets of contrasts are now possible, the figure includes one set that may be of interest.

The first contrast compares the sum of the CW scores with the sum of the CCW scores for a test of direction. The second contrast compares acceleration with deceleration under the CW direction and the third compares acceleration with deceleration under the CCW direction.

If, instead of the above comparisons, the research interest were in: 1) comparing the two levels of direction; 2) comparing the two levels of speed; and 3) determining if an interaction existed between direction and speed, then the contrast matrix would have the following form:

$$C = \begin{bmatrix} 1 & 1 & -1 & -1 \\ 1 & -1 & 1 & -1 \\ 1 & -1 & -1 & 1 \end{bmatrix}$$

Multiple Group Repeated Measures Designs

A design on the subjects may be introduced in any of the five examples given above. Multivariate hypotheses would then be tested on the occasions, the groups, and on group-by-occasion interactions. Assuming these were significant, subsequent univariate hypotheses would be considered to answer specific research questions about the occasions and the groups.

Example 9-5. Returning to the wheelchair study in Example 9-1, suppose it was desirable to compare spinal cord injured adults with different forms of paralysis to determine if there was an appropriate match between type of disability and type of wheelchair. Now, instead of a single group of 15 quadriplegics, suppose that three different groups, with ten subjects in each group, are used: quadriplegics, paraplegics, and hemiplegics. The design is given in Figure 9-6. From the multivariate analysis perspective, this design is treated as a one-factor case, because technically, there is only one independent factor (i.e., types of groups). The measures taken under levels of type of wheelchair are considered to be three dependent variables.

The same transformation process that was outlined under the discussion of Example 9-1 is applied to create new variates. Under the one-group situation, two pair-wise contrasts were used and it was stated that a third possible contrast (the mean of the scores) was of no interest. Now, this also is included in the transformation, and may be used as the dependent variable in tests of group differences.

In the same manner that transformations were used to create contrasts across the occasion, similar transformations may be used to create contrasts across the groups. This is analogous to using a priori contrasts in a univariate analysis of variance. In this example, suppose pair-wise contrasts also were used on the groups to provide comparisons between quadriplegics and

Group	Subj.	Wheelchair Activation Devices		
		Joystick	Voice	Light Beam
Quadriplegic	1 . . . 10			
Paraplegic	11 . . . 20			
Hemiplegic	21 . . . 30			

Figure 9-6. Three groups of spinal cord injured adults repeatedly measured on ease of mobility under three levels of wheelchair activation devices.

paraplegics, and between paraplegics and hemiplegics. Rather than illustrating the manner in which these various transformations are accomplished and how they are used in the analysis, the focus will be on interpretation of the results of such an analysis.

The first thing to be considered is the multivariate test of the group by occasion interaction. If this is significant, the implication is that types of wheelchairs are differentially useful to adults with different types of paralysis. The next appropriate step is to graph the cell means and to interpret the nature of the interaction based on these graphs.

If the interaction effect is not significant, then we examine the multivariate tests for groups and occasions. First consider the test on the occasions and assume that this is significant. Recall that this is a test of the hypothesis that the vector of transformed variates, which represent the contrasts of interest, is equal to zero. This test ignores the grouping structure and functions exactly like the one-sample care. As before after finding significance on the multivariate test, the univariate tests of the specific contrasts are used to determine where the differences lie.

The multivariate test on the groups tests the null hypothesis that the three groups differ on the vector of means across the occasions. If this is significant, subsequent univariate tests on the pair-wise contrasts between group means will inform the researcher of exactly where the differences lie in exactly the same manner as for the occasion tests. These tests use the mean of scores over the occasions as the dependent measure, which was the variate created as a result of the first contrast on the occasions.

Robustness of Multivariate Techniques

It was stated earlier that the sphericity assumption was of no concern in a MANOVA of RM analysis. While this is true, the 3 multivariate assumptions must hold for valid results of a multivariate analysis. That is, groups must be independent, and the data must be multivariate normal and have equal variances and covariances across groups. Unlike the univariate F-test, which is generally robust to violations of the normality and homogeneity of variance assumptions whenever groups are of equal size, the multivariate test statistics may suffer under similar violations.

In a MANOVA of RM analysis, multivariate tests for group differences are identical to usual MANOVA tests, where several dependent measures are involved. Although these multivariate test statistics are relatively robust to violations of normality, it has been shown (Hopkins and Clay, 1963) that they are robust to violations of homogeneity only with two equal groups (the most robust case with univariate F-tests). However, departure from nominal significance levels increases with any of the following occurrences: a) an increase in the number of dependent measures; b) a decrease in the total number of subjects; or c) an increase in heterogeneity. For more than two groups, even equal sample sizes do not protect against the effects of heterogeneity (Korin, 1972; Olson, 1976).

The assumption of equal variances and covariances across groups may be tenable in certain occupational therapy research situations. For example, suppose the design in Example 9-4 was extended to include a group of 40 normal children. It might be reasonable to assume that, although the means may differ, the variability in the dependent measure (eye movement) is comparable for both normal and learning disabled children under the various testing conditions. It also may be reasonable to assume normality of eye movement in both groups. However, considering Example 9-5, it may not be reasonable to assume that the variability in the amount of mobility within a group is equivalent across quadriplegics, paraplegics, and hemiplegics. Also, mobility may not be normally distributed in these groups.

Statistical tests are available to test the viability of the homogeneity assumption. A frequently used test is Box's M. It has been shown (Ceurvorst, 1980) that this test may be unreliable in exactly the cases where it is needed most (i.e., where the above assumption is violated in such a way as to lead to inflated significance levels). While this may seem like an unresolvable problem with many clinical data sets, a simple strategy can be used to overcome the problem. This strategy is based on the fact that, while the multivariate tests of between-group differences may not be robust to assumption violation, multivariate tests of within-group differences are fairly robust in most cases where samples are of equal size. Belli (1984) showed that overall multivariate within-group tests for trends across up to five time points tend to be fairly robust even in cases where one group is four times as variable as the other groups. Follow-up tests for specific trends would be even more robust in these cases. Such discrepancy in variability across groups is generally rather dramatic in practical situations, so these tests generally may be used with confidence. This is not the case for multivariate tests of between-group differences, which tend not to be robust even with smaller violations such as one group being twice as variable.

Therefore, whenever the researcher suspects that his or her data may not meet the multivariate assumptions, an appropriate analysis strategy is to use a two-step approach. First, use a MANOVA of RM analysis to test the hypotheses on the occasions. Then, use a single dependent measure that consists of the average of the repeated measures (i.e., the variate from the first contrast in any transformation of the repeated measures) in an ANOVA to test for group differences.

In this way, the potential problems for within-group tests on the occasions in a mixed-model analysis are avoided through the use of a multivariate analysis of these hypotheses. Likewise, any potential problems for within-group tests in a multivariate analysis are avoided through use of univariate analyses of hypotheses about group differences.

Computer Analysis of Repeated Measures Data

A variety of computer analysis packages are available to handle repeated measures data. Among the most commonly used for mainframe computers are the Statistical Package for the Social Sciences (SPSSX), Statistical Analysis System (SAS), and the Biomedical Computer Program (BMDP). Each provides a full range of data analysis procedures, as well as both univariate and multivariate analyses for repeated measures. Manuals that outline how to use these packages are available (SPSS, 1986; SAS, 1985a and 1985b; and Dixon, 1981, for BMDP). These manuals provide some information about the way repeated measures analyses procedures are handled in each package. However, in all cases, the information is rather limited. More detailed discussions about how to run these analyses, including models of actual programs and outputs with appropriate explanations, may be found in other sources that deal with these packages. Along with examples of other data analysis procedures, a chapter on repeated measures analysis is included in each of the following: Barcikowski (1983a) for BMDP, (1983b) for SAS, and (1983c) for SPSS and SPSSX; and Norusis (1985) for SPSSX.

Although limited in availability, a very useful analysis program is Finn's (1980) MULTIVARIANCE. This is a little more complex than the above packages in terms of the program specifications, but the output is exceedingly clear and logical. A comprehensive discussion of the procedures, with accompanying programs and outputs, may be found in Finn and Mattsson (1978). The large- scale mainframe packages mentioned above have comparable versions for use on personal computers. With the growth of the personal computer industry, many other statistical analysis software packages are becoming readily available. While there are too many to detail here, a potential user should examine the manuals to these software products to determine if they are capable of performing a multivariate analysis of repeated measures. Because this is an advanced procedure, statistical software that is limited in scope would generally not provide these capabilities. SYS-TAT (Wilkinson, 1986) is one example of a statistical package that provides a wide range of both univariate and multivariate repeated measures analyses.

Given the generally wide availability of the SPSSX mainframe data analysis package, a simplified discussion of programs associated with the examples presented in this chapter is provided in Appendix D.

Summary

This chapter presented a detailed overview of the analysis of data in repeated measures designs. Such designs are an appropriate means of managing time-ordered data. For factorial designs over measures, they provide the benefit of decreasing the within-group variability as well as of decreasing the total number of subjects needed.

Although the univariate mixed-model approach to analysis is more powerful if the sphericity assumption is met, in most clinical or "real life" data sets, a multivariate approach would be indicated. Whenever multiple groups are involved and violations to multivariate assumptions are likely, a two-step procedure that uses univariate analyses for between-group tests and a multivariate analysis for within-group tests is an appropriate strategy.

The analysis of repeated measures data may not be the most straightforward, because there are a variety of concerns that a researcher must deal with to correctly analyze the data. However, the utility of repeated measures designs dictate their increased use in clinical research.

References

Anderson, T.W. (1958). *An introduction to multivariate statistical analysis.* New York: John Wiley and Sons.

Anderson, L.J. and Anderson, J.M. (1986). A positioning seat for the neonate and infant with high tone. *The American Journal of Occupational Therapy, 40,* 186-193.

Barcikowski, R.S. (1983a). *Computer packages and research design, Vol. I: BMDP.* New York: University Press of America.

Barcikowski, R.S. (1983b). *Computer packages and research design, Vol. II: SAS.* New York: University Press of America.

Barcikowski, R.S. (1983c). *Computer packages and research design, Vol. III: SPSS and SPSSX.* New York: University Press of America.

Belli, G.M. (1984). Robustness of repeated measures multivariate tests. Paper presented at the annual meetings of the American Educational Research Association, New Orleans, April 23-27.

Bock, R.D. (1963). Multivariate analysis of repeated measures. In C.W. Harris (ed.). *Problems in Measuring Change.* Madison, Wisconsin: University of Wisconsin Press, pp. 85-104

Bock, R.D. (1985). *Multivariate statistical methods in behavioral research.* Mooersville, Indiana: Scientific Software, Inc.

Box, G.E.P. (1954). Some theorems on quadratic forms applied in the study of analysis of variance problems, II: Effects of inequality of variance and of correlation between errors in the two-way classification. *Annals of Mathematical Statistics*, 25, 484-498.

Ceurvorst, R.W. (1980). Robustness of MANOVA under heterogeneity of variance and correlation. Unpublished doctoral dissertation. Arizona State University.

Dayton, C.M. (1970). *The design of educational experiments*. New York: McGraw Hill Book Company.

Dixon, J.W. (Ed.). (1981). *BMDP statistical software*. Los Angeles: University of California Press.

Edwards, A.L. (1985). *Experimental design in psychological research*. New York: Harper and Row.

Finn, J.D. (1980). *MULTIVARIANCE IV: Univariate and multivariate analysis of variance, covariance, regression and repeated measures; user's guide*. Chicago: National Educational Resources, Inc.

Finn, J.D. and Mattsson, I. (1978). *Multivariate analysis in educational research: Applications of the MULTIVARIANCE program*. Chicago: National Educational Resources, Inc.

Geisser, S. and Greenhouse, S.W. (1958). An extension of Box's results on the use of the F distribution in multivariate analysis. *Annals of Mathematical Statistics*, 29, 885- 891.

Gilfoyle, E. (1986). Professional directions: Management in action Presidential Address. *The American Journal of Occupational Therapy*, 40, 593-596.

Glass, G.V., Peckham, P.D., and Sanders, J.R. (1972). Consequences of failure to meet assumptions underlying the fixed- effects analysis of variance and covariance. *Review of Educational Research*, 42, 237-288.

Greenhouse, S.W. and Geisser, S. (1959). On methods in the analysis of profile data. *Psychometrika*, 24, 95-112.

Hopkins, J.W. and Clay, P.P.F. (1963). Some empirical distributions of bivariate T^2 and homoscedasticity criterion M under unequal variance and leptokurtosis. *Journal of the American Statistical Association*, 58, 1048-1053.

Huck, S.W., Cormier, W.H., and Bounds, W.G. (1974). *Reading statistics and research*. New York: Harper and Row.

Huynh, H. and Feldt, L.S. (1970). Conditions under which mean square ratios in repeated measurements designs have exact F- distributions. *Journal of the American Statistical Association*, 65, 1582-1589.

Huynh, H. and Feldt, L.S. (1980). Performance of traditional F tests in repeated measures designs under variance heterogeneity. *Communications in Statistics: Series A*, 9, 61-74.

Keppel, G. (1982). *Design and analysis: A Researcher's handbook* (2nd ed.). Englewood Cliffs, New Jersey: Prentice- Hall, Inc.

Kirk, R.E. (1982). *Experimental design: Procedures for the behavioral sciences* (2nd ed.). Belmont, California: Brooks/Cole Publishing Company.

Korin, B.P. (1972). Some comments on the homoscedasticity criterion M and the multivariate analysis of variance tests T^2, W, and R. *Biometrika*, 59, 215-216.

Lindquist, E.F. (1953). *Design and analysis of experiments in psychology and education.* Boston: Houghton Mifflin Company.

Lunneborg, C.E. and Abbott, R.D. (1983). *Elementary multivariate analysis for the behavioral sciences: Applications of basic structure.* New York: North Holland Publishing Company.

Norusis, M.J. (1985). *SPSSX advanced statistics guide.* New York: McGraw Hill Book Company.

Olson, C.L. (1976). On choosing a test statistic in multivariate analysis of variance. *Psychological Bulletin, 83,* 579- 586.

Polatajko, H.J. (1985). A critical look at vestibular dysfunction in learning-disabled children. *Developmental Medicine and Child Neurology, 27,* 283-292.

Potthoff, R.F. and Roy, S.N. (1964). A generalized multivariate analysis of variance model useful especially for growth curve problems. *Biometrika, 51,* 313-326.

SAS Institute Inc. (1985a). *SAS user's guide: Basics.* Cary, North Carolina: SAS Institute, Inc.

SAS Institute Inc. (1985b). *SAS user's guide: Statistics.* Cary, North Carolina: SAS Institute, Inc.

Scheffe, H. (1959). *The analysis of variance.* New York: John Wiley and Sons.

Searle, H.R. (1982). *Matrix algebra useful for statistics.* New York: John Wiley and Sons.

SPSS Inc. (1986). *SPSSX: User's guide* (2nd ed.). New York: SPSSX, Inc.

Timm, N.H. (1975). *Multivariate analysis with applications in education and psychology.* Monterey California: Brooks/Cole Publishing Company.

Warren, M.L. (1984). A comparative study on the presence of the asymmetrical tonic neck reflex in adult hemiplegia. *The American Journal of Occupational Therapy, 38,* 386-392.

Wilkinson, L. (1986). *SYSTAT: The System for statistics.* Evanston, Illinois: SYSTAT, Inc.

Winer, B.J. (1971). *Statistical principles in experimental designs* (2nd ed.). New York: McGraw Hill Book Company.

APPENDIX A

EXAMPLE OF COMPUTATION OF GENERALIZABILITY COEFFICIENT

Theodore R. Cromack

This is an example, using fictitious data, to demonstrate the computation of a reliability coefficient using Analysis of Variance methods and generalizability theory. The data is presented in Table A-1. In this example there are ten clients, rated by three observers on a five item rating scale with values ranging from 0 to 9.

Table A.1
Table of Observations

P e r	Observer X Items					Observer Y Items					Observer Z Items					Totals			Total Obs
	1	2	3	4	5	1	2	3	4	5	1	2	3	4	5	ObX	ObY	ObZ	Obs
1	8	6	9	3	0	7	5	7	3	5	8	4	8	2	1	26	27	23	76
2	7	8	8	4	4	7	7	8	3	4	7	8	8	4	3	31	29	30	90
3	9	5	9	3	1	8	6	9	4	2	9	5	8	2	1	27	29	25	81
4	6	4	7	2	1	6	3	6	2	0	7	5	6	2	2	20	18	22	60
5	9	8	9	6	5	8	9	8	7	6	9	9	9	5	4	37	38	36	111
6	7	7	8	3	2	6	5	7	2	4	7	5	7	3	1	27	24	23	74
7	9	8	8	4	2	9	8	9	4	3	8	7	8	3	2	31	33	28	92
8	7	6	8	3	2	6	5	7	4	2	7	6	8	3	1	26	24	25	75
9	6	8	7	2	0	7	6	7	4	1	5	7	8	3	0	23	25	24	72
10	9	7	9	3	1	6	7	7	5	4	8	6	8	2	2	29	29	26	84
Tot	77	67	82	33	18	70	61	75	39	31	76	62	78	29	17	227	276	262	815
Total all items across all Obs						223	190	235	101	66									

For the purposes of notation, it will be convenient to designate the facets of the analysis of variance as i individual clients or persons, j items, and k observers or raters. The following sums of squares are needed to compute the analysis of variance:

$\Sigma(X_{ijk})^2$ = 5504		squares of single observations (Square each single observation and sum them.)
$\Sigma(X_{.jk})^2$ = 52117		squares of sums over persons (Square the total observations for each item for all persons for each rater and sum them.)
$\Sigma(X_{i.k})^2$ = 22781		squares of sums over items (Square the total observations for each rater for each person for all items and sum them.)
$\Sigma(X_{ij.})^2$ = 16075		squares of sums over raters (Sum each item for each person, square those sums and total them.)
$\Sigma(X_{.j.})^2$ = 155611		squares of sums over both persons and raters (Square total observations for all items across all raters and sum them.)
$\Sigma(X_{..k})^2$ = 221549		squares of sums over both persons and items (Square the total observations for each rater and all items and sum them.)
$\Sigma(X_{i..})^2$ = 68163		squares of sums over both items and raters (Square the total rating for each person and sum them.)
$\Sigma(X_{...})^2$ = 664225		square of the grand sum (Square the grand total, 815.)

These sums are the raw material from which one may now calculate sums of squares for each component of the model. The sums of squares are necessary to estimate the mean square for each component, which is the basis for estimating variance components. Using the above information the sums of squares for each component is as shown:

Total sum of squares = 5504 − 664225/150	=	1075.83
Persons sum of squares = 68163/15 − 664225/150	=	116.03
Items sum of squares = 155611/30 − 664225/150	=	758.86
Raters sum of squares = 221549/50 − 664225/150	=	2.81
P × I = 16075/3 − 664225/150 − 116.03 − 758.86	=	55.27
P × R = 22781/5 − 664225/150 − 116.03 − 2.81	=	9.19
I × R = 52117/10 − 664225/150 − 758.86 − 2.81	=	21.86
P × I × R = 1075.83 − (116.03 + 758.86 + 2.81 + 55.27 + 9.19 + 21.86)	=	111.81

With these data, it is now possible to proceed to compute the mean square for each component by dividing the sum of squares by the degrees of freedom. This step is shown in Table A-2.

Table A.2
Analysis of Variance

Source	Sum of Squares	Degrees of Freedom	Mean Square
Persons	116.03	9	12.89
Items	758.86	4	189.72
Raters	2.81	2	1.40
P × I	55.27	36	1.54
P × R	9.19	18	0.51
I × R	21.86	8	2.73
P × I × R	111.81	72	1.55

Each of the mean square components can be used to calculate variance components using the model shown below. The Greek letter sigma squared represents variance and the subscripts identify the components: p for persons, i for items, and r for raters. In each instance, n represents the number of cases and MS the mean square from the table above.

$$\sigma_{pir}^2 = MS_{pir}$$
$$\sigma_{pi}^2 = 1/n_r(MS_{pi} - MS_{pir})$$
$$\sigma_{pr}^2 = 1/n_i(MS_{pr} - MS_{pir})$$
$$\sigma_{ir}^2 = 1/n_p(MS_{ir} - MS_{pir})$$
$$\sigma_p^2 = 1/n_i n_r(MS_p - MS_{pi} - MS_{pr} + MS_{pir})$$
$$\sigma_i^2 = 1/n_p n_r(MS_i - MS_{pi} - MS_{ir} + MS_{pir})$$
$$\sigma_r^2 = 1/n_p n_i(MS_r - MS_{pr} - MS_{ir} + MS_{pir})$$

Substituting the values for each component from the analysis of variance table, above, the value for each component is as shown:

$$\sigma_{pir}^2 = 1.55$$
$$\sigma_{pi}^2 = 1/3(1.54 - 1.55) < 0$$
$$\sigma_{pr}^2 = 1/5(0.51 - 1.55) < 0$$
$$\sigma_{ir}^2 = 1/10(2.73 - 1.55) = 0.118$$
$$\sigma_r^2 = 1/50(1.40 - 0.51 - 2.73 + 1.55) < 0$$

The fact that some components are less than or approximately zero is caused by the small number of observations and the fact that the entire data set is a sample. When a variance is equal to or less than zero, that component may be ignored.

Computation of the coefficient of generalizability proceeds from first examining the estimate of true score and observed score variance. The best estimate of true score variance from the table of variance components is in the persons variance. In this instance, it may be noted that it is rather small, particularly when compared with the item variance. The large variance component representing items indicates that the instrument is quite heterogeneous: not at all what would normally be desired. In looking at the table of observations, Table A-1, it may be noted that there is certainly more variance across items than across persons.

To proceed with computing the coefficient of generalizability, the formula for expected true and expected observed variance is first needed. The expected true variance is given by:

$$\sigma_{true}^2 = (n_i n_r) \sigma_p^2$$

Where σ_p^2 is the estimate of the persons variance component. The expected observed variance is given by:

$$\sigma_{obs}^2 = (n_i n_r)(n_i n_r \sigma_p^2 + n_i \sigma_r^2 + n_r \sigma_i^2 + n_i \sigma_{pr}^2 + n_r \sigma_{pi}^2 + \sigma_{ir}^2 + \sigma_{pir}^2)$$

With appropriate divisions in the numerator and denominator (simple algebra) and substitution of the numbers from above:

$$r = \frac{\sigma_{true}^2}{\sigma_{obs}^2}$$

$$r = \frac{0.826}{0.826 + \dfrac{623}{5} + 0 + 0 + 0 + \dfrac{0.118}{15} + \dfrac{1.55}{15}}$$

$$r = \frac{0.826}{2.183} = 0.378$$

Examination of the denominator will show where most of the error variance occurs. It is in the second component, the items. If the number of items were doubled (assuming items of similar type) the error variance attributed to items would be halved.

$$\frac{6.23}{5} = 1.246 \quad \text{and} \quad \frac{6.23}{10} = .623$$

This assumes that the original five questions are randomly selected from the same universe from which the second five questions would be randomly selected, thereby retaining the same amount of variance per item. By increasing the number of items by a factor of two, the coefficient of generalizability is increased from 0.378 to 0.549: a substantial increase, but barely sufficient for consistent measurement. It might be more profitable to examine the existing items and determine whether it is necessary to measure all of the dimensions now represented, because the major problem seems to be that one or two of the items assess a different dimension than the others.

APPENDIX B

EXAMPLES OF EXPLORATORY DATA ANALYSES

Charlotte Brasic Royeen

Example B-1

Exploratory data analysis was conducted with data analyzed by using a paired t-test within a study conducted by Nelson, Weidensaul, Anderson, and Shih (1984).

Their investigation sought to determine if there is a significant difference between the duration of nystagmus as measured by the Southern California Postrotary Nystagmus Test (SCPNT) during bright light and dim light conditions. Null and alternative hypotheses were tested.

H_o: There is no significant difference.
H_a: There is a significant difference.
The data set is presented in Table B-1.

Table B.1
Duration of Nystagmus for Each Condition by Subject

Subject	No. Seconds Bright	No. Seconds Dim	Difference Scores
1	24	23	1
2	26	26	0
3	16	10	6
4	22	19	3
5	23	22	1
6	19	20	−1
7	16	20	−4
8	13	12	1
9	19	21	−2
10	19	20	−1
11	15	16	−1
12	16	17	−1
13	8	8	0
14	20	21	−1
15	16	17	−1
16	23	18	5
17	21	19	2
18	14	14	0

The data (scores of the difference between the nystagmus duration between bright and dim light conditions) were subjected to exploratory data analysis. A boxplot of the difference scores is presented in Figure B-1.

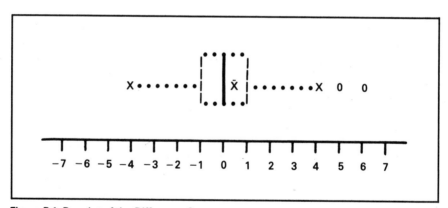

Figure B.1. Boxplot of the Difference Scores

Figure B-1 reveals that this distribution may be slightly skewed since the mean and median are not coincident. Also, there are two mild outliers associated with the right tail of the distribution. Considering the presence of two outliers in the right tail, the distribution of the data set is mildly asymmetrical.

Table B-2 presents results of more formal tests used for exploratory data analysis. The distributional testing presented indicates that the data set tests as normally distributed, but just marginally so (W = .912587, p = .095), and the data set is mildly skewed beyond the absolute value criterion of .5 (Walburg, Stykowksi, Rovai, and Hung, 1984).

Table B.2 Distributional Testing for Difference Scores Between Bright and Dim Light Conditions	
Test	**Value**
Normality	W = .912587 p = .095
Skewness	.845092

In summary, the data set tests as marginally normal but is skewed and has two mild outliers.

Example B-2

Data analyzed using an independent t-test was obtained from an investigation by Slavik (1982), and is presented in Table B-3.

Table B.3 Duration of Nystagmus for Each Subject by Group	
Group	**Total Score in Seconds**
1	53
1	41
1	45.5
1	61.5
1	40.5
2	21
2	14
2	15
2	17
2	22
2	26
2	21
2	27
2	25
2	25

The investigation studied duration of postrotary nystagmus as measured by the Southern California Postrotary Nystagmus Test (SCPNT) in normal and strabismic children. Null and alternative hypotheses were tested.

H_o: There is not a significant difference in duration of nystagmus between normal and strabismic children.

H_a: There is a significant difference in duration of nystagmus between normal and strabismic children.

The subjects were from two different settings. Ten normal children were from a Montessori Day School, whereas the five children with strabismis were from an optometrist's clinic.

Figure B-2 presents the boxplots of the data sets from normal and strabismic children, and reveals that the data set from the normal group (n = 10) appears symmetric. However, the data set from the strabismic group (n = 5) is positively skewed; furthermore, the left tail is almost nonexistent and the mean and median are divergent.

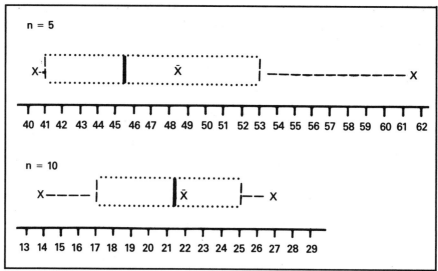

Figure B.2. Boxplots of Data from Normal and Strabismic Children

Table B-4 presents the results of more formal testing for distributional characteristics. The results indicate that the two data sets test as normally distributed. The data set from the normal children is not skewed, but the data set from the strabismic children exceeds the absolute value of .5 in terms of degree of skewness and is therefore a mildly skewed distribution, as was indicated by the boxplot.

Table B.4
Distributional Testing for Data from Normal and Strabismic Children

Test	Data by Group	
	Normal Children	Strabismic Children
Normality	W = .914503	W = .892229
	p = .363	p = .385
Skewness	− .454793	.891195

In addition, since equality of variance between the two groups is an assumption underlying the two sample t-test, testing for variances was executed. The results of an F test were equivocal (F = 3.67, df = 4/9, p = .0962). Due to the small sample sizes involved (5 and 10) and due to the skewness of the strabismic sample, a distribution-free test of variances, the Two-Sample Squared Ranks Test of Variances, was calculated (Conover, 1980). Conover and Iman (1981) report the asymptotic relative efficiency of this test to the F test to be .76 for a normal distribution. The Squared Ranks Test did not support the assumption of homogeneity of variances (T = 3.2266, p < .01).

References

Nelson, D. L., Weidensaul, N.K., Anderson, V.G., and Shih, S-R (1984). The Southern California Sensory Integration Postrotary Nystagmus Test and electronystography under differing conditions of visual input. *American Journal of Occupational Therapy*, 38(8), 535-540.

Slavik, B. (1982). Vestibular functions in children with nonparalytic strabismus. *Occupational Therapy Journal of Research*, 2(4), 220-233.

SPSS Inc. (1983). *SPSSX: User's guide*. New York: McGraw Hill.

Walburg, H.J., Strykowski, B.F., Rovai, E., and Hung, S.S. (1984). Exceptional performance. *Review of Educational Research*, 54(1), 87-112.

APPENDIX C

CRITICAL VALUES

<table>
<tr><th colspan="8">Appendix C-1
Critical Values of the T in the Wilcoxon Matched-Pairs Signed-Rank Test
n = 5(1)50</th></tr>
<tr><td colspan="8">Reprinted with permission from W.H. Beyer (Ed.), Handbook of Tables for Probability and Statistics, 2nd ed., Copyright CRC Press, Inc., Boca Raton, FL.</td></tr>
<tr><th>One-sided</th><th>Two-sided</th><th>n = 5</th><th>n = 6</th><th>n = 7</th><th>n = 8</th><th>n = 9</th><th>n = 10</th></tr>
<tr><td>p = .05</td><td>p = .10</td><td>1</td><td>2</td><td>4</td><td>6</td><td>8</td><td>11</td></tr>
<tr><td>p = .025</td><td>p = .05</td><td></td><td>1</td><td>2</td><td>4</td><td>6</td><td>8</td></tr>
<tr><td>p = .01</td><td>p = .02</td><td></td><td></td><td>0</td><td>2</td><td>3</td><td>5</td></tr>
<tr><td>p = .005</td><td>p = .01</td><td></td><td></td><td></td><td>0</td><td>2</td><td>3</td></tr>
<tr><th>One-sided</th><th>Two-sided</th><th>n = 11</th><th>n = 12</th><th>n = 13</th><th>n = 14</th><th>n = 15</th><th>n = 16</th></tr>
<tr><td>p = .05</td><td>p = .10</td><td>14</td><td>17</td><td>21</td><td>26</td><td>30</td><td>36</td></tr>
<tr><td>p = .025</td><td>p = .05</td><td>11</td><td>14</td><td>17</td><td>21</td><td>25</td><td>30</td></tr>
<tr><td>p = .01</td><td>p = .02</td><td>7</td><td>10</td><td>13</td><td>16</td><td>20</td><td>24</td></tr>
<tr><td>p = .005</td><td>p = .01</td><td>5</td><td>7</td><td>10</td><td>13</td><td>16</td><td>19</td></tr>
<tr><th>One-sided</th><th>Two-sided</th><th>n = 17</th><th>n = 18</th><th>n = 19</th><th>n = 20</th><th>n = 21</th><th>n = 22</th></tr>
<tr><td>p = .05</td><td>p = .10</td><td>41</td><td>47</td><td>54</td><td>60</td><td>68</td><td>75</td></tr>
<tr><td>p = .025</td><td>p = .05</td><td>35</td><td>40</td><td>46</td><td>52</td><td>59</td><td>66</td></tr>
<tr><td>p = .01</td><td>p = .02</td><td>28</td><td>33</td><td>38</td><td>43</td><td>49</td><td>56</td></tr>
<tr><td>p = .005</td><td>p = .01</td><td>23</td><td>28</td><td>32</td><td>37</td><td>43</td><td>49</td></tr>
<tr><th>One-sided</th><th>Two-sided</th><th>n = 23</th><th>n = 24</th><th>n = 25</th><th>n = 26</th><th>n = 27</th><th>n = 28</th></tr>
<tr><td>p = .05</td><td>p = .10</td><td>83</td><td>92</td><td>101</td><td>110</td><td>120</td><td>130</td></tr>
<tr><td>p = .025</td><td>p = .05</td><td>73</td><td>81</td><td>90</td><td>98</td><td>107</td><td>117</td></tr>
<tr><td>p = .01</td><td>p = .02</td><td>62</td><td>69</td><td>77</td><td>85</td><td>93</td><td>102</td></tr>
<tr><td>p = .005</td><td>p = .01</td><td>55</td><td>61</td><td>68</td><td>76</td><td>84</td><td>92</td></tr>
</table>

			Appendix C-1 (continued)					
One-sided	**Two-sided**	n = 29	n = 30	n = 31	n = 32	n = 33	n = 34	
p = .05	p = .10	141	152	163	175	188	201	
p = .025	p = .05	127	137	148	159	171	183	
p = .01	p = .02	111	120	130	141	151	162	
p = .005	p = .01	100	109	118	128	138	149	
One-sided	**Two-sided**	n = 35	n = 36	n = 37	n = 38	n = 39		
p = .05	p = .10	214	228	242	256	271		
p = .025	p = .05	195	208	222	235	250		
p = .01	p = .02	174	186	198	211	224		
p = .005	p = .01	160	171	183	195	208		
One-sided	**Two-sided**	n = 40	n = 41	n = 42	n = 43	n = 44	n = 45	
p = .05	p = .10	287	303	319	336	353	371	
p = .025	p = .05	264	279	295	311	327	344	
p = .01	p = .02	238	252	267	281	297	313	
p = .005	p = .01	221	234	248	262	277	292	
One-sided	**Two-sided**	n = 46	n = 47	n = 48	n = 49	n = 50		
p = .05	p = .10	389	408	427	446	466		
p = .025	p = .05	361	379	397	415	434		
p = .01	p = .02	329	345	362	380	398		
p = .005	p = .01	307	323	339	356	373		

Appendix C-2

Areas of the Standard Normal Distribution

Second decimal place in z

z	0.00	0.01	0.02	0.03	0.04	0.05	0.06	0.07	0.08	0.09
0.0	0.0000	0.0040	0.0080	0.0120	0.0160	0.0199	0.0239	0.0279	0.0319	0.0359
0.1	0.0398	0.0438	0.0478	0.0517	0.0557	0.0596	0.0636	0.0675	0.0714	0.0753
0.2	0.0793	0.0832	0.0871	0.0910	0.0948	0.0987	0.1026	0.1064	0.1103	0.1141
0.3	0.1179	0.1217	0.1255	0.1293	0.1331	0.1368	0.1406	0.1443	0.1480	0.1517
0.4	0.1554	0,1591	0.1628	0.1664	0.1700	0.1736	0.1772	0.1808	0.1844	0.1879
0.5	0.1915	0.1950	0.1985	0.2019	0.2054	0.2088	0.2123	0.2157	0.2190	0.2224
0.6	0.2257	0.2291	0.2324	0.2357	0.2389	0.2442	0.2454	0.2486	0.2517	0.2549
0.7	0.2580	0.2611	0.2642	0.2673	0.2704	0.2734	0.2764	0.2794	0.2823	0.2852
0.8	0.2281	0.2910	0.2939	0.2967	0.2995	0.3023	0.3051	0.3078	0.3106	0.3113
0.9	0.3159	0.3186	0.3212	0.3238	0.3264	0.3289	0.3315	0.3340	0.3365	0.3389
1.0	0.3413	0.3438	0.3861	0.3485	0.3508	0.3531	0.3554	0.3577	0.3599	0.3621
1.1	0.3643	0.3665	0.3686	0.3708	0.3729	0.3749	0.3770	0.3790	0.3810	0.3830
1.2	0.3849	0.3869	0.3888	0.3907	0.3925	0.3944	0.3962	0.3980	0.3997	0.4015
1.3	0.4032	0.4049	0.4066	0.4082	0.4099	0.4115	0.4131	0.4147	0.4162	0.4177
1.4	0.4192	0.4206	0.4222	0.4236	0.4251	0.4265	0.4279	0.4292	0.4306	0.4319
1.5	0.4332	0.4345	0.4357	0.4370	0.4382	0.4394	0.4406	0.4418	0.4429	0.4441
1.6	0.4452	0.4463	0.4474	0.4484	0.4495	0.4505	0.4515	0.4535	0.4535	0.4545
1.7	0.4554	0.4564	0.4573	0.4582	0.4591	0.4599	0.4608	0.4616	0.4625	0.4633
1.8	0.4641	0.4649	0.4656	0.4664	0.4671	0.4678	0.4686	0.4693	0.4699	0.4706
1.9	0.4713	0.4719	0.4726	0.4732	0.4738	0.4744	0.4750	0.4756	0.4761	0.4767
2.0	0.4772	0.4778	0.4783	0.4788	0.4793	0.4798	0.4803	0.4808	0.4812	0.4817
2.1	0.4821	0.4826	0.4830	0.3834	0.3838	0.4842	0.4846	0.4850	0.4854	0.4857
2.2	0.4861	0.4864	0.4868	0.4871	0.4875	0.4878	0.4881	0.4884	0.4887	0.4890
2.3	0.4893	0.4896	0.4898	0.4901	0.4904	0.4906	0.4909	0.4911	0.4913	0.4916
2.4	0.4918	0.4920	0.4922	0.4925	0.4927	0.4929	0.4931	0.4932	0.4934	0.4936
2.5	0.4938	0.4940	0.4941	0.4943	0.4945	0.4946	0.4948	0.4949	0.4951	0.4952
2.6	0.4953	0.4955	0.4956	0.5947	0.4959	0.4960	0.4961	0.4962	0.4963	0.4964
2.7	0.4965	0.4966	0.4967	0.4968	0.4969	0.4970	0.4971	0.4972	0.4973	0.4974
2.8	0.4974	0.4975	0.4976	0.4977	0.4977	0.4978	0.4979	0.4979	0.4980	0.4981
2.9	0.4981	0.4982	0.4982	0.4983	0.4984	0.4984	0.4985	0.4985	0.4986	0.4986
3.0	0.4987	0.4987	0.4987	0.4988	0.4988	0.4989	0.4989	0.4989	0.4990	0.4990
3.1	0.4990	0.4991	0.4991	0.4991	0.4992	0.4992	0.4992	0.4992	0.4993	0.4993
3.2	0.4993	0.4993	0.4994	0.4994	0.4994	0.4994	0.4994	0.4995	0.4995	0.4995
3.3	0.4995	0.4995	0.4995	0.4996	0.4996	0.4996	0.4996	0.4996	0.4996	0.4997
3.4	0.4997	0.4997	0.4997	0.4997	0.4997	0.4997	0.4997	0.4997	0.4997	0.4998
3.5	0.4998									
4.0	0.49998									
4.5	0.499997									
5.0	0.4999997									

Reprinted with permission from *Standard Mathematical Tables,* 15th ed., Copyright CRC Press, Inc., Boca Raton, Fl.

Appendix C-3
Critical Values for the Wilcoxon Rank Sum Test
$m = 3(1)25$ and $n = m(1)m + 25$
$P = .05$ one-sided; $P = .10$ two-sided

n	m = 3	m = 4	m = 5	m = 6	m = 7	m = 8	m = 9	m = 10	m = 11	m = 12	m = 13	m = 14
n = m	6,15	12,24	19,36	28,50	39,66	52,84	66,105	83,127	101,152	121,179	143,208	167,239
n = m + 1	7,17	13,27	20,40	30,54	41,71	54,90	69,111	86,134	105,159	125,187	148,216	172,248
n = m + 2	7,20	14,30	22,43	32,58	43,76	57,95	72,117	89,141	109,166	129,195	152,225	177,257
n = m + 3	8,22	15,33	24,46	33,63	46,80	60,100	75,123	93,147	112,174	134,202	157,233	182,266
n = m + 4	9,24	16,36	25,50	35,67	48,85	62,106	78,129	96,154	116,181	138,210	162,241	187,275
n = m + 5	9,27	17,39	26,54	37,71	50,90	65,111	81,135	100,160	120,188	142,218	166,250	192,284
n = m + 6	10,29	18,42	27,58	39,75	52,95	67,117	84,141	103,167	124,195	147,225	171,258	197,293
n = m + 7	11,31	19,45	29,61	41,79	54,100	70,122	87,147	107,173	128,202	151,233	176,266	203,301
n = m + 8	11,34	20,48	30,65	42,84	57,104	73,127	90,153	110,180	132,209	155,241	181,274	208,310
n = m + 9	12,36	21,51	32,68	44,88	59,109	75,133	93,159	114,186	136,216	159,249	185,283	213,319
n = m + 10	13,38	22,54	33,72	46,92	61,114	78,138	96,165	117,193	139,224	164,256	190,291	218,328
n = m + 11	13,41	23,57	34,76	48,96	63,119	80,144	100,170	120,200	143,231	168,264	195,299	223,337
n = m + 12	14,43	24,60	36,79	50,100	65,124	83,149	103,176	124,206	147,238	172,272	199,308	228,346
n = m + 13	15,45	25,63	37,83	52,104	68,128	86,154	106,182	127,213	151,245	177,279	204,316	234,354
n = m + 14	15,48	26,66	39,86	53,109	70,133	88,160	109,188	131,219	155,252	181,287	209,324	239,363
n = m + 15	16,50	27,69	40,90	55,113	72,138	91,165	112,194	134,226	159,259	185,295	214,332	244,372
n = m + 16	17,52	28,72	42,93	57,117	74,143	94,170	115,200	138,232	163,266	190,302	218,341	249,381
n = m + 17	17,55	29,75	43,97	59,121	77,147	96,176	118,206	141,239	167,273	194,310	223,349	254,390
n = m + 18	18,57	30,78	44,101	61,125	79,152	99,181	121,212	145,245	171,280	198,318	228,357	260,398
n = m + 19	19,59	31,81	46,104	62,130	81,157	102,186	124,218	148,252	175,287	203,325	233,365	265,407
n = m + 20	19,62	32,84	47,108	64,134	83,162	104,192	127,224	152,258	178,295	207,333	237,374	270,416
n = m + 21	20,64	33,87	49,111	66,138	86,166	107,197	130,230	155,265	182,302	211,341	242,382	275,425
n = m + 22	21,66	34,90	50,115	68,142	88,171	109,203	133,236	159,271	186,309	216,348	247,390	280,434
n = m + 23	21,69	35,93	52,118	70,146	90,176	112,208	136,242	162,278	190,316	220,356	252,398	285,443
n = m + 24	22,71	37,95	53,122	72,150	92,181	115,213	139,248	166,284	194,323	224,364	257,406	291,451
n = m + 25	23,73	38,98	54,126	73,155	94,186	117,219	142,254	169,291	198,330	229,371	261,415	296,460

Appendix C-3 (continued)

$m = 3(1)25$ and $n = M(1)\ M + 25$

$P = .025$ one-sided; $P = .05$ two-sided

n	$m = 3$	$m = 4$	$m = 5$	$m = 6$	$m = 7$	$m = 8$	$m = 9$	$m = 10$	$m = 11$	$m = 12$	$m = 13$	$m = 14$
$n = m$	5,16	11,25	18,37	26,52	37,68	49,87	63,108	79,131	96,157	116,184	137,214	160,246
$n = m + 1$	6,18	12,28	19,41	28,36	39,73	51,93	66,114	82,138	100,164	120,192	141,223	165,225
$n = m + 2$	6,21	12,32	20,45	29,61	41,78	54,98	68,121	85,145	103,172	124,200	146,231	170,264
$n = m + 3$	7,23	13,35	21,49	31,65	43,83	56,104	71,127	88,152	107,179	128,208	150,240	174,274
$n = m + 4$	7,26	14,38	22,53	32,70	45,88	58,110	74,133	91,159	110,187	131,217	154,249	179,283
$n = m + 5$	8,28	15,41	24,56	34,74	46,94	61,115	77,139	94,166	114,194	135,225	159,257	184,292
$n = m + 6$	8,31	16,44	25,60	36,78	48,99	63,121	79,146	97,173	118,201	139,233	163,266	180,301
$n = m + 7$	9,33	17,47	26,64	37,83	50,104	65,127	82,152	101,179	121,209	143,241	168,274	194,310
$n = m + 8$	10,35	17,51	27,68	39,87	52,109	68,132	85,158	104,186	125,216	147,249	172,283	198,320
$n = m + 9$	10,38	18,54	29,71	41,91	54,114	70,138	88,164	107,193	128,224	151,257	176,292	203,329
$n = m + 10$	11,40	19,57	30,75	42,96	56,119	72,144	90,177	110,200	132,231	155,265	181,300	208,338
$n = m + 11$	11,43	20,60	31,79	44,100	58,124	75,149	93,177	113,207	135,239	159,273	185,309	213,347
$n = m + 12$	12,45	21,63	32,83	45,105	60,129	77,155	96,183	117,213	139,246	163,281	190,317	218,356
$n = m + 13$	12,48	22,66	33,87	47,109	62,134	80,160	99,189	120,220	143,253	167,289	194,326	222,366
$n = m + 14$	13,50	23,69	35,90	49,113	64,139	82,166	101,196	123,227	146,261	171,297	198,335	227,375
$n = m + 15$	13,53	24,72	39,94	50,118	66,144	84,172	104,202	126,234	150,268	175,305	203,343	232,384
$n = m + 16$	14,55	24,76	37,98	52,122	68,149	87,177	107,208	129,241	153,276	179,313	207,352	237,393
$n = m + 17$	14,58	25,79	38,102	53,127	70,154	89,183	110,214	132,248	157,283	183,321	212,360	242,402
$n = m + 18$	15,60	26,82	40,105	55,131	72,159	92,188	113,220	136,254	161,290	187,329	216,369	247,411
$n = m + 19$	15,63	27,85	41,109	57,135	74,164	94,194	115,227	139,261	164,298	191,337	221,377	252,420
$n = m + 20$	16,65	28,88	42,113	58,140	76,169	96,200	118,233	142,268	168,305	195,345	225,386	256,430
$n = m + 21$	16,68	29,91	43,117	60,144	78,174	99,205	121,239	145,275	171,313	199,353	229,395	261,439
$n = m + 22$	17,70	30,94	45,120	61,149	80,179	101,211	124,245	148,282	175,320	203,361	234,403	266,448
$n = m + 23$	17,73	31,97	46,124	63,153	84,184	103,217	127,251	152,288	179,327	207,369	238,412	271,457
$n = m + 24$	18,75	31,101	47,128	65,157	84,189	106,222	129,258	155,295	182,335	211,377	243,420	276,466
$n = m + 25$	18,78	32,104	48,132	66,162	86,194	108,228	132,264	158,302	186,342	216,384	247,429	281,475

Reprinted with permission from W.H. Beyer (Ed.) Handbook of Tables for Probability and Statistics, 2nd ed Copyright CRC Press, Inc., Boca Raton, Fl.

Appendix C-3 (continued)

$m = 3(1)25$ and $n = m(1)\ m + 25$

$P = .01$ one-sided; $P = .02$ two-sided

n	m = 3	m = 4	m = 5	m = 6	m = 7	m = 8	m = 9	m = 10	m = 11	m = 12	m = 13	m = 14
n = m	5,16	10,26	16,39	24,54	34,71	46,90	59,112	74,136	91,162	110,190	130,221	153,253
n = m + 1	5,19	10,30	17,43	26,58	36,76	48,96	62,118	77,143	94,170	113,199	134,230	157,263
n = m + 2	6,21	11,33	18,47	27,63	38,81	50,102	64,125	80,150	97,178	117,207	138,239	161,273
n = m + 3	6,24	12,36	19,51	26,68	39,87	52,108	66,132	83,157	101,185	120,216	142,248	166,282
n = m + 4	6,27	12,40	20,55	30,72	41,92	54,114	69,138	85,165	104,193	124,224	146,257	170,292
n = m + 5	7,29	13,43	21,59	31,77	43,97	56,120	71,145	88,172	107,201	128,232	150,266	174,302
n = m + 6	7,32	14,46	22,63	32,82	44,103	58,126	74,151	91,179	110,209	131,241	154,275	179,311
n = m + 7	7,35	14,50	23,67	34,86	46,108	60,132	76,158	94,186	113,217	135,249	158,284	183,321
n = m + 8	8,37	15,53	24,71	35,91	48,113	62,138	79,164	97,193	117,224	138,258	162,293	188,330
n = m + 9	8,40	16,56	25,75	36,96	49,119	64,144	81,171	100,200	120,232	142,266	166,302	192,340
n = m + 10	9,42	16,60	26,79	38,100	51,124	66,150	83,178	102,208	123,240	146,274	170,311	196,350
n = m + 11	9,45	17,63	27,83	39,105	53,129	68,156	86,184	105,215	126,248	149,283	174,320	201,359
n = m + 12	9,48	18,66	28,87	40,110	55,134	71,161	88,191	108,222	130,255	153,291	178,329	205,369
n = m + 13	10,50	18,70	29,91	42,114	56,140	73,167	91,197	111,229	133,263	157,299	182,338	210,378
n = m + 14	10,53	19,73	30,95	43,119	58,145	75,173	93,204	114,236	136,271	160,308	186,347	214,388
n = m + 15	10,56	20,76	31,99	45,123	60,150	77,179	96,210	117,243	139,279	164,316	190,356	219,397
n = m + 16	11,58	20,80	32,103	46,128	61,156	79,185	98,217	120,250	143,286	168,324	194,365	223,407
n = m + 17	11,61	21,83	33,107	47,133	63,161	81,191	101,223	122,258	146,294	171,333	198,374	228,416
n = m + 18	12,63	22,86	34,111	49,137	65,166	83,197	103,230	125,265	149,302	175,341	203,382	232,426
n = m + 19	12,66	23,89	35,115	50,142	67,171	85,203	106,236	128,272	152,310	179,349	207,391	236,436
n = m + 20	12,69	23,93	36,119	51,147	68,177	87,209	108,243	131,279	156,317	182,358	211,400	241,445
n = m + 21	13,71	24,96	37,123	53,151	70,182	90,214	111,249	134,286	159,325	186,366	215,409	245,455
n = m + 22	13,74	25,99	38,127	54,156	72,187	92,220	113,256	137,293	162,333	190,374	219,418	250,464
n = m + 23	14,76	25,103	39,131	56,160	74,192	94,226	116,262	140,300	165,341	193,383	223,427	254,474
n = m + 24	14,79	26,106	40,135	57,165	75,198	96,232	118,269	143,307	169,348	197,391	227,436	259,483
n = m + 25	14,82	27,109	41,139	58,170	77,203	98,238	121,275	145,315	172,356	201,399	231,445	263,493

Appendix C-3 (continued)

m = 3(1)25 and n = m(1) m + 25

P = .005 one-sided; P = .01 two-sided

n	m = 3	m = 4	m = 5	m = 6	m = 7	m = 8	m = 9	m = 10	m = 11	m = 12	m = 13	m = 14
n = m	5,16	9,27	15,40	23,55	33,72	44,92	57,114	71,139	88,165	106,194	126,225	148,258
n = m + 1	5,19	10,30	16,44	24,60	34,78	46,98	59,121	74,146	91,173	109,203	130,234	152,268
n = m + 2	5,22	10,34	17,48	25,65	36,83	47,105	61,128	76,154	94,181	113,211	133,244	156,278
n = m + 3	5,25	11,37	18,52	27,69	37,89	49,111	63,135	79,161	97,189	116,220	137,253	160,288
n = m + 4	6,27	11,41	19,56	28,74	39,94	51,117	65,142	82,168	100,197	119,229	141,262	164,298
n = m + 5	6,30	12,44	19,61	29,79	40,100	53,123	68,148	84,176	102,206	123,237	144,272	168,308
n = m + 6	6,33	12,48	20,65	30,84	42,105	55,129	70,155	87,183	105,214	126,246	148,281	172,318
n = m + 7	6,36	13,51	21,69	31,89	43,111	57,135	72,162	89,191	108,222	129,255	152,290	176,328
n = m + 8	7,38	13,55	22,73	32,94	45,116	59,141	74,169	92,198	111,230	133,263	156,299	180,338
n = m + 9	7,41	14,58	23,77	34,98	46,122	61,147	77,175	95,205	114,238	136,272	159,309	185,347
n = m + 10	7,44	15,61	24,81	35,103	48,127	62,154	79,182	97,213	117,246	139,281	163,318	189,357
n = m + 11	8,46	15,65	25,85	36,108	49,133	64,160	81,189	100,220	120,254	143,289	167,327	193,367
n = m + 12	8,49	16,68	26,89	37,113	51,138	66,166	83,196	103,227	123,262	146,298	171,336	197,377
n = m + 13	8,52	16,72	26,94	38,118	52,144	68,172	86,202	105,235	126,270	150,306	175,345	201,287
n = m + 14	9,54	17,75	27,98	40,122	54,149	70,178	88,209	108,242	129,278	153,315	178,355	205,397
n = m + 15	9,57	17,79	28,102	41,127	55,155	72,184	90,216	110,250	132,286	156,324	182,364	210,406
n = m + 16	9,60	18,82	29,106	42,132	57,160	74,190	93,222	113,257	136,293	160,332	186,373	214,416
n = m + 17	9,63	19,85	30,110	43,137	59,165	76,196	95,229	116,264	139,301	163,341	190,382	218,426
n = m + 18	10,65	19,89	31,114	45,141	60,171	78,202	97,236	118,272	142,309	167,349	194,391	222,436
n = m + 19	10,68	20,92	32,118	46,146	62,176	80,208	99,243	121,279	145,317	170,358	197,401	224,446
n = m + 20	10,71	20,96	33,122	47,151	63,182	82,214	102,249	124,286	148,325	173,367	201,410	231,455
n = m + 21	11,73	21,99	33,127	48,156	65,187	83,221	104,256	126,294	151,333	177,375	205,419	235,465
n = m + 22	11,76	21,103	34,131	49,161	66,193	85,227	106,263	129,301	154,341	180,384	209,428	239,475
n = m + 23	11,79	22,106	35,135	51,165	68,198	87,233	109,269	132,308	157,349	184,392	213,437	243,485
n = m + 24	12,81	23,109	36,139	52,170	70,203	89,239	111,276	134,316	160,357	187,401	216,447	247,495
n = m + 25	12,84	23,113	37,143	53,175	71,209	91,245	113,283	137,323	163,365	191,409	220,456	252,504

APPENDIX C-4
PERCENTAGE POINTS, CHI-SQUARE DISTRIBUTION

$n\backslash P_p$	.005	.010	.025	.050	.100	.250	.500	.750	.900	.950	.975	.990	.995
1	.0000393	.000157	.000982	.00393	.0158	.102	.455	1.32	2.71	3.84	5.02	6.63	7.88
2	.0100	.0201	.0506	.103	.211	.575	1.39	2.77	4.61	5.99	7.38	9.21	10.6
3	.0717	.115	.216	.352	.584	1.21	2.37	4.11	6.25	7.81	9.35	11.3	12.8
4	.207	.297	.484	.711	1.06	1.92	3.36	5.39	7.78	9.49	11.1	13.3	14.9
5	.412	.554	.831	1.15	1.61	2.67	4.35	6.63	9.24	11.1	12.8	15.1	16.7
6	.676	.872	1.24	1.64	2.20	3.45	5.35	7.84	10.6	12.6	14.4	16.8	18.5
7	.989	1.24	1.69	2.17	2.83	4.25	6.35	9.04	12.0	14.1	16.0	18.5	20.3
8	1.34	1.65	2.18	2.73	3.49	5.07	7.34	10.2	13.4	15.5	17.5	20.1	22.0
9	1.73	2.09	2.70	3.33	4.17	5.90	8.34	11.4	14.7	16.9	19.0	21.7	23.6
10	2.16	2.56	3.25	3.94	4.87	6.74	9.34	12.5	16.0	18.3	20.5	23.2	25.2
11	2.60	3.05	3.82	4.57	5.58	7.58	10.3	13.7	17.3	19.7	21.9	24.7	26.8
12	3.07	3.57	4.40	5.23	6.30	8.44	11.3	14.8	18.5	21.0	23.3	26.2	28.3
13	3.57	4.11	5.01	5.89	7.04	9.30	12.3	16.0	19.8	22.4	24.7	27.7	29.8
14	4.07	4.66	5.63	6.57	7.79	10.2	13.3	17.1	21.1	23.7	26.1	29.1	31.3
15	4.60	5.23	6.26	7.26	8.55	11.0	14.3	18.2	22.3	25.0	27.5	30.6	32.8
16	5.14	5.81	6.91	7.96	9.31	11.9	15.3	19.4	23.5	26.3	28.8	32.0	34.3
17	5.70	6.41	7.56	8.67	10.1	12.8	16.3	20.5	24.8	27.6	30.2	33.4	35.7
18	6.26	7.01	8.23	9.39	10.9	13.7	17.3	21.6	26.0	28.9	31.5	34.8	37.2
19	6.84	7.63	8.91	10.1	11.7	14.6	18.3	22.7	27.2	30.1	32.9	36.2	38.6
20	7.43	8.26	9.59	10.9	12.4	15.5	19.3	23.8	28.4	31.4	34.2	37.6	40.0
21	8.03	8.90	10.3	11.6	13.2	16.3	20.3	24.9	29.6	32.7	35.5	38.9	41.4
22	8.64	9.54	11.0	12.3	14.0	17.2	21.3	26.0	30.8	33.9	36.8	40.3	42.8
23	9.26	10.2	11.7	13.1	14.8	18.1	22.3	27.1	32.0	35.2	38.1	41.6	44.2
24	9.89	10.9	12.4	13.8	15.7	19.0	23.3	28.2	33.2	36.4	39.4	43.0	45.6
25	10.5	11.5	13.1	14.6	16.5	19.9	24.3	29.3	34.4	37.7	40.6	44.3	46.9
26	11.2	12.2	13.8	15.4	17.3	20.8	25.3	30.4	35.6	38.9	41.9	45.6	48.3
27	11.8	12.9	14.6	16.2	18.1	21.7	26.3	31.5	36.7	40.1	43.2	47.0	49.6
28	12.5	13.6	15.3	16.9	18.9	22.7	27.3	32.6	37.9	41.3	44.5	48.3	51.0
29	13.1	14.3	16.0	17.7	19.8	23.6	28.3	33.7	39.1	42.6	45.7	49.6	52.3
30	13.8	15.0	16.8	18.5	20.6	24.5	29.3	34.8	40.3	43.8	47.0	50.9	53.7

Reprinted with permission from W.H. Beyer (Ed.), *Handbook of Tables for Probability and Statistics*, 2nd ed, CDC Press, Boca Raton, Fl.

APPENDIX D

USING SPSSX TO ANALYZE REPEATED MEASURES DATA

Gabriella M. Belli

Although a number of statistical analysis packages are available to analyze repeated measures data using a multivariate analysis of variance (MANOVA) approach, the Statistical Package for the Social Sciences (SPSSX) has been selected for use in this brief demonstration. This is a fairly commonly used package that is quite powerful and generally available to most occupational therapy researchers. The programs presented here are for examples from Chapter 9. They are intended to provide an introduction to the use of the SPSSX MANOVA procedure to analyze repeated measures data. For more detailed descriptions of SPSSX programs, with corresponding outputs, see references given in Chapter 9.

SPSSX Programs for Simple Repeated Measures Designs

A sample SPSSX program for Example 9-1 is given in Figure D-1. Recall that this represents a single-group situation with repeated measures under three types of wheelchair activating devices: joystick (J), voice (V), and light beam (L), where pair-wise contrasts are used to transform the repeated measures. All statements that are in upper case are exact SPSSX commands, keywords, or specifications. Statements that are in lower case are specific to the example.

General SPSSX Commands. The DATA LIST command (line G-1) provides the necessary information about the structure of the data matrix, providing variable names and their column location. For this example, there is a subject

```
G-1.    DATA LIST        /id 1-2 group 3 joy 4-6 voice 7-9 light 10-12
G-2.    COMMENT          Repeated measures data with:
                         Design on occasions = one-way with three measures,
                              where pairwise contrasts are used
                         Design on subjects = three groups of subjects
G-3.    VAR LABELS       group 'type of paralysis'
                         joy 'joystick activated'
                         voice 'voice activated'
                         light 'light beam activated'
G-4.    VALUE LABELS     group 1 'paraplegic' 2 'quadriplegic' 3 'hemiplegic'
G-5.    BEGIN DATA
G-6.       .
           .
           .
G-7.    END DATA
G-8.    COMMENT          Single group repeated measures analysis for Example
                         9.1, ignoring grouping structure.
G-9.    MANOVA joy voice light
G-10.                        /WSFACTOR = device (3)
G-11.                        /CONTRAST (device) = REPEATED
G-12.                        /RENAME = mean j-v v-1
G-13.                        /WSDESIGN = device
G-14.                        /PRINT = HOMOGENEITY (BARTLETT COCHRAN BOXM)
G-15.                           CELLINFO (MEANS COV)
G-16.                           TRANSFORM
G-17.                           ERROR (SSCP COR)
G-18.                           SIGNIF (HYPOTH MULTI AVEF)
G-19.                        /METHOD = SSTYPE (UNIQUE)
G-20.                        /ANALYSIS (REPEATED)
G-21.                        /DESIGN
G-22.   FINISH
```

Figure D.1. SPSSX program for Example 9.1, a single-group repeated measures analysis.

identification variable, a group membership variable, and three variables for the scores under different wheelchair types. The COMMENT keyword (lines G-2 and G-5) allows the analyst to personalize a program by inserting helpful comments. These may appear anywhere in the program. Comments may be several lines long; the only stipulation is that subsequent lines cannot begin in column one. The VAR LABELS command (line G-3) is an option that provides for assigning descriptive labels (of up to 40 characters), which are more informative than the eight character variable names. The VALUE LABELS command (line G-4) provides for similar descriptive labeling (of up to 20 characters each) for numerical values of categorical variables.

Lines G-5 to G-7 represent the raw data matrix along with the BEGIN DATA and END DATA commands, which must go before and after the data listing. The final command in any SPSSX program is the FINISH statement (line G-22).

MANOVA Commands. The main MANOVA command (line G-9) lists the dependent variables to be used in the analysis. The next four subcommands define the structure of the repeated measures and provide for appropriate transformations and labels.

The WSFACTOR (within subject factor, line G-10) subcommand defines one occasion factor, which is labelled "device," that has three levels (i.e., three repeated measures). The CONTRAST (line G-11) requested for this within-subject factor is REPEATED, which transforms the original variables into new variates reflecting successive pair-wise differences. The RENAME subcommand (line G-12) provides names for the new transformed variates: a mean over the repeated measures and two pair-wise differences (joystick score minus voice-activated score and voice-activated score minus light beam score). The WSDESIGN (within-subjects design, line G-13) subcommand specifies the design on the occasions, which in this case is a single factor, "device."

The PRINT subcommand has a number of specifications for the printed output, which may appear in the program in any order following the keyword PRINT. In this example, HOMOGENEITY (line G-14) requests three tests of equality of variance: Bartlett-Box F, Cochran C, and Box's M criterion. CELLINFO (line G-15) requests a summary of cell means and a covariance matrix. TRANSFORM (line G-16) causes the coefficients of the orthonormalized transformation matrix used to transform the repeated measures to be printed. This shows how the dependent variables are transformed to create the within-subjects effects and is useful to check that the intended transformation was performed. The sums of squares and cross-products (SSCP) and correlation matrices are requested by ERROR (line G-17). This subcommand also produces Bartlett's test of sphericity, which tests whether the sphericity assumption is tenable. The three keywords after SIGNIF (line G-18) request the printing of three statistics: 1) the hypothesis sums of squares and cross products matrix; 2) multivariate F-tests for group differences (printed only if multiple groups are present); and 3) averaged F-tests, which are the univariate results for a repeated measures analysis.

The METHOD subcommand (line G-19) controls computational aspects of the MANOVA analysis. The keyword SSTYPE relates to the method of partitioning the sums of squares. The ANALYSIS subcommand (line G-20) with the keyword REPEATED produces the within-subjects effects defined by the WSDESIGN and WSFACTOR subcommands. This also causes the repeated measures effects to be labeled nicely.

The DESIGN subcommand (line G-21) relates to any design on the subjects. Because this is a one-group analysis, nothing is specified here. However, this subcommand must appear in the MANOVA procedure.

Modifications of the SPSSX MANOVA Procedure

Only slight modifications to the above MANOVA procedure are needed for the following examples: a) a multiple group analysis with one between-subjects factor; b) a single-group analysis with special contrasts on the repeated measures; and c) a single-group analysis with repeated measures are taken over time.

Modifications for Multiple Groups. Example 9-5 was an extension of the above wheelchair example, where measures on the three types of wheelchairs were repeatedly taken on separate groups with three different types of

```
G-9.    MANOVA joy voice light by group (1,3)
G-21.        /DESIGN group
```

Figure D.2 Modifications to MANOVA procedure from Figure D.1 for Example 9.5 with one between-subjects factor.

```
G-9.       MANOVA horizon vertical light
G-10.          /WSFACTOR = device (3)
G-11.          /CONTRAST (device) = SPECIAL   ( 1  1   1
                                                .5 .5 −1
                                                 1 −1   0)
G-12.          /RENAME = mean J-L H-V
```

Figure D.3. Modifications to MANOVA procedure from Figure D.1 for Example 9.3 using special contrasts.

paralysis. As shown in Figure D-2, only two MANOVA commands need to be changed to use the grouping structure in the analysis.

The main MANOVA command now lists the three dependent variables (i.e., the repeated measures), followed by the grouping variable. The values in parenthesis are the lowest and highest values of this categorical variable. Because the DESIGN subcommand is for the design on the subjects, the single factor "group" is listed here.

Modifications for Special Contrasts. Example 9-3 was a variation of the wheelchair example, where comparisons were made between two types of wheelchairs (joystick and light beam-activated) and between two types of joysticks (horizontal and vertical). This required non-standard contrasts to be created so that the average of the two joystick scores are compared with the light beam score, and then the two joystick scores are compared with each other. The coefficients for the transformation matrix must be supplied by the researcher for any non-standard set of contrasts.

With appropriate changes in the DATA LIST command so that the variables are now called "horizon" "vertical" and "light," Figure D-3 gives the modifications for the MANOVA procedure.

The WSFACTOR is given as a single factor with three levels. The coefficients in the CONTRAST subcommand create the variates of interest to test the within-subject effects. As before, specifications after RENAME reflect the nature of the new variates.

Modifications for Time-Ordered Data. Again, with appropriate modifications in the data definition commands and comments in Figure D-1, only slight changes are needed in the MANOVA procedure commands to analyze time-ordered data. Using Example 9-2, where one group of subjects was measured at three equally spaced intervals over time, suppose the variable names for the three scores are given as "time1" "time2" and "time3." Then, the five lines in the previous MANOVA sequence corresponding to the relevant changes required are given in Figure D-4.

As before, the main MANOVA command lists the variables to be used. The

```
G-9.      MANOVA time1  time2  time3
G-10.        /WSFACTOR = time(3)
G-11.        /CONTRAST (time) = POLYNOMIAL
G-12.        /RENAME = contrast linear quad
G-13.        /WSDESIGN = time
```

Figure D.4. Modifications to MANOVA procedure from Figure D.1 for Example 9.2, a single-group analysis of time ordered data.

```
G-23.     DATA LIST /id 1-3 group 4 gender 5 cwa cwd ccwa ccwd 6-13
G-14.     COMMENT design on subjects = 2×2, where:
                      factor A = group (LD or normal)
                      factor B = gender (male or female)
                      design on occasions = 2×2, where:
                      factor C = direction (cw or ccw)
                      factor D = speed (accel or decel)
G-25.     VAR LABELS  cwa 'clockwise, accelerating score'
                      cwd 'clockwise, decelerating score'
                      ccwa 'counter-clockwise, accelerating score'
                      ccwd 'counter-clockwise, decelerating score'
G-26.     VALUE LABELS   group 1 'learning disabled' 2 'normal'
                      /gender 1 'male' 2 'female'
G-27.     BEGIN DATA
G-28.        .
             .
             .
G-29.     END DATA
G-30.     MANOVA cwa cwd ccwa ccwd by group gender (1,2)
G-31.        /WSFACTOR = direct(2) speed(2)
G-32.        /REMAME = constant d s dbys
G-33.        /WSDESIGN = direct speed direct by speed
G-34.        /PRINT = HOMOGENEITY (BARTLETT COCHRAN BOXM)
G-35.           CELLINFO (MEANS COV)
G-36.           TRANSFORM
G-37.           ERROR (SSCP COR)
G-38.           SIGNIF (HYPOTH MULTI AVEF)
G-39.           DESIGN (ONEWAY OVERALL SOLUTION)
G-40.        /METHOD = SSTYPE (SEQUENTIAL)
G-41.        /ANALYSIS = constant d s dbys
G-42.        /DESIGN group gender group by gender
G-43.     FINISH
```

Figure D.5. SPSSX program for a modification of Example 9.4, with 2×2 designs on both subjects and occasions.

single WSFACTOR is "time" with three levels. The CONTRAST requested for this within-subject factor is POLYNOMIAL, which transforms the original variables into new variates reflecting constant, linear, and quadratic trends over time. The RENAME subcommand provides appropriate names for the new transformed variates. The WSDESIGN subcommand specifies the factor "time" as the design on the occasions.

SPSSX Program with Factorial Designs on Subjects and Occasions

Example 9-4 described a group of learning disabled children being tested on eye movement under four conditions, which were the result of a 2×2 design on the occasions of testing. These resulted from crossing two factors: a) direction, with two levels: clockwise (cw) and counter-clockwise (ccw); and b) speed, with two levels: accelerating and decelerating.

Assume that there was also a crossed, two-factor design on the subjects and that these factors were: a) group, with two levels: learning disabled and normal; and b) gender, with two levels: male and female. The complete SPSSX program listing is given in Figure D-5.

Lines G-23 through G-29 and most of the MANOVA subcommands are comparable with corresponding lines in Figure D-1. The main MANOVA command (line G-30) lists four dependent variables and two independent factors. According to the WSFACTOR subcommand (line G-31), the four dependent measures represent two factors with two levels each. Given the WSDESIGN subcommand (line G-33), scores for the two within-subject factors are transformed to a full factorial model consisting of effects for the two factors (direction and speed) and their interactions (direction by speed). The labels for these effects are provided with the RENAME specifications (line G-32). The DESIGN subcommand (line G-42) gives the full factorial model for the between-subjects design, and the DESIGN specification under the PRINT subcommand (line G-288 39) provides for the printing of this between-subjects design. Use of ANALYSIS (REPEATED), as in the previous examples, would produce only univariate results in this case. The ANALYSIS specification used here (line G-41) produces both multivariate and univariate results for all relevant hypotheses.

Index

You'll also want a copy of these other Slack books:

RESERACH TRADITION IN OCCUPATIONAL THERAPY: PROCESS, PHILOSOPHY AND STATUS. Dr. Royeen's companion book is written to familiarize the interested occupational therapist with the values, attitudes, and concepts underlying both general research and specifically, research in occupational therapy. Contents include.

- Guidelines for quality research
- Research in relation to the clinical role
- Definition of current research traditions
- Recommendations of necessary statistical knowledge
- Politics and impact of research
- Discussion of the humanistic approach
- Future trends

ANATOMY OF CLINICAL RESARCH: AN INTRODUCTION TO SCIENTIFIC INQUIRY IN MEDICINE, REHABILITATION AND RELATED HEALTH PROFESSIONS — Franklin Stein, PhD, OTR. This book is designed to help health care researchers plan and implement a research project and then communicate and use the results effectively. This revised edition addresses the rapidly changing developments in health care delivery by offering new statistics and reference sources. Contents include:

- Historical overview
- Data analysis and statistics
- Application of scientific research to allied health and rehabilitation
- Eight expanded research models
- Literature review
- Research design
- Methodology